KENILWORTH

SUNSET?

A Luton Town supporter's journal

Tim Kingston

The Book Castle

This book is dedicated to:
Brian Swain - Luton News football correspondent 1971 – 1997
and Michael Flaherty (the Australian Hatter, not the Irish dancer)

First published August 1998 by:
The Book Castle
12 Church Street
Dunstable
Bedfordshire LU5 4RU

Cover design features a selection of the author's memorabilia and tat both past and present (or at least relevant to the 1995/96 season).

ISBN 1 871199 83 2

Computer typeset by D. Goodman.
Printed by Progressive Printing (U.K.) Ltd., Leigh-on-Sea, Essex.

CONTENTS

A Limerick by Mr John Hegley, Luton Town fan:

This testament by a supporter
of Luton Town I found it brought a
few drips to my cheeks
with its pits and its peaks
it'll kill in the Kenilworth quarter

About the Author

A third-generation Town fan, Tim Kingston has frequented Kenilworth Road, on and off, since boyhood nearly twenty years ago. He was co-editor of TOWN magazine which he sold to, amongst some others, Eddie Large and Nigel Kennedy, the formerly known violinist. Sadly, his passion for watching the game he loves is not equalled by his own natural flair on the pitch.

During the nineteen nineties he has written a weekly column for the Luton News, in which football looms large (and theatre reviews in which it normally doesn't). In this book we have the full unexpurgated horror of Tim and pals, revelling in their fraught lives as fans of the Hatters.

FOREWORD

Timothy Kingston is slightly more of a football fan than I am, which for years has caused me no small amount of concern and annoyance. He's definitely a better supporter of the Town, which is less irksome. In the pages of this book he will probably wax on and on, in a witty and funny way, about how his "affair with the game and the modest team from South Beds" has led him through a gamut of emotions and is more important to him now than, say, remembering to wash regularly. No doubt the story will start with Dave, our Dad, who used to take us to reserve games. Here, I'm sure, is where you'll read how young Tim caught "the bug" but as Dave, our Dad, always likes to tell family and friends, he didn't. Tim's appreciation of football in the mid 70's was driven by boredom, which was probably relieved by teasing our younger brother, Simon, so that he'd cry and his particularly fine "Kingston upper lip" would jut out a mile to stop the tears and snot running down his chin. Or he'd run up and down the empty rows, slamming chairs down as he went, before setting them up carefully and repeating the process about a dozen times.

Still, I digress. Tim stopped being bored with football in the early 80's. Dave, our Dad, had lost interest in football a few years beforehand but would take us to selected first team games which promised absolutely no hint of visiting fans or hooliganism. "Fancy seeing Luton play Orient in the Primula Glasswear Southern Area and District Cup, First Leg?" he might ask out of parental duty, whilst thinking about where to park and getting to the ground in time to buy armloads of chewing gum and sweets. Somehow, in this period, Dad took us to see a few crackers – Newcastle and Birmingham for example.

Chubby kid in LTFC top, the author aged about 11.

Inexplicably, we'd be subjected to watching from the Kenilworth Road end, which was, of course, where all the away fans used to stand. Dad hated football violence – this is why he stopped going to matches (he told us), but football dealt him a few more blows. Dad was (and probably still is) shocked and upset about George Best being on telly after having been proven to be a drunkard and a criminal. He saw England in the 70's a few times, when they'd grind out nil-nils against awful sides and so never qualify for any proper tournament whatsoever. He also had to pay off the long standing debts for the damage caused to seats in the main stand by member(s) of his family.

I think it was really in the early 80's that Tim "got into" football. He'd enjoyed going to matches before, but I knew he'd had fads before. On the other hand, it took me about five years of finely tuned teenage moodiness, threats, sulks and tantrums before I grew up sufficiently for my parents to allow me to go with my chums to see Luton play. For five years, during the football season, every other Friday would bring the same humiliation. For the whole week I'd be daft enough to wear a Luton scarf to school and write things like "Hill for England" and "Alan West's quite good" on my schoolbooks. Then Friday lunchtime would come.

"Going to the game tomorrow Andy?"

"No. I've got to, er ……. pick the wings off a few daddy long-legs…"

Which was a very silly thing to say, aged 15, but I couldn't very well admit that "No, Mum and Dad won't let me….."

But, as I say, my day came. And for the first and second matches, my joy at supporting my team in a melting pot of swearing and cigar smoke was easily enough to compensate for getting chronic back ache. Those two games, I forget who they were against, who played and what the results were – were by far and away the best I have ever seen. Because, unbelievably, on the third game, my day was ruined about an hour before I left home, on being informed that Tim was not only interested in the game again, but that he was allowed to come with me. My golden days of being an LTFC fan had come to an abrupt end.

A few years later, I stopped going. I was becoming interested in other things – like being a full-time, sulky, late developing adolescent – and I thought that if going to a football game didn't always guarantee excitement, it wasn't worth it (very mislaid sentiments for a Town fan). My lack of interest was triggered by three different occassions. First was the time Tim was allowed to come. Second, and one home game later, Simon joined us. I'd turned my tantrums down by then, but was piqued by the five year war I'd waged being so successfully won by Tim in two weeks and Simon in one.

The final straw came in the 1985 FA Cup Semi-Final against Everton, when the buggers went up to Birmingham without me. I can't remember exactly, but the circumstances and the cruel result made me hang up the orange, white and blue for a while. In a recent chat with the author, he confirmed that I wasn't welcome to go with them to Villa Park, because I hadn't let him go with me to Liverpool a few seasons before; which was particularly upsetting as that wasn't the one where Kirk Stephens heroically kept goal in a 3-3 stunner, but it was the occasion where Ian Rush scored a hat-trick within about 10 minutes and we ran out 6-0 losers – Rush got four, and after the game the Scousers we met were as friendly as the legend suggests.

For a while I had no interest in football, and managed to miss Luton at Wembley in the 1988 Final against Arsenal. A couple of years after that, I moved to Gillespie Road, about two yards from Highbury, but I still wasn't interested. Odd though, that one of the first things I did was to walk by the main entrance of the ground thinking, "God, this is a huge club, but we had ya!".

Fast forward to 1998. I can't wait to read nice things about me, and assuming Tim's memory is better than my own (most people's are), I might well catch up on a few games I've forgotten. The current season is drawing to an end, and has been awful. I have made it to a few games, managing to see us battle back against Northampton and hold Fulham to four. These truly dreadful displays have somehow inspired me to "come back home" and buy my first season ticket for the 1998/99 season. I hope it gets a whole lot better. If we get a rich benefactor, we could be in the Premier in time for the 2000/01 season. Then we might be in a better position to challenge for silverware, and I can be there. And if I can wreak some sort of revenge over Timothy and Simon Kingston then so much the better.

Andrew John Kingston,
London April 1998

PREFACE

Late `90's Lutonia

From its source in a park in the town, near the Marsh Farm estate and inside the ancient site of Waulud's bank, the River Lea meanders slowly, as if the water therein feels hard done by with its latest manifestation in the H_2O cycle, into town. The river on which the town was originally built is in a sorry state in Luton now. It passes right through the centre of town but years of building around, and on top of, the river, renders it now almost invisible. In those places where it is still on show, notably in the ditches that run alongside New Bedford Road, the river is noted for the shopping trolleys which are chucked in it. In the places where it isn't so well known to townsfolk and trolley dumpers, we occasionally hear bad press stories from places we didn't even know the it passed through; a body found in the river, behind a nightclub.... scientists warn of the dangers of the increasing number of rats urinating in the Lea.

The River Lea trickles slowly into the town centre, though it often appears stagnant in the summer, and under Bridge Street where there used to be a ford (and not, curiously enough, a bridge). By this time the river is out of sight, long since out of mind. Well informed rat piss dowsers might know where to find traces of the river underneath The Arndale, but to the naked eye it makes its next public appearance on the other side of a brick wall at the edge of a roundabout, passing the rear of The Herald & Post building on Church Street. Here the river is apparently gushing, three or four times wider and faster than on the other side of the town centre. A cynic might put this down to the busy Arndale toilets, a more romantic cynic might wonder if having got through Luton town centre the river isn't in a hurry to get right out and into the countryside to the South of the town. The rest of its journey through the outer reaches of South Luton is hidden away from public view by estate housing, a retail park, the railway and Vauxhall Motors. It is only truly visible again from the new dual carriageway that links the airport to the M1.

An elevated section of the road looks over the Luton Hoo estate. Our own stately home, detached almost completely from Luton and the Lutonians. Once (apparently) the home of the world's largest collection of Fabergé. Much of that has now been sold and the estate is now slowly dying from outstanding debts, like the rest of the English aristocracy. The estate continues to earn a bit from the film industry (the house was the reception venue for one of the four weddings) and the grounds have recently held rave festivals, but the debts remain massive and Luton Hoo slowly crumbles.

Still, as Luton goes, it's pretty. You can't actually see the house from the road but the grounds look nice and the river Lea, in all its glory, forms part of the scene. It actually looks like a river in the Luton Hoo estate, tree lined, complete with wooded island; the sea scouts use this part of the river for their exercises as they await NATO mobilisation.

From Luton Hoo, the river runs through the pleasant countryside and villages between Luton and Wheathampstead, past the East Hyde sewage works; a last lingering whiff from the town it left behind

If you're still reading you may ask the point of this tale from the riverbank. A prelude to an environmental message maybe? Or an excuse to slag off the town from a different angle than the rest of the world usually does? Well, no. But the river, and the town's treatment of it, is indicative of the way that Luton has grown over the years, blindly disregarding its heritage in favour of industrial and/or economic progress

In this respect the town of Dunstable, to the west of Luton, has the opposite viewpoint. For a town of its size Dunstable has quite a long and interesting history. Pre-historic man had a settlement on its outskirts. The Romans had a site there. Queen Eleanor's funeral cortège passed through Dunstable in the 13th Century, a cross being built to commemorate the visit - like the one in Northampton (unlike the one in Northampton it was later demolished). Dunstable's Priory church used to be the centre of a huge monastery. Henry VIII's marriage to Catherine of Aragon was annulled in Dunstable, a decision that angered the Pope and necessitated the formation of the Church of England.

Dunstable's centre, the ancient crossroads of the prehistoric Icknield Way and Roman Watling Street, is marked by an ugly little double roundabout. The townsfolk cling to Dunstable's illustrious past, many of the townsfolk view Luton as an ugly urban sprawl, while their own town faces a future which is at best uncertain. In the meantime the Dunstable townsfolk fight to save what they already have - be that local businesses looking furtively elsewhere or the Queensway Hall - the 60's white elephant designed as a municipal events venue - gradually exposed as being useless for each of the events it was supposed to stage.

It would be nice to say that a healthy rivalry exists between the townsfolk of Luton and Dunstable. The Dunstablians are well known for their open suspicion and dislike of Luton. Unfortunately the trend is for Lutonians to agree with almost everything they say.

Luton is a town with an unhealthy lack of civic pride. For many who live in the town the only redeeming feature is that, situated where it is, it has good travel connections. Luton is "handy" for elsewhere. It's handy for London. Handy for Birmingham. Handy for the airport. Handy for I-bloody-biza. The town has the charm of an oversized motorway service station (the shopping facilities are bigger, but so is the crime problem) and it's no surprise. The British media has long portrayed Luton as a blot on the landscape. Luton Airport's stock trade is cheap package holidays to the Spanish Sun – lads' and slags' holidays in the sun. Our most valuable cultural ambassador over the years has been Lorraine Chase as the vacuous Campari quaffing beauty with the catchphrase "Naaah, Luton Airport". Even our biggest and proudest manufacturers, Vauxhall, are having a hard time impressing the likes of Jeremy Clarkson, God of the Company Rep, on Top Gear.

Luton is widely regarded as a dump. But the real shame is that so many of its townsfolk are all too prepared to slag off their own town - to shrug their shoulders and agree with Luton's detractors before shuffling back under their stone and trying to carry on with life in their own little nuclear families. If Luton is crap then these people (typically unwittingly) help make it so. There was a "Luton's Looking Up" scheme a few years ago, trying to promote the town to outside business. In this aim it claimed modest success, but was continually put down and rubbished by the townsfolk. And every time the council spends money for the town's entry in the Britain's in Bloom competition, there is no shortage of people on hand whinging "What's the point?".

Putting a finger on why Luton is held in such low esteem in the eyes of its people is a complex question. It possibly has quite a lot to do with the changing local social and economic situation in the town during the last three decades. In the early sixties Luton, and the thousands of Vauxhall workers employed there, was researched in a study of the new affluence in working class Britain. During the same time Luton's population increase bought about the building of tower blocks on some of the town's estates. As with many similar estates in urban Britain, the effects of recession, unemployment and crime have had a detrimental effect on the quality of life for those living there. But, in Luton's case, the Sixties planners (who should have been locked up for crimes against humanity years ago) went a step further by designing the Luton Arndale Centre. The biggest shopping centre in the country (apparently) at the time, it was built smack bang in the middle of the town and at a stroke effectively killed the town centre. The Arndale, especially since its renovation a couple of years ago, is a bright and pleasant shopping centre during the day; but at night it is a huge concrete monolith surrounded by eerily deserted multi-storey carparks around which the pubs and clubs try to operate with some semblance of town centre normality. Luton town centre can be eerily quiet on a late weekend evening. Inside the nightclubs the chat up lines, which will eventually lead to spawning the kids of a new generation, are shouted loud to be heard over the deafening noise from the amps. Outside booze, malice and paranoia reign. Reports of muggings, stabbings and street brawls are not uncommon. There are some in Luton, and certainly in Dunstable, who are so scared by the threat of crime in Luton town centre that they wouldn't dream of going out there.

But, try as we might to hide the fact, Luton does have redeeming qualities. For one thing Luton is a town with a rich cultural mix. Apart from the indigenous English, there are large and vibrant Irish and Asian communities (and a growing student population in the town's new university - in the building formerly known as Luton Technical college). The Irish and English communities, by and large, get on fine - with hardly any tension. The Asian community, although seemingly insular in their community which centres around Bury Park (where the football ground is), provide the town with some of it's best eateries and most exotic and exciting food stores. Meanwhile the, even more insular, student community huddle themselves together in the student bar. Even so, the courting of the students by the local business community is starting to pay dividends to the town. We now have two decent bookshops and some half decent specialist market stalls. And new pubs, clubs and restaurants are opening up in what's left of the town centre. Luton will, I am assured, benefit from its new status as a University Town.

At the risk of reading like a "Luton's Looking Up" promo leaflet, we've got our half decent shopping centre, some second rate leisure facilities (new leisure emporium currently being built in the town centre), parks (not overly dog shit blighted, except People's Park), good travel connections and, of course, LTFC.

Luton Town FC have never been a trendy club, even in Luton. Maybe this is because the population believe they live in a hole, so they're unlikely to support the local team. Even so, as a focal point for what civic pride there is in the town, the football club is invaluable to Luton.

Deep down, I know that, I love the town. For no other reason than that it's home. I know it's not the greatest place in the world, but I know it better than any other town in the country. It has its bad points, even a few good ones, but on the whole it remains a town always on the look out to improve itself. Luton will never be seen as one of the country's prettiest towns but, as soon as it can persuade its own people that it isn't such a bad place to live, if they can be persuaded to look to the future in expectation rather than cynicism and resignation, then it will really begin to look up.

INTRODUCTION

Hello and welcome to this, my entry into the Nick Hornby football special library. Fantastic book though it is, Hornby's "Fever Pitch" failed (in all but two chapters) to go on about Luton Town FC. And the chapter about the 1988 Littlewoods Cup Final simply didn't ring true - he wrote it up as if it *wasn't* the greatest Cup Final that Wembley has ever seen.

Apart from the opportunity to jump on to the football book bandwagon, there are other reasons why I've written this book. Firstly, I want to make a ton of money out of it. True, it's not as well written as "Fever Pitch", the subject Club aren't glamorous and the appeal might be limited. Even so, naïve fool that I am, I'm aiming at making a million quid or so out of royalties.

Then there's the desire to write a book based on my Club that doesn't follow the hoary old hooligan line. Sadly, the "Hooliebook" genre prospered in the wake of new interest in football related books. As long as football hooliganism is portrayed as dangerous and sexy, then there will always be numskull subscribers to the attitude. In general football supporters had had enough hooliganism after the Heysel and Hillsborough tragedies but sadly, and especially at lower league clubs effectively disenfranchised from meaningful competition, there are still groups of blokes who use football as a means to impress (and hopefully frighten) each other with great shows of machismo.

The vast majority of football fans have, and want, nothing to do with the hooligan following. However, as football supporters, one of the most irresponsible things we can do is to ignore the fact that there remains a problem. Unless we want to end up in the same sorry situation as the `80's, where all football supporters were tarred with the same brush (especially, and ashamedly, by the Luton Town away fan ban), the hooligan element has to be individually identified and action taken to stop them attending further. Anyway, as far as this book goes, I don't want Luton Town to be associated with another boring hooligan publication.

Whilst I count myself as part of "the majority" of football fans, I won't pretend that (by writing this book) I'm Luton Town's most loyal supporter. There are quite a few hundred Luton Town fans who have shown more loyalty towards the cause - there are those whose lives are devoted to the Club. Players, managers, coaches and chairman come and go; league position is won and lost; but these people will still turn up to support the team. Their loyalty is, as far as I can see, beyond reproach. These people include the doyen of the Supporters Club, John Pyper - the bloke they call "Beano" (or "Albino" or "Seamarks" depending on who you talk to) - another bloke called Pat and, if Nick Hornby is right, Neil Kaas (I don't know the bloke, I'm sure he's a good sort). Apart from John, an affable obsessive who makes it his business to know anyone with any interest in the Club (including smart arse columnists, like my good self, in the local press), I only really know these people by reputation. To engage them in conversation about Luton Town might all too easily involve their embarrassing me twice over, with their superior knowledge on the subject, and the passion with which they talk about it.

My own position in the Luton Town fans' fantasy league is way below these people. By my reckoning in the `96/97 season, as a season ticket holder attending a few away games, I'd make about 2900th place. In season `86/87 I'd have been one of the top few hundred Town fans, between `88/89 and `89/90 I left the scene altogether (becoming a Man U type "first score I look for" fan), before re-establishing myself in the top 1000 up until a couple of seasons ago when successive relegations took their toll on my interest. Sad though it might seem that I've actually spent valuable seconds working out such estimates (and that you've presumably wasted time reading them) I make the point because Football Clubs apparently still look at their support base in terms of a "hardcore" support who, supposedly, turn up to every match. In fact every football fan, however loyal, has a breaking point - be it emotional, health related or financial - after which the reasonable thing to do is to give the game up. In the meantime football continues to take blind loyalty for granted by taxing the pockets and the patience of its traditional supporter base.

I can remember regarding money spent on football (£1.50 in the Oak Road during the '80's) as a small basic commodity. I remember the abhorrence at having to pay a full £5 to stand at Oxford United, barely a decade ago. The decision to go to an away game these days is more financial than loyalty inspired. Football seems hell bent on pricing itself out of the traditional working class market. The whole league seems comfortably resigned to agree with the big Club mantra that football "is big business now". However, whilst the statement rings true (to the glorious sound of the overworked till) for Man Utd, Liverpool, Chelsea, Arsenal and other Premiership Clubs where the Club shop has been replaced by multi-branch megastores, it is the smaller Clubs who will die as a result of hiking prices to the new "going rate" of admission.

The '96/97 season is one that will live in the memory of Luton Town fans for approximately nine months, if that. It was a season during which, for the first time in ages, the club was fighting for promotion; but the quality of Second Division football, and the eventual failure to actually get straight back into Division 1, made it a season of ultimate frustration. We're used to that; it's nothing new.

However, by marking out exactly what we were up to at the time I hope that I've managed in some way to highlight the fickle world of football fandom. The big issues in any one season are the race for promotion/against relegation and cup runs. But, during the 90 minutes of any one match, the result that afternoon or evening is paramount. Other attitudes towards the game at large change too. The 96/97 season, for example, was the first, hopefully the last, in which I've had the opportunity to feel an acute aversion toward the way Bury play football. Then there's the way that my personal attitude, and level of parochial hostility, towards our rivals Watford has changed over the years; as has one's opinion of Luton's own players, managers and chairmen.

By the time of writing this introduction, I have long forgotten feelings felt during our match this year against, for example, Shrewsbury Town, but my write up at the time (however irrelevant it now seems) might help to encapsulate what was going on at the time.

It might not be ever so inspiring but, if the truth be known, the seasoned football supporter has long since learned not to be over impressed. The season around which this book is based was by no means outstanding. It ended, as it couldn't fail to, with Luton in the lowest position I'd ever seen them finish, but its unexceptional nature makes it more representative of the supporting lives of the average fan than a list of Cup Final anecdotes. Not that these aren't included too...

When you're sitting through a tedious midweek fixture, there's always the past for your imagination to slip back into. I've put on rose tinted spectacles and written up some of the matches in Luton Town's `80's heyday, interjected after research which was a little more painstaking than I'd have liked. I spent hours in the library, trying to match my guesstimates with evidence from the microfilmed Luton News archives. Thankfully, I later called upon the invaluable help of club statistician/historian Roger Wash - and later bought the newly published Definitive LTFC record book, which was a real boon. My book runs like a calendar from June to May (with matches in, for example, March `84 alongside those in March `97). It's a bit confusing, but see the notes on format. I'm trying a new slant on the football book formula, and have one or two decent reasons for doing it this way. OK?

Of course the past wasn't great at the time. I hated school, retained a morbid fear of nuclear war into my early teens (I still wouldn't be too delighted now, to be honest) and took time to take in quite a few of the traditional childhood and teenage problems. When I wasn't imagining hearing the four minute warning before the match, the Oak Road terrace at Kenilworth Road provided my brothers and me with a temporary *angst* retreat and a place where we could happily rip our adolescent voices to shreds in support of our team.

The traditional folk hero of the Luton crowd these days is Micky Harford, the hard man centre forward who did the Club great service in the mid to late eighties. However, looking back, most of my memories of the good times seem to centre around Ricky Hill - the best Luton Town player I've ever seen; and Brian Stein - who scored so many important goals for the Club. Both were ever present from the time I started going to matches in 1980, right through to the end of the decade.

They were my heroes. Both England internationals. Players of the like that, in this day and age, Luton Town would never be allowed to keep. But fifteen years ago, the small crowds at Kenilworth Road wowed at their skills.

As far as my own football skills go - my dreams of representing my team and my country were dashed early on by cruel twists of fate. Firstly, from my very early days playing for Slip End Scouts, it was clear that I was useless. Undaunted, I continued to play where and when I could - but faced a further setback when I badly twisted my right ankle during a match in a Southampton park. The ankle has remained weak, and was later exacerbated by an injury incurred during a drunken impression of David Pleat's famous jig on the Maine Road pitch. However, when my brother's mate asked for players for a 5-a-side competition I was delighted to sign for AC Meringue. This book also details our own lamentable "season".

Apologies to those who are likely to be offended by the bad language (whether actual or implied) in this book. Swearing, in most cases, displays a doltish lack of vocabulary. In normal society swearing is only really of any effect, and only remains shocking, if used as an expletive. But life inside the football ground does not reflect normal society. In a football ground, after all, the supporters are encouraged, nay expected, to be emotionally and (more importantly) financially involved in a game in which 22 men kick a ball about a park for 90 minutes. The escapism element of supporting a football Club is perhaps the most attractive thing about going along to the match. Breaking free from society's code, if only for a couple of hours a week, is extremely enjoyable - and can quite possibly be therapeutic. For the most part swearing at football matches isn't a show of "being hard", but in a heady atmosphere, when a match is exciting and engrossing, one's ability at witty and informed comment is severally compromised. Of course some idiots go way too far by resorting to violence, but swearing has always been part and parcel of going to the football. That said, there are, of course, times when it isn't on - like if one is unlucky enough to find oneself surrounded by family units. In those cases it's better to keep oneself in check, but by doing so one is holding back emotionally and missing out on quite a bit of the experience.

So we probably care, and swear, too much. I'd also like to take the opportunity to point out that the people (i.e. my pals) in this book are unavoidably portrayed as exaggerated comic versions of their true selves, highlighting the sides of their character which only see the light of day during match days. It's a Jekyll and Hyde transformation, from upstanding member of society to foaming partisan, that probably affects the majority of football fans to a certain extent. Outside Kenilworth Road my football-going pals are some of the nicest people I know. Inside the ground, they get worked up a bit - and swear lots. But then don't we all?

Anyway, so there it is. If you enjoy reading this book half as much as I enjoyed, say, the fourth goal against Crewe in the league last season - I'd be well chuffed. If you enjoy it as much as I enjoyed the winning goal in the 1988 Littlewoods Cup Final then keep calm, stop kissing your mates, and find out about getting some education.

April 1998

The main characters in this book, from left to right: Andy Whiting, Michael Flaherty, Chris Johnson, your author and his brother Simon, wearing a suit.

FORMAT NOTES

This book is written in a specific time structure. It's not strictly chronological from 1980 (when I started supporting the Hatters) through to 1997, listing memorable games along the way. Instead the book is built around the `96/97 football season - with recollections popping up on the same day as they happened way back when. Thereby, for example, the account of the rather impressive home win against Preston North End on the 22/2/97 is followed by my recollections of the second leg of the Littlewoods Cup Semi-Final against Oxford on the 28/2/87. I reckon the style gives the book a certain depth. But there are a couple of other reasons for writing it this way viz.:-

1. Because, had I written it in strict chronological order, it would have read like a sad wistful story of a club in decline. Whereas this is in many ways accurate, it certainly isn't the feeling that fans necessarily take with them when they watch the Town. They certainly don't need a book telling them that things were so much better 15 years ago.

2. With "the good times" in mind, I feel it's important to also record just how boring most games are. Football matches on a cold Tuesday night, against Wycombe Wanderers, with a full time score of 0-0, wouldn't find their way into a football fan's memoirs. But they should. Most football games are, in the most part, dull. Live second division football, unlike a Man Utd highlights video, is like that. I felt it was important to write up a season for posterity. The intersecting "highlights" from days of yore are there, if

anything, to hopefully fend off rigor mortis as the reader trawls through accounts of bore draws at Kenilworth Road.

For those who would still rather read the book in chronological order, I have put the "next" dates in brackets at the bottom of each account which doesn't follow on to the next in the book. From there you can flick from page to page at your leisure - and read the book a bit like one of those old "Dungeons and Dragons" (training) books for kids. In this way you might incorporate a dice and make it more interesting; 1-2 Luton win, go to next entry, 3-4 score draw, go back one page, 5-6 killed by ork, start again. Blasts from the past are printed *in italics*, enclosed betwixt lines of nostalgic boaters and include an hourglass graphic, all of which should help denote "flashback".

It won't take an eagle eyed expert to notice that most of the historic recollections are from Luton Town's days in the First Division from `82 to `92. Whilst run of the mill matches make up the vast majority of a football fan's life, the highlights are obviously going to correspond with his/her Club's own halcyon days. Nineteen ninety five, on the other hand, isn't covered at all. The same reasoning explains why there are more recollections of matches in April and May than there are those of September and October. Important matches tend to occur at the end of the season.

Even so, as the `96/97 coverage might show, there is usually no more important match in the club's history than the next (this manager's cliché is almost true, until he starts using it in the context of the midweek league match before the Cup Final at the weekend).

The strict chronologist can start the book here.

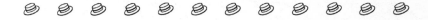

THE MID TO LATE 70'S.....

70's

Luton Town are, for the most part, rubbish at the moment (in the late `90's, we've not gone back yet, wait for it); although we've got some small reason for hope, in the shape of the new stadium proposals, in the future. But, to my young eyes, the

Football Club was in a terrible state when I was first introduced to football matches at Kenilworth Road.

If this was a ploy by my Dad to turn us off football, it worked in my case, if not for my brothers. Perhaps they were better informed than I was. At that time, having taken in the news that football crowds were down due to hooliganism, I believed that this was it at Luton Town - football played out in a run down ground where the fans no longer attend. I had no notion of reserve team football and no idea that this was what Dad was dragging us along to see.

In the absence of any interest whatsoever we used to spend our time running up and down the deserted main stand, putting all the seats up so we could slam them down again, being told via tannoy announcement to stop, trying to scrounge tea from Dad's thermos and my pestering him that I wanted to go home. Two hours out in the cold is a long time when you're bored witless. That, and being made to accompany him to the allotment of a Sunday afternoon, were formative excuses to hate my Dad. He made matters worse a few years later by making us go to church every Sunday. The very idea! It's not as if we're even Roman Catholic. We're C of E; the church that rarely requests loyalty from its congregation, past asking newly baptised infants to bear them in mind for their wedding.

These days (especially since I left home) it's difficult not to love the old fella.... however much I try.

Back in the 1970's I would, on every possible occasion, decline the invitation to go and see Luton play - even when Dad started taking Andrew and Simon to see the first team, on the quiet, during the 79/80 season (26/4/80).

That was a long long time ago, but please, read on..................

JUNE

29/6/96: Seasoned Freshers' Season Ticket Purchase.

It was barely half nine in the morning but already Saturday 29th June 1996 was turning into a right swine of a day. Our plans to buy our season tickets before the end of June, thus cashing in on the maximum "early bird" discounts, were all over the place, right at the last minute. England's progress in the European Championship had excited us far more than the publication of the Luton Town fixture list for '96/97, and now it was almost too late. I couldn't get hold of my brother Simon , his working in Chelmsford and living in St. Albans had recently made him extremely elusive. Meanwhile our mate Andy, not to mention my good self, was moaning about being skint.

I'd eventually got hold of Simon, having got him turfed out of bed, at 9.45am....we were supposedly meeting Michael and Chris at the ground at 10. Simon sulkily moaned that there was no way he was going to be able to afford the season ticket this year and wouldn't be able to get hold of the student passes either. Great.

Meanwhile Andy was next door trying to sort out a busy day with his fiancée Maxine. He'd allocated a miserly time window for the season ticket purchase and was threatening to talk himself out of it. But he figured that, if he didn't get a season ticket, he'd end up going to ten or so games at £12 a time and would end up out of pocket. Such financial dilemmas haunt those of us who still don't truly accept the fact - we get Luton Town season tickets because we're a bit sad. Even if we can't enjoy the football, there's something fatefully enjoyable about being in the pub on a Saturday afternoon or

Tuesday evening, drinking two pints and fretting about the match to come.

Stopping at the bank to replace the allocated money I'd spent at the pub the night before, and to get a further £100 out for Simon's ticket, we eventually got to the ground about 20 minutes late to find Michael and Chris waiting leaned up against the portacabin club shop. Simon used to work with Michael.

Michael and Chris used to frequent the public house in town where we once spent Saturday nights (before it was ruined by a kitsch-Irish theme refit). These days we only really see them during the football season and, football bores though they (and we) are, I realised I'd missed them during the short close season.

So we met, in full view of the ticket office, and discussed the situation; before deciding to carry on hatching our nefarious plot in the privacy of Andy's car.

We planned to purchase student tickets for two excellent reasons. Firstly, at £99, the student ticket represented a saving of £108. Secondly there was no way we could afford £207, and no way a season watching Luton Town FC is worth that anyway. There was a time when we all had student ID cards but our friends at Exeter University Student Union have, sadly for us, long since graduated. Andy was the only person actually to be featured on any of the three cards we had, and that was a year out of date (apart from being another fake). The others belonged to my cousin, a student at Leeds University, and a girl at Luton Uni who was apparently the girlfriend of a bloke that Michael works with. Very nice too....that's the glamour of the season over with.

Andy would have to blag his way into getting the other two; meanwhile Michael's suggestion of getting two full price tickets and dividing the cost was unceremoniously chucked out. We'd done the same the season before, in the really cheap seats - £89 students, £139 full - but decided this year that, if we were going to con the club we might as well do it the best we could. This year we had a contingency plan whereby, if five cards were needed, we'd dash to Simon's original source or hang around the halls of residence offering students £10 for the use of their cards and faces for half an hour ("No, look, we promise this isn't a town v gown abduction plot mate"); failing that Andy was under instruction to tell the ticket office staff to "Bugger it then". We hoped the big wad of cash he was carrying would be incentive enough to encourage the staff to progress the transaction.

He took ages. Meanwhile we waited in the car like undercover cops on a stakeout, attracting suspicious looks from the Club shop staff - but out of the way of the ticket office. We imagined that Andy's cover had been blown, that he was being interrogated by LTFC stewards. We talked a small amount about next season, about the Kohlerdome inquiry and about the disgraceful Watfordesque yellow third kit hanging in the window of the shop. Eventually Andy came running out of the office carrying two forms on which we had to make up the names of the other two students. He ran back and was another age (I used the time to have a look in the shop and purchase a signed picture of Marvin Johnson for 50p) until he finally came back to the car grinning and carrying five books of brand new season tickets. Simon, due to the fact that he wasn't there - and had been a tremendous pain in the arse - was allocated the girl ticket and we all went our separate ways; Michael to Debenhams to meet his Mum, Chris to buy a lottery ticket, Andy to meet up with Max and take her (and her Mum) to Milton Keynes to shop, and I to get a curry pattie in the market before wandering back home.

When I got in, Simon was on the phone to my girlfriend Claire. He had apparently been faffing about since he came off the phone to me in the morning and was furiously trying to raise cash and student cards. He had driven from his home in St. Albans to our flat and to the football club trying to find us. I told him I'd got a ticket for him and he could pay in instalments if he liked. He came round later with the £100 in cash. We used £20 to go out that night, and he took £20 back the day after.

30/6/96: European Championship Final
Germany v Czech Republic

With England out of the competition, this match is decidedly anticlimactic. I want the Czech Republic to win because I like Prague, I like their beer, because they're the underdogs and because someone's got to beat Germany surely....... not, as it happens.

Possibly just as bad as penalties, I don't know 'cause I didn't really care, Germany win on the "Golden goal" rule whereby the first scorer in extra time wins anyway. It seems a bit stupid, but there you go, as I say - I didn't really care.
Score: 2-1

JULY

Pre season friendlies

Watching your team trot around in the summer sun, playing meaningless matches before the start of the season doesn't normally set the heart racing. If you do bother turning up at all it's:-

1) Because you're keen for the start of the new season. Not necessarily to be confused with "optimistic". But, for quite a few football fans, the brief summer break between seasons is an aimless period without the comforting structure of the league fixture list to adhere to and fall back on. The week of the ardent football supporter revolves around Saturday afternoon. Having that focus taken away for a couple of months usually means that, however pessimistic he or she is about the coming season, they're keen for the season to start.

2) Out of curiosity. Hopes are always high for the start of the season. The local press display colour centre spreads of the new season's squad photo. Your team is beaming - maybe wearing the new kit - even possibly including the new star signing, which at Luton is likely to be an ex-Wolves reserve who earned his valuable first team experience whilst on loan at Torquay. The new kit looks good, new signing says he's pleased (and "just wants to get Luton back to Division 1"). If by the end of the friendlies you're still clinging onto the hope that new lad just "needs time" it'll eventually

dawn on you that he - like the rest of the team and like the replica shirt you paid £35 for - is just plain poor quality.

3) Other factors. You're on holiday in the area (of Luton's pre-season tour of Scotland or Devon).

30/7/96: Hitchin Town v Luton Reserves

How Martin Thurlow and I became friends is a long story - involving his late '80's conversion from dodgy geezer into indie pop kid and my going around with Thrilled Skinny, my brother's band. Previous to that, during our school years, he had beaten up my then best friend, Brian, quite badly. When Mick Sheridan (our mutual friend, mine through the 6th form, Martin's through outside life) told me Thurlow wanted to come to a gig, I was somewhat dubious of the idea that he had indeed turned his back on violence since becoming a disciple of Morrissey. However, when he did eventually come along he was as charming a bloke as one could wish to meet and, though he's still regarded as "something of a character" (Mick has around eight thousand "Furlow" anecdotes) he's been a great pal for years now.

Martin had got a couple of tickets from his mate Ian Scott who plays for Hitchin. Scotty was in our year at school. Clearly the school's best footballer he was a trialist, and later a pro, at Luton Town. But, by a twist of fate, his emergence on the brink of first team selection was at the very time that Luton Town were at their First Division height. Eventually Scott went six miles up the road to Hitchin Town of the Isis league - recent FA Cup giantkillers and traditional stop off for ex-Luton pros. And currently on their books is the ex-Spurs player Micky Hazard. Scotty says that Hazard is "class".

Having been talked into going to the match by Martin I had picked him up from IBC Motors, where he was working a knackering twelve hour shift in the paint shop. At the turnstiles, where the tickets were to have been waiting, Martin was told that Scott wasn't allowed guests until he had signed a new contract at the Club. So we ended up paying £4.

The Luton side was an unrecognisable bunch of twelve year olds from the reserves playing alongside the ancient Trevor "Pops" Peake - now wearing a goatee beard, presumably to show off to the kids. Keith Hayward from the fanzine (and Dave, and the bloke known as "Mr Boring") turn up and we started talking/moaning/airing

6

pre-season pessimism. The friendly tour of Scotland, apparently, was awful.

Bored of the game, and probably more of the conversation, Martin decided to have another word with the bloke on the gate. He was unsuccessful again but returned with a story of a couple of young blokes coming in behind him. "We're Luton players" they apparently said. The turnstile man, in jobsworth mode having been hassled by Furlow, isn't initially convinced. "Look mate," say the kids "we wouldn't lie about it would we?". The gateman saw their point and let them in. And then sent Thurlow packing again.

Ten minutes before the end of the match we went into the bar to play pool. Later we met Scotty who moaned about having only played fifteen minutes (in which time he came closest of anyone to scoring). Apparently Hitchin played a lot of their youngsters in an attempt to catch the eye of attending scouts. He gave us the admission money back and arranged a night out to get lashed with Thurlow. Scotty and Thurlow's friendship is very much a throwback to our schooldays - I think Scotty remains a bit confused as to why Martin is seen out with the fat, stiff kid from school.

Score: 0-0
Attendance: dunno, hundreds rather than millions

AUGUST

3/8/96: St. Albans City v Luton Town (reserves...ish)

A far stronger Town side than the one at Hitchin took a two goal lead in the first half with goals from Guentchev and new signing Showler. From his picture in the paper Paul Showler, from Bradford, looks like Trevor Peake's older brother - but on the field he doesn't look too bad.

After picking Michael up before the match, we drove to Simon's St. Albans abode. Simon had been to St. Albans for a couple of friendlies and reckoned they weren't a bad side.... Meanwhile Michael expected trouble from Watford fans, and he told us the chilling story of the last time the Town played here - a Watford fan had apparently smashed a bottle on the terraces. Simon, who was at the same match, couldn't remember the incident - but it was enough to get Michael's adrenaline going. Keith was on the terrace, this time accompanied by the Ivinson brothers (who I'm on occasional nodding terms with). I'm sure they're nice blokes when you get to know them.

At half time we swap ends to be behind the goal Luton are attacking, getting away from the old fellows who are happily talking to us and slagging off our team. It's OK, we're generally agreeing with them, but Michael is adding a few interjections which could eventually lead to him cheeking the two old fellas a little bit more than is socially acceptable. All the goalscoring action was at the end we left as the Town are beaten 3-2 with a last minute penalty. I've never seen the Town lose after being 2-0 up but Keith reminds me, as if I cared, that it doesn't matter until August 17th.....

Score: 3-2. Town scorers – Guentchev, Showler
Attendance: a few hundred.

5/8/96: Julian James Testimonial. Luton Town v West Ham.

West Ham apparently ran out with seven first team regulars and were still well beaten. I don't go to the match despite a last bid attempt by Michael Flaherty, on behalf of Julian James.

It's difficult; yes, James has been a "good servant to the club" but happy Julian James memories are few and far between. The defences he's appeared in have all too often seemed of the headless chicken variety. There is also the fact that he hasn't signed a new contract yet, although the local press is full of him saying that that is what he wants. Unfortunately Luton fans had the same situation with David Preece (a far better player) a year or two back - apparently eager to sign in the days leading up to his lucrative testimonial v Man Utd (for which Kenilworth Road was full of bloody Lutonian Red Devil kids) - he seemingly couldn't wait to get out afterwards.

Loyalty is something that fans and players shouldn't take for granted....and less than 3000 for a testimonial is terrible, even if the player is too.   If James really does sign for the Town again I might send him a cheque for the £5.50 I would've spent to see the match.
Score: 4-2 Town scorers dunno, they probably let Jules score one
Attendance: Low. Sorry

7/8/96: Luton Town v Norwich City

Trying to get any information about pre-season friendlies is next to impossible. Too skint and/or disinterested to go. Teletext eventually shows the result the day after. Results are looking good - hopefully I shall tap into some pre-season optimism down the pub at the weekend.

That optimism, through Keith and Steve from the fanzine, was evident but well guarded. I suppose what I wanted was fiery eyed, alcohol promoted renditions of "Here we go, here we go, here we go". But these blokes are too wise - they've been around too long. So far.....we just don't know....(*17/8/96*)
Score: 2-0 Town scorers ?
Attendance: I'm sorry, I haven't a clue.

17/8/85: Plastic Fantastic!
Luton Town v Nottingham Forest

The opening match of the `85/86 season was the first on Luton Town's new En-tout-cas synthetic playing surface. We got to the ground early to look at the lovely new pitch and were

1985 *treated to a myriad of different sporting mini events - the full scale versions of which would all be made possible on the versatile new surface. The pitch had been divided up into quarters (at least) and on each slot a different team or teams were strutting their diverse sporting stuff. We had American football, gymnastics, five-a-side football and, I can't remember, The Royal Tournament or something....*

Every so often a whistle would blow and the action would move round one square, so that the whole ground would get a taste of the different games. Very interesting, for a couple of minutes; rather like a cheap Christmas Games Compendium, bought by a well meaning but short sighted relative. The big question was - how would the Town get on on it? And, what's the bounce like? The second question was soon answered. The ball bounced alright (the surface was obviously far better than QPR's plastic pitch) but the surface was strangely covered in loads of sand. The Hatters seemed to be doing OK. The slick pitch seemed perfect for our slick passing play. Steiney scored to put us up 1-0, and it was a little disappointing that the Town couldn't add to that score and eventually let in an equaliser. Still, we couldn't help but agree, what a marvellous playing surface...(5/10/85)

Score: 1-1.   Town scorer - Brian Stein
Attendance: 11,318

17/8/96: Start of the season
Luton Town v Burnley

The pub was sliding back into football season stride. The fanzine on sale meant that the lads involved with its sale were off early. Andy and I sat in the "garden" (it's a carpark, although the hanging baskets do make it quite pleasant in the summer) waiting for Slim. Michael and Chris (and Martin) were off watching Pulp in Chelmsford.

Alison, our friendly neighbourhood landlady, comes out a couple of times to say that the pub is full of "bleedin' Northerners". When we go in to wait for my brother inside we see she is indeed right. We talk to a group who have been faxed with a list of half decent Luton pubs - I tell them that the other two listed pubs are no nearer the ground than where they're at and not to bother going for a drink at the pubs near Kenilworth Road anyway. When we try and talk football they blast my downbeat attitude towards my club (having not had a good season for a number of years) and tell me that over the last 20 years we've been lucky. We've sunk to the level of the perennial downtrodden now folks. Burnley fans feel it worse than most, with the success of their hated rivals Blackburn.

To the tune of the summer Euro96 hit "Football's coming home" they sang of Alan Shearer, the Geordie striker sold by Blackburn to Newcastle for £15m after top scoring for England in the competition, "Shearer's f***ed off home". A good away day for those fans as Luton proved they could adapt to a (much) lower standard of football and stay on losing ways. Blackburn lost at home. Watford won away.

Score: 1-2. Town scorer – Thorpe
Attendance: 7,064

20/8/96: League Cup First Round
Luton Town v Bristol Rovers

Glory night...(?) Michael had, as usual, faffed about (admirably) over ticket arrangements - the post-away fan ban procedures at Luton still make it more than a little difficult to see a game which is only going to attract 3000 people anyway. I asked him to get tickets in "the Kenny" - the Kenilworth Road stand - which affords a much better view than that from our season ticket seats from which a stanchion pillar completely obliterates the goal at the Kenilworth end. We'll be doing a lot of leaning back and forth this year.

Martin comes along and Andy and Simon don't. But Andy, living next door, comes down the pub beforehand. It's amazingly quiet there for a mid-week match. Only three or four of the regular "Mad as a Hatter" boys show and, for this match, there are just two Rovers fans (boyfriend and girlfriend dressed up in away shirts) -

making their presence felt via the jukebox. I make out my "fantasy Luton Town seven" team and give it to Keith (it's the fanzine's own fantasy football and could prove too complicated for its own good). Martin introduces himself to Michael and Chris and we talk pop....it's a fair discussion - I reckon Pulp are poor and Paul Weller is ace, they disagree (and they, eventually, win the argument).

The first half of ther match is terrible - before the penalty at the stroke of time - the second half is really quite good. Bristol Rovers are in our league - if we can beat teams like this then we'll be alright......but then Bristol Rovers might turn out to be the worst team in the country.

Afterwards I ring Claire, who has good news on the job front (she's getting paid more than me now, for a six day week at a cafe), and with Martin we go and have a curry. It's too hot and too expensive, but it's been a good night.

It was once worked out that the performance of a local football team directly affects the performance of local industry. A factory on the Monday after a win will work better than after a loss etc. Whether that theory can still be measured at Vauxhall motors is questionable. The percentage of Town fans must have receded, along with the workforce, over the years - and those die-hard Hatters must surely be used to it all by now. A much clearer indication that this theory still holds true would be in the attitude to children at school, up and down the country, on a Monday morning after Man Utd have lost. It's quite embarrassing the effect that Luton's results have on my attitude to work. Quite simply when they lose I'm liable to sulk a lot - when they win I'm walking around the office singing.......and probably working better too (more likely to offer to make the tea anyway). This is only an early stage win in a competition much degraded over the years, but I can still wear a cheesy grin the day after.

Score: 3-0. Town scorers - Thorpe (p), Grant, Oldfield
Attendance: 2,643

24/8/96: Brentford v Luton Town

The plan is that I'm to meet Martin, Mick and Andrew in London. We have a drink, go to the match, then meet Claire off the train from St. Albans where she works. In the evening there is a Northern Soul

Club. Andy and Max are going to see Steve in Weston-Super-Mare so they can't come. The plans are laid on Friday night. But Claire is none too confident about travelling on the train alone....she can't work out an underground map.....and I don't want to go to either the football match or the night out and not the other. It's All or Nothing, as The Small Faces sang, for me.

It ends up as Nothing and I tell my brother, Mick and Michael (which would've required another planned rendezvous) to "give them a cheer for me". Obviously they didn't cheer loud enough and the match was lost after we'd been ahead twice.

It turns out that Andrew, Mick and Martin didn't get to the match; getting within five miles of the ground before the lack of a taxi foiled their plans. So they went back to the pub instead. Had I been there I'd more than likely have ruined the day by adamantly making my, and their, way to the game.

Score: 3-2. Town scorers - Thorpe (pen), Hughes
Attendance: 5,409

27/8/96: Bristol City v Luton Town

No chance - of my going or of the Town winning. I was watching the episode of The Prisoner where they almost fool him by bringing in an exact double ("The Schizoid Man" its called), but switched it off; I've seen it all before. I've seen Luton thrashed too. It's not as painful when it's only via wincing glimpses of the latest score through Teletext. Radio 5 mentioned Luton were down to 10 men and I flicked on the text again to find out if it was that hotheaded idiot Hughes again. No - it was Tony Thorpe, for violent conduct. So, probably our best player is a suspension glutton too. Oh good.
Score: 5-0
Attendance: 7,028

31/8/96: Luton Town v Rotherham United

The teams in this division are so *bleedin' awful* but Luton Town have managed to adapt to the change in quality and have seemingly stepped down a gear following last year's relegation campaign. Rotherham were particularly dour......but at least we beat them.

Good point - Keith and the Mad as a Hatter boys have their new 1973 away shirt on sale. Which he sells down the pub (away supporter count - one apparently, I didn't see him) like hot cakes.

Bad point - The fact that our seats are so terrible. A stanchion post totally obliterates the Kenilworth Road goal - so we end up not seeing Mitchell Thomas's matchwinner until Anglia News on Monday. Luckily we're not stupid - we join in the celebrations knowing, by crowd reaction alone, that we'd won more than a corner. Even so Andy, who chose the seats, should really be sued by the rest of us.

Score: 1-0. Town scorer – Thomas
Attendance: 5,112

SEPTEMBER

4/9/96: Coca-Cola Cup, 1st Round 2nd Leg
Bristol Rovers v Luton Town

League/Fizzypop Cup. First look at Teletext is appalling - 2-0 down
after 20 minutes (with a 3-0 first leg lead). It seems we're pretty
likely to go out but when I find out that Oldfield has made it 2-1. I sit
and watch the screen in our bedroom for an inordinately long time
expecting the score to suddenly flash to 4-1. In fact I watched until
the clock in the corner showed the match should surely be over, at
which time I thought the sad evening I had made myself could be
made even more pathetic if I whistled impatiently at the telly until
"Result" appeared by the scoreline. Thankfully I didn't sink quite that
low.

A pattern is emerging here right? Author doesn't go to away
games - especially evening matches (in Bristol). Well, at the moment
results are poor and the football is usually terrible. If, later on in the
year/my life, we're pushing for promotion then I'll be straining at the
leash to follow the rip-roaring Hatters. (*7/9/96*).
Score: 2-1 (2-4 on aggregate). Town scorer - Oldfield
Attendance: 2,320

6/9/86: Great Expectations/Having a word with oneself
Chelsea v Luton Town

1986 *Not surprisingly, if you've ever been to Kenilworth Road, playing in the top flight (or the second flight, in some cases even the third flight) meant that away games usually presented the chance to see a good ground. There were some grounds, even in the pre-Taylor Report eighties, which were very impressive. Villa Park, with the massive Holte End terrace was one. Highbury another (even if the Clock End was no fun in the rain). White Hart Lane used to be an excellent football ground. However, with one's idea of a football ground created through Match of the Day pictures, which always made grounds look huge, there was often an initial disappointment when entering a new, but famous, ground for the first time. Anfield was somewhat smaller than I had thought, the Kop not nearly as loud, even for the visit of Luton, as the media had led me to expect. Goodison's three tiered stand was mightily impressive, but you needed a periscope to view play from the away end. Old Trafford, circa `86, seemed a charmless concrete "hate bowl".*

Maybe the only ground where a sense of enormity immediately struck me was Stamford Bridge. The "new" stand stood out, but the grandeur of the stadium was in the steep terraces and ramshackle West stand that made up the rest of the ground. It was plain to see how, in days gone by, tens of thousands of fans could easily have been accommodated in Stamford Bridge. It was, as I said at the time, vast. I don't know, other than by TV pictures, what it's like now. It looks to be more enclosed.

Old Trafford (see 18/10/86) wasn't a pleasant place to visit. At Chelsea the away support in the eighties was lucky that the Chelsea fans were far away in "the shed" and the West stand. Even so, there were plenty there who were up for baying at the away supporters, even at such a distance, even against Luton Town. It wasn't somewhere where it was advisable to wear your colours outside; although, as an away fan, I found it didn't have the menace of the walk back to Upton Park tube station.

This was my first visit to Stamford Bridge and the Town won 3-1 after being 1-0 down to a Kerry Dixon goal. Two goals from Mick Newell, one from Steiney. This was the season after Pleat left. He was replaced by the promotion of John Moore, the big honest Scottish ex-defender, who loved (and loves) working with the players but hated the administration side of the job. Admittedly Pleat had left the Town with a good squad (even after he stole Mitchell Thomas back for Spurs) but Moore introduced a defensive resolve lacking in Pleat's cavalier teams. Under John Moore, although he was only manager for one season, Luton Town finished 7th in the First Division - our best placed finish ever.

It was a great result at Chelsea although my day was a little bit spoilt, not by the Chelsea fans, but by my own brother Simon. Newell had just scored his second or third goal and I was gleefully leaping around a terrace only lightly populated by the travelling support. Perhaps my celebrations were somewhat more animated than those of my fellow Town fan, because my brother (who had given up the leapin' and had settled back into hearty applause), called me to one side and requested I "have a word with yourself " and consider whether my post goal frenzy was maybe a touch over played. The little git. Being told to calm down, by your younger brother, isn't something you want to happen. Suitably chastised, I spent much of the rest of the game in a sulk. (4/10/86).

Score: 1-3.   Town scorers - Newell (2) Brian Stein
Attendance: 13,040

7/9/96: Wycombe Wanderers v Luton Town

First away game I've been to this season - and the first away win. A tidy little ground, a large (1500 strong) Town following and something to bloody cheer about for a change. The Wycombe fans - who have seen their club progress from non-league obscurity to full league status, and promotion in that - are keen to make new rivals (as their old, stunted, adversaries don't play with them anymore). Their small knot of chanting fans - one of whom has a drum - apparently "Hate Watford". The Loves. Of course they only have the one song at the moment (and not many of their fans seem to want to join in) but they might have picked up a few new ones from the Luton end. Indeed, the Town fans are singing the new "Cheer up Graham Taylor" song (from the Monkees' "Daydream Believer" via Sunderland fan's

"Cheer up Peter Reid"). Whether or not the song will catch on in time for the October derby is questionable - the sentiments are popular enough but the name "Graham Taylor" just has one too many syllables.

Town play well although need to sort out the attack. David Oldfield scores during a goalmouth scramble in the second half. Ray Wilkins plays, square balls aplenty, for Wycombe after leaving QPR earlier in the week. One of the linesmen is a lady. We stand up at pitchside for the game, because we found we could, without looking for our £12 seats.

Michael, Martin and myself met up with Mick Sheridan and Paul O'Mally at the ground. They're extremely good blokes and (Mick and Martin in particular) friends. But when three or four of them get together then they become an extraordinary clique. The pace and pitch of their humour is sometimes difficult to keep up with and understand - and if you do see the joke then it's hard to find it as funny as they do or to offer anything to their conversation. Their bond is amazingly strong, they will talk to each other about anything......Thurlow's gonads, we were reliably informed, resemble two large grey and red pomegranates. Each has a seemingly endless supply of anecdotes, involving the others, to tell (we once suggested Mick bought out a collection of books entitled "The time that Me and Thurlow..." or "Me and Mally..." or "Me and Kieron..." etc).

I went to school with all three but, though I was quite friendly with Mick in the 6th form when all his other pals had deserted him, really got to be friends with them during the time we all ended up touring with my brothers band Thrilled Skinny between '88-92. Anecdotes number 16024 to 16330.

Whether it is a result of a Catholic upbringing, a warped sense of humour or the fact that they're probably quite a bit cleverer than me, I miss the closeness of the friendship they've got. With the best friends I've got - the four members of Thrilled Skinny (Andy Whiting, Andrew my brother, Simon Bishop, Steve Whiting), my brother Simon, Saul Branston, Martin and Mick - we have a more distant, C of E type relationship.. We don't hug each other on meeting, probably because of deep-rooted homophobia, but we never argue about whose round it is or whether it's OK to kip over. And we have a laugh, when we see each other (I haven't seen Simon B for ages) and have our own line in anecdotes - almost all of which revolve around the days touring around Britain and Germany in a VW Camper van or Ford Transit. Still, hey, I love those guys.

Score: 0-1.   Town scorer – Oldfield
Attendance: 6,471

8/9/90 TOWN Magazine Launch
Luton Town v Leeds United

1990

Even though we'd only been back in the fold for a few games, Steve and I decided that it would be a good idea to put a fanzine together. Steve had been writing his own (decidedly strange) fanzine, "Clod", for a year or so and I had been doing the Luton News column for a good few months, plus the Thrilled Skinny fans' club mag. And we'd both got a wealth of experience (albeit dated, but nostalgia was in) in being fans of the Hatters.

We had three plans at the outset. Firstly, we saw the fanzine movement as an opportunity to get rich quick – especially if we charged £1 a go. Secondly, because we charged twice as much as the other fanzines ("Mad as a Hatter" and "Depleated" at the time) we would make our mag twice as good as the the the competition. Thirdly, if point two was a bit dodgey, we'd have gimmicks. Issue one came out with a "Jimmy Ryan's orange, blue and white army" badge on. Issue two had a No Frills white on black "Luton Town FC" badge. Another issue offered a free red card to help the fans advise the ref after tackles on Phil Gray. (Ours was, to the best of my knowledge, the first red card for fans – it has been copied loads of times since by fans on "sack the board" campaigns). Other gimmicks included a free tea bag, a free balloon with the message "Everyone loves Luton Town FC" on (the return of away fans had, by our reckoning, turned the tables to make LTFC the most popular club in the League) and a draw to win a bottle of Chivas Regal.

PG TIPS with Phil 'Earl' Gray

Always the ones to carry on joke onto another issue. In conjunction with the LTFC refreshment bars* TOWN magazine present YOU the fan with just what you want at half-time. Phil 'the Earl' Gray, the man for whom tea is not just a drink - it's a way of life presents you with the tea so tasty you'll be as happy as a bloody chimp. As Phil says "It's the taste".

Directions - Take the tea-bag out of the magazine carefully. At half-time wander to your nearest refreshment kiosk. Ask the nice lady/gent serving for a cup, some hot water, milk, sugar (if desired) and some sort of stirring implement. If lucky thank the lady/gent warmly. If told "piss off you cheeky bugger" don't despair, simply take the tea-bag home and enjoy the Beverage there whilst watching Brucie on the television.

Get the L-U-T-ON

mmmm aaa

* NOT REALLY.

Tea Bag give-away from TOWN 7
featuring "High Class Wit"

Issue 1 came out at the Town's match against Leeds United. It was the third match of the last season of the away fan ban, so we didn't expect (or get) any trouble from Leeds fans. Indeed, we didn't get any hassle the season afterwards when TOWN 7 came out on the same fixture the next, away fan welcoming, season. What we did get, whilst trying to sell TOWN 1, was hassle from the police. Whilst I was at the corner of Oak Road and Beech Hill path a young copper walked up to me, not saying anything whilst I was selling but staring straight at the side of my head from a distance of about three inches.

Once I'd served the customer (my last of the day as it turned out), the policeman asked me whether I "had a permit". The short conversation which followed, ended in my being taken to meet the officer in charge and, having rounded up the rest of the sales team, being given an overlong lecture on the potential dangers of our publication being racist, pornographic, blasphemous and/or highly flammable – and that we'd need permission from the council to sell *our wares on the streets of Luton anyway. On the condition that we stopped selling, and gave gratis copies to all the coppers hanging around like kids after free sweets , he let us go free.*

Score 1-0. Town scorer – Black.
Attendance 10185.

At the next match, armed with a photocopied notification that the council effectively couldn't give a damn what we sold on the streets, we started vending again – and we enjoyed a healthy relationship with the police from then on. I sold a copy of TOWN 2 to Nigel Kennedy at the Aston Villa match that season. He was with Brix Smith of The Fall – I made a point of appearing to recognise her and not him.

TOWN mag lasted 7 or 8 issues after Steve decided to move on. Simon and I did another copy – but by then we'd run out of ideas. Since then I've written, on average, an article every other issue, for those fine fellows at Mad as a Hatter fanzine. (11/5/91)

NEXT PAGE: KENILWORTH THE CAT (TOWN 7)

A mainstay of TOWN mag was the further adventures of Kenilworth the Cat who was the official mascot, along with Rowdy Rat, of the Hatters during the late 80's. He and Rowdy used to join the players in the kick-in in those days – but the costume heads were too heavy and the bloke inside had to hold the head up....which looked a little strange.

8/9/96: I'm sent, via The Luton News, four cans of a new beer from America (brewed under licence etc, etc,) by some promotion agency. All I've ever written in the paper about beer is sarcasm about town centre pubs turning kitsch-Irish overnight, but this is what I want. Free booze. Makes doing the column all worth while.

10/9/96: Luton Town v Gillingham

A fine passing display by the Town leads to a 2-0 lead (through Bontcho and Oldfield) but a Gillingham goal with ten minutes to go means a frantic last few minutes. Our boys do tend to panic. Gillingham have a small, but vociferous, following. From what I could catch of their songs they are A) a little bit racist and B) fancy themselves as rough tough football hooligan types. Watch out Millwall fans - me reckons they'll be looking to skirmish outside the New Den.

They sing "Will you come to Gillingham" (on Boxing Day) - we all shout "Nooooo" and other Town fans sing "Where the f*** is Gillingham?" (which, fascinatingly, really annoys several Gillingham fans). One of my all-time favourite bands, The Prisoners, came from Chatham and I know the area. In fact there's an area to the south of Gillingham (or maybe within, my local knowledge isn't that good) called Luton. So a few of those Gillingham fans, one imagines, must live and work in Luton. Funny eh? No?

Ex-Watford captain Andy Hessanthaler is booed quite a bit, although I've seen the fans give harder times. So, Luton win at home but - dagnabbit - Watford win 3-2 at Notts County and are now.....well, above us anyway.

Score: 2-1. Town scorers - Guentchev & Oldfield
Attendance: 5,171

14/9/91 The return of Micky Harford
Luton Town v Oldham Athletic

1991 *The sacking of Jimmy Ryan at the end of the 90/91 season, in favour of David Pleat (aka Judas '86), certainly left a bad taste in the mouth. Pleat succeeded, at least in part, to get the fans onside by signing up a couple of old favourites – Micky Harford and Brian Stein, the shooting stars of the 80s, charged with leading the Hatters attack of the 90s. If the fact that Steiney had lost almost all of his (never spectacular) pace was noticeable, it was countered by evidence that big Mick could still put himself a bit. In any case both players, unlike the manager, could do no wrong in the eyes of the fans.*

Typically Mick Harford made his mark in his very first match back, The Town were losing 1- 0, and playing appallingly, against newly promoted Oldham when he scored a simple tap in with about five or six minutes left. Hardly a vintage Harford goal, but the crowd went wild anyway.

And then, in injury time, he won the ball in the area and, with his back to goal, sent a spectacular overhead kick searing into the back of the net. Surely one of the best goals he ever scored for Luton Town – and the crowd went bananas. Oh yes, Micky Harford was back.

The feeling of optimism that his return (and especially that match) inspired was slow to melt away, but the fact remains that neither he (with 12 goals in 29 games), Stein (a sad 3 goals in 39 games), or "The Old Master" David Pleat could save Luton Town from relegation at the end of the season. (2/5/92)

Score 2-1. Town scorer – Harford (2).
Attendance 9,005.

14/9/96: Luton Town v Chesterfield

I've seen Luton beat all the big Clubs at Kenilworth Road - Man Utd, Liverpool, Spurs, Arsenal. The lot. It's surely come to something getting beaten by Chesterfield at home. Town supporters in the late

`50's and early `60's must have felt the same as the club plunged from the First to the Fourth Division.

Luton return to form, muscled out of it by a team armed with a big boot and a modicum of interest. Because of the (gaping) gaps in the crowd Andy, Slim and Chris move up a few seats to get a better view - their places are taken by two longhaired heavy metal types. Cut off from most of my pals I sit with Michael, who is in poor form and shouts "GET IT ON THE BLOODY FLOOR LUTON" (and pleas to that effect) again and again and again. After the game one Town supporter is giving all the Luton players grief in turn as they go up the tunnel (which our seats are next to). Looking around I see it is Andy, who is uncharacteristically giving stick aplenty, especially to Julian James and with particular regard to his tenuous links with Watford FC. According to what we heard in the pub, James' Dad is a steward at Vicarage Road and Julian himself has apparently been seen kicking a football about wearing a Watford shirt. "JAMES - YOU WATFORD SCUMMER" is Andy's candid opinion.

The few Chesterfield fans who are there are also a racist bunch - following up a "Paki" song with the hilarious "Let's all have a curry".

It could be that the paranoia of supporting a lower league club manifests itself through racism and/or hooliganism among a higher proportion of supporters than you'd normally expect. Racism in football is so unfashionable that most fans won't touch it with a bargepole (even the racists, as a minority group, don't want to appear silly). However, when an individual club is also unfashionable it would be quite easy for NF or BNP reps to make quite an impression within their fanbase. Then they turn up at England matches and everyone wonders where they come from.

As a club with aspirations (to build Jerusalem off junction 10 of the M1) Luton hasn't yet fallen foul of racists to a great degree - although just how long that will continue is questionable, especially if the Kohlerdome plans are chucked out.

Score: 0-1
Attendance: 5,292

Contrary to what some London clubs' supporters believe, Luton is very much urban and its townsfolk are no country hicks from the sticks. As if to disprove this theory Andy, Max, Claire and myself went to a Northern Soul night at the Jazz Bistro in London on Saturday to meet my brother Andy and our old mate Saul Branston, believing that we would be OK to leave at 2.30am because the trains ran to Luton all night.... God knows where I picked up that idea. After wasting time and money on taxi-cabs going to closed up stations (having ignored my brother's advice that "you won't get home") we ended up spending yet more on taxis to Andy's and Saul's houses. And had to buy another ticket to Luton on Sunday. And our table were accused of smoking pot in the club, when we weren't (we got an apology later). And it wasn't Northern Soul.

OK - so we passed pretty much as bumpkins......but there are loads of people in town who really are cool - and go to raves and that......and support Spurs. (*17/9/96*).

15/9/92: The Devil's own.
Anglo-Italian Cup First Round. Watford v Luton Town

1992 *Gnash. Perhaps the only perceived good thing about being relegated to First Division (post Premier League), was the resumption of traditional hostilities towards Watford. The Luton/Watford rivalry had been quite intense up until the time of Luton's away fan ban - but throughout both clubs' forays into the top flight there was too much similarity between our plight (that of little club out of depth) for most rival fans to subscribe wholeheartedly to the whole hatred bit. The derbies in the First Division had an edge - but more than anything they presented, for both teams, a chance to get points against one of the division's weaker clubs. When Watford eventually got relegated from the old First Division, they did so with barely a whimper at the end of the same season that Luton gloriously won the Littlewoods Cup. It was dereliction of duty on the part of Luton fans, we hardly turned a hair when we should have been heartily mocking.....*

Anyway, whereas the "M1 derby" is small fry in the top flight - it's a passionate, if lowly attended, rivalry well suited to the Second division.

And so we looked back and remembered (or imagined) just how much we hated those 'orrible 'ornets. The first match against the old enemy was a regional tie in the atrocious Anglo-Italian Cup. But the match served its purpose. It was still an opportunity to go back to the hated Vicarage Road. The crowd was small (though at over 5000, bigger than the vast majority of the competition's gates) but the atmosphere was electric..... and not very pleasant.

It's not at all a healthy thing to walk up to a football ground, grimacing with self induced hatred for the place, but it seemed appropriate at the time. There is a strange air of disquiet on the streets around the Vicarage Road allotments on derby days - and especially nights. It's not necessarily a violent thing - I've never felt the need to hit a Watford fan, although polite conversation about the game never seems very appealing either - but both sets of fans have enormous interest in winning (or, more importantly not losing) a match against the enemy. This game was under floodlights and, as I say, was particularly charged.

When the Watford team ran onto the pitch, amidst ear piercing catcalls from the Luton end, I felt a mixture of joy and disgust. Disgust as they appeared, dressed up in their hideous yellow, red and black kits. Blood, coal and custard. Watford, the team of the devil. It's the same sort of abhorrence, albeit concentrated and uglier, with which kids greet the pantomime villain. The joy was that, even at this lower level, football would still mean something.

The game was the typical furious, no quarter given, type affair which - if it wasn't for the inherent hype - would hold nobody's attention.

The same feeling of nastiness at the derby matches has continued, to a certain extent. I don't like it. I try these days to keep the bile of hatred in check (there is, in truth, not that much to hate about Watford - but we manage); mentally stepping back sometimes to review the situation and ask myself if the barking of "SCUM SCUM SCUM SCUM" at some spotty kid taking a Watford throw-in nearby is actually doing my team any good.

Probably not.

But that night at Watford it didn't matter. It was a 'hate fest'. By the end of the night my throat was hoarse and I had a splitting headache. Watford's fault.

Score: 0 - 0
Attendance: 5,197

With recognition to fervent Watford fans/ex thugs (they've given it up in the interests of world peace) Doug and Dinsdale Piranha's hooliebook "Bad boys, Testosterone on the terraces", which gives a lists of things that Watford fans would *never* do/allow in their hatred of Luton; there follows a list of things that Luton fans would NEVER do/allow:-

1. We would *never* allow an ex-Watford player to play for Luton.....until one signs in the future. Doug and Dinsdale make a similar claim for Watford fans but, since their first book came out at least two ex-Town players (Kerry Dixon and current keeper Alec Chamberlain) have signed for the Horns.

2. We *never* buy records by Elton John or George Michael.

3. Ginger Spice, because she's a Watford fan, is Scum Spice in Luton. We would NEVER allow her scarves and hats in our homes during a tempestuous love affair.

4. We *never* drink Benskins ale.

5. We NEVER *never* pass up the chance to blame England's failure to qualify for the World Cup in '94 not only on Graham Taylor, but also on the club with which he made his name with appalling kick and run tactics.

6. On Microsoft Windows there's a colour scheme called "Hotdog Stand"; a garish mix of yellow, black and red. Luton fans would *never* use Hotdog Stand on their PCs.

7. We *never* allow our wives and girlfriends to shop at the Harlequin Centre in Watford, although on the odd occasion when they do want to go they don't tend to ask our permission. *(20/2/94).*

17/9/96: Coca-Cola Cup 2nd round, 1st leg
Luton Town v Derby County

On Saturday, after the Chesterfield game, we all said that we wouldn't bother going to the cup game. The season ticket doesn't cover cup games and we'd have had to pay - but there were other reasons. First and foremost, Steve Whiting was in town prior to moving to Cheltenham to start a degree in painting. Andy and Max were jetting off to bloody Florida on Friday, so Tuesday was one of the only nights we could get together for a drink. Secondly, we thought we might get beat - if not on the night almost certainly over two legs.

But crucially it was the money thing. I phoned Michael on the day and he decided that, if the price was right, we'd be prepared to go for the £7.50 cheapest seats. Then I found out from the club that the cheapest seats were £8. The extra 50p was the straw that broke the camel's back. Worse still was the news that the second leg (which would be good to go to if the Town had a half decent lead to defend) would be £18 for away fans.

One line of conversation in the pub was that, if Luton Town had retained top flight status, we would not be able to see them anymore. Football clubs make as much money as they can on the loyalty of the fans, but every individual has a financial limit. There was a time, not very long ago, when fans didn't think about the money spent watching their team - like a commodity it was just something you did. As prices go up (and, in Luton's case, the quality goes down) there comes a point when you decide that there are other things, better things, to do with your money - that your Club, god bless 'em, are taking the piss.

In the case of this match it was Derby County, not Luton Town, who priced us out of the market. If the option of attending both matches is no longer open (the second leg, of course, is the real match) then why bother going to the first? The awful gate figure, for what should have been a prestigious cup tie, and a notable scalp, seemed to suggest we weren't the only ones disillusioned.

Score: 1-0. Town scorer – James
Attendance: 4,459

21/9/96: Bury 0 Luton Town 0

In the pub on Friday night, at last orders or thereabouts, Ian (the Scotsman) asks if I want to go to Bury and share the petrol costs. Having never been to Bury before, and being perverse enough that that sort of thing matters ("ground required" as the fanzine boys say), I would have been tempted - especially being quite drunk. I have also long suffered under the illusion that snap decisions on Friday nights about going to see Luton away (preferably up in the grim North) the next day make me something of a flamboyant character, and a hit with the chicks. With scant evidence that this has ever been the case one wonders why my sub-conscious is still so turned on by the idea.

Luckily, for my nerves (in relation to Ian's driving) and my pocket, I have an excuse - I'm going, with a group of workmates, to race go-karts at Silverstone that evening. So can't go to Bury. Listen out for the Town score on the radio. There is none.

The go-karting was a disaster. I had previously been on go-karts at the little two corner circuit next to the Palace Pier in Brighton. On our last visit I showed off to great effect by passing Claire and nudging Andy out of the way. At Silverstone it was different. This track, nothing to do with the Grand Prix circuit - but you do go through the main gates (and get to tell people you've raced at Silverstone), wasn't brilliant but it was certainly more challenging than the one at Brighton. It quickly became apparent that, being something of a fat git, my weight was going to be a handicap. There were teams of bloody hot-shots, equipped with their own personalised helmets, cheering on their team-mates from the sidelines when they weren't racing, generally taking it all very seriously. Six races each, starting at every one of the six grid positions, I came in last in all but two of my races (including the one I started in pole......last place by the end of lap one). I counted it a moral victory that, over six four lap races, I was never lapped.

The rest of our team weren't brilliant, but our coming last overall must have been largely down to me. We laughed about it afterwards. But not much. On Monday at work it seemed that Bill and Simon, from my team, weren't speaking to me. Bill agreed that my weight had something to do with my performance but added that you also need some amount of skill to race a go-kart.

Well sod them, sod the bloke Russ who had "Russ" painted on the back of his helmet and won just about all his races, sod soddin' Silverstone and sod bloody Frank Williams - I don't want the bloody job.

25/9/96: Coca-Cola Cup, 2nd round 2nd leg
Derby County v Luton Town

What of the chances of this match being the highpoint of the season after I vowed (see 17/9) not to attend. Missed this match because of the cost. I'm skint and wouldn't have paid £18 if I did have the money. Instead I went bowling with workmates.......this going out with workmates thing is getting to be a trend as well isn't it? You'll get to the vital Christmas fixtures in this book and I'll be going on about the hi-jinks of our traditional office "do" (it's traditionally disappointing - talking shop is shunned but, once it's clear none of the women want to embark on an affair, it's often very dull). Anyway, bowling was OK. Got two strikes....

The match, I found out much later, was something of a stormer too. Grant scoring first, Derby score two, then Thorpe finishes Derby off. Saw the match report on Sky - Luton playing in the bloody horrible yellow third strip.....I don't know if I could cheer them heartily on when they're wearing Watford colours. The sound effects from the match suggest that more than a couple of Town fans made the trip - Hats off to these, the most loyal supporters.

Score: 2-2. Town scorers – Grant, Thorpe
Attendance: 13,569

28/9/96: Luton Town v Blackpool

The new fanzine is out! So, when the fanzine sellers go fanzine selling, the Hatters fans in the pub are soon greatly outnumbered by their Blackpool counterparts. However, they prove to be a much more amicable bunch than we've had so far this year (Burnley fans were OK).

Inside the pub it was getting to the critical point when a group of the Blackpool fans would get a donkey ride business going (ho ho, a bit of regionalist "humour", hope it doesn't offend. I love Blackpool) but, when we got to the ground, there was only really a small away following. They must have all gone to just the one public house before the match.

Match was alright. Luton should have won by more and the referee denied both teams clear penalties (an obvious Blackpool handball in the first half, a blatant foul by Feuer in the second). A victory made all the better for Watford having lost at Shrewsbury.

Score: 1-0. Town scorer - Grant
Attendance: 5,785

OCTOBER

1/10/96: The away match at Wrexham is called off because of Welsh international call ups (from Wrexham, not Luton). As if I was planning to go to the match anyway.... On the radio is a drab first division match and news that Brighton fans hold pitch invasions in protest against their apparently terrible chairman. There is a BBC reporting team on the spot who are full of distaste and admonishment at the (comparatively small scale and peaceful by the sound of it) actions of the fans. "There must be another way" adds Alan Brazil.... Another example of the strange relationship between football fans and the media. The "other way", that Alan Brazil talks about, might be to write letters to the local press and to sign petitions. Neither will attract the national media. However, if the word is that the fans are going to break the law then the press will be there and the fans will get the exposure they wanted. Why else would a BBC team be at a lowly Third Division match?

Over the past few years the BBC has been instrumental in changing media attitude towards football supporters, we're now no longer necessarily thought of as morons - they've even successfully promoted the laddish (non-aggressive) side of being a football supporter. However, the media in general still likes to flirt with the stereotypical yob and squirms with uncomfortable glee every time there is a new hooligan tale to tell. (*5/10/96*).

4/10/86: Pleat Hatred
Tottenham Hotspur v Luton Town

A match of little importance to the home fans but, as it was the first Luton/Spurs game since David Pleat did a run for the money, of immense importance to the big Luton following. I

1986 *was pretty unhappy about Pleat's move, but even I was struck by the vehemence when Pleat came out before the match to smile and wave in the centre circle with his new signing.*

I remember it was a match that the Luton team seemed determined not to lose, whilst the Spurs fans seemed genuinely taken aback and bemused by the noise, passion and downright hatred that the Town following aimed towards the home dugout.

In retrospect it seems that Luton fans were whipped up in the personal argument between our then chairman, the infamous David Evans, and David Pleat. Evans made sure that Pleat left Kenilworth Road, for the more illustrious job, on bad terms - telling any hack prepared to listen how disgusted he, the club and the fans were by Pleat's appalling show of disloyalty. When Pleat left all he took was Mitchell Thomas - David Evans' parting gesture was to sell the ground.

But, at the time, we were convinced that it was Pleat who was enemy number one. The Town won the Kenilworth Road fixture 3-1; and many Town supporters, myself included, delighted (along with our Arsenal counterparts) at Pleat's dramatic fall from grace and eventual resignation following seedy revelations in The Sun. (18/10/86)

Score: 0-0
Attendance: 22,738

5/10/85: Record denied
Luton Town v Manchester United

The start of the '85/86 season saw an amazing run from Manchester Utd who, up until October, had won each and every one of their games. This fact meant that they had a

1985 *chance to beat the all time winning start record held by Spurs since the days of Jimmy Greaves.*

A win at Luton would be the record equaliser and, even though it was on the Kenilworth Road plastic, United were expected to roll on. A big crowd of over seventeen thousand was made up of a packed Kenilworth Road end – full of Man Utd fans hoping to witness history in the making, and Hatters fans throughout the rest of the ground hoping that our lads could upset the form book.

The first half was a tense affair, but goal less – which, given the situation, suited us down to the ground. Early in the second half a shot by Mark Hughes took a horrendous deflection and ballooned over Sealey and into the Oak Road goal. It was, as I remember it, very much like, and as welcome as, the opening goal for West Germany in the 1990 World Cup Semi-Final. Cue scenes of wild excitement on the Kenilworth Road terrace – full of delirious Man U fans, who probably expected Luton to follow the script and promptly cave in.

The flood gates, gloriously, stayed very closed and Luton came roaring back into the game. It was no surprise when Steiney scored a well earned equaliser – the cue for equally animated scenes on the packed Oak Road terrace.

To this day I can't really see how the score stayed at 1-1, but Manchester United managed to salvage a point after an amazing open goal miss by Paul "Leroy" Elliott (nicknamed after the kid from "Fame"). All he needed was to side foot it in.... He didn't, and, in the end, it didn't really matter.

*Its was, perhaps, a hollow victory – but a victory for the underdog all the same. The form book, the media and thousands of Man Utd fans had wanted the Hatters to lose – but Luton Town heroically refused to comply. "You can stick your f****** record up your arse" we were delighted to sing.*

A good day, and the long running Manchester United joke was especially funny that year when, even after such a good start, they once again failed to win the title. (19/10/85).

Score: 1-1. Town scorer - Brian Stein
Attendance: 17,454

5/10/96: Luton Town v Walsall

Missing key players Grant and Oldfield - this convincing win wasn't as well played by the Town as the Blackpool match. Feuer kept us in it in the first half before Thorpe put the Town ahead right at the end of the first half. The second half was all Luton - if I remember right.

The Walsall fans were quite entertaining. They had quite a wide repertoire of songs (including Minnie the Moocher, which was novel but not altogether successful) which could have been brought out on record - possibly on the Pickwick label.

They spoilt it rather with the first rendition of "You're going to get your f***ing heads kicked in" I've heard in over ten years. Extraordinary. Thankfully the song was laughed at by most Luton fans. The charge toward the Luton fans that followed was even funnier. The offending Walsall fans congregated in a small group at the top of the Oak Road terrace, by the exits. They attempted to surge threateningly toward the Luton fans but, beaten back by ridicule, most of them simply popped out of the ground instead. In the end we witnessed the terrifying spectacle of a sole Saddlers fan attempting a malicious crowd surge. He body-popped his way for a few yards but, realising he was on his own, decided to cut his losses, stick his fingers up and walk out too. It was a lucky escape - although bars and a line of bemused policemen and stewards stood between him and the rival set of supporters - he was within twenty metres of swearing at the girl in the away end refreshment stand.

Score: 3-1. Town scorers - Thorpe, Showler, Fotiadis.
Attendance: 5,456

My girlfriend Claire has bought the guide to football league grounds. She was going to give it to me at Christmas but didn't want to wait. She is currently working at a shopping mall cafe in St. Albans and, through some of her workmates there, has been touched by the romance of the Luton/Watford rivalry. Bless her cotton socks, she is now calling Watford "Scum" and recounting to me stories she has heard at work about fights between the two sets of supporters. I tell her I'm not really interested in that sort of carry-on.... Even so, she is now keen to come to the Watford v Luton derby game. (*12/10/96*).

6/10/87: The long and winding road.....(sorry)
Littlewoods Cup, 2nd Round. Luton Town 4 (5) Wigan 2 (2)

1987 *It sounds like a lie, but in 1987/88 it was true, the Littlewoods (League) Cup run was more exciting for Town fans than the FA Cup run of the same year. There are a couple of good reasons for this. Firstly Luton Town, because of the away fan ban, had been chucked out of the competition before they started the previous year by the Football League (who were perfectly happy to let us play in their league competition week in, week out - but were cajoled by the other clubs to make a stand). In 87/88 Luton were allowed back, on the understanding that away fans would be let in, but David Evans made it clear that - rather than allow hordes of hooligans (i.e. away support) to descend on Luton - home games would, if a large away following was expected, be transferred to a neutral ground. That pronouncement meant that the 87/88 Littlewoods Cup run would, if nothing else, be interesting. In later stages of the cup, as Luton won through to the quarter final and then the semi-final, the FA Cup campaign really did seem like a bonus. There was the feeling, during the FA Cup ties, that, if we lost, as least we had the Littlewoods Cup to fall back on.*

Such considerations were certainly not on the mind during our first match at home against Wigan. The Town had won the first leg 1-0 with a Micky Weir goal (ace Scots player for the Town for just a few months until he got homesick for Hibs). Whatever division Wigan were in at the time, we were certainly not up for a Cup shock at the time. Even so, Wigan gave Luton quite a few problems before Micky Harford scored a hat-trick and the Town eventually won 4-2.

I can't remember anything about the game - other than it was cold. There was also the added excitement of an away following (albeit a titchy one) on the left side of the Kenilworth Road terrace. Their behaviour was very much as I remember a small, well behaved away following - failing in choice and endeavour to wreak havoc upon the town and its people. Still, with Luton safely into the next round, David Evans was to have his say.

And, yes, we got the big home tie we wanted in the next round. Coventry City. FA Cup holders at the time - but altogether unlikely to bring a massive, hooligan based, away support. Even so the match was switched to Craven Cottage, Fulham's ground. Then that plan

37

was scrapped - and the match was switched to Filbert Street Leicester.
(27/10/87).
Score: 4-2 (5-2 on aggregate). Town scorers - Harford (3)
McDonough.
Attendance: 4,240

12/10/96: Shrewsbury Town v Luton Town

Claire and I have decided to go to Prague in November. We went a
couple of years ago during the same time of year, loved the city, quite
liked to experience the cold. The only worry is that we really can't
afford it. Until after we come back away football, Watford aside, is
out until after November (I'll also more than likely miss the
"glamour" Coca-Cola game against Wimbledon at Selhurst Park -
although those are two more very good reasons to give the game a
miss). Shrewsbury was one game I'd have liked to have gone to and
one that I was trying, a few weeks ago, to get Michael to drive to. No
chance.   Radio 5 told of the first goal - then nothing until the
videprinter. What a great result......maybe things really are looking up
for LTFC....

Go to the pub later with Claire and, on the back of her new
found interest in the game and charged with optimism and booze,
make plans to go to Stockport on Tuesday night. Wake up on Sunday
morning and my cool financial head informs me that the beer has been
talking again - making commitments that my wallet can't possibly
keep.
Score: 0-3. Town scorers - Showler, Thomas, Grant
Attendance: 3,357

14/10/96: AC Meringue - Five-a-Side

Simon has got together a five-a-side team out of friends and
colleagues and Steve Nash (from Slip End) came up with the excellent
name.

Sadly our first couple of games aren't as good as we'd have
hoped. I know just about all the blokes - Michael is in the team,

Steve, Simon, Italian Tony and a bloke called Pete - who I don't really know but seems a good bloke. Martin has also expressed a bit of interest - and it should be a good laugh. Unfortunately Simon has also asked a bloke called Paul into the team because he's supposedly good in goal (apparently he "had a trial" at some club or other). No-one except Michael and Simon know Paul, but he is quickly stamping his self-imposed "authority" on the team - screaming foul mouthed orders - and generally pissing everyone off. And, as a Home Counties Newcastle supporter, taking the time to slag off Luton Town. On top of that, he refuses to go in goal for the first match (and flies about in the second, without actually stopping much).

AC Meringue lose 6-2 in the first game against "Boys with Attitude" ("they'll be jumped up little 14 year olds" Simon suggests. They turn out to be geezers in their late 20's). Then 3-0 in the second game against a bunch of arrogant swine all wearing '94/95 Newcastle away shirts.

Because of the complicated substitution rule I missed the first game and only played the second. Even though the halves are only 6 minutes long, it is amazing the difference that going to the gym has made to my fitness. None apparently. After twelve minutes I'm knackered, the worst moment of the match was when I foolishly tried to talk free kick technicalities with Steve during the match - only to find I didn't have nearly enough breath available for coherent discussion. Meanwhile Paul barked his orders, which I ignored, "Tim...**Tim**...are y' fookin' deaf or what?".

15/10/96: Stockport County v Luton Town
Another Teletext "funny". I switch on to see that Luton have taken the lead from Davis. But the time I've clenched me nashers and whispered "YES" through them, accompanied of course by instinctive fist clench, the equaliser flashes up. (*19/10/96*).
Score: 1-1. Town scorer - Davis
Attendance: 5,352

18/10/86 Small hope in the theatre of wet dreams.
Manchester United v Luton Town

 Looking back to our days in the old First Division it seems amazing that, season after season, I'd find it easy to dismiss the thought of following Luton Town to Old Trafford. I

1986 *suppose it's the hype surrounding Man Utd now I expect that, for those who can get tickets in the away section, the Man Utd day out is a highlight of other Premiership club fans.*

At the time I just knew there was little or no chance of getting a result, I knew how far Manchester was (and there are thousands of Man Utd fans who haven't got a clue, other than it's vaguely Northern). Bryan Robson would, as often as not, put his shoulder out in matches against Luton in Manchester, but it was too far to go to see that.

I've only been to Old Trafford the once, before it was the theatre of dreams, in the days when Man Utd's fruitless ambition for the championship title (which their fans seemed to believe was theirs by right) was the best and most enduring joke in the league. But we went up to Old Trafford because I thought that there was a chance of the Town getting a result.

We (my brothers and I) went up on one of the various travel club coaches. It wasn't long on the M6 before the Luton buses were outnumbered by the various national Man Utd supporters club buses from around the country. Man Utd have supporters all around the country, and abroad. Supporters willing to travel thousands of miles to see their heroes, and/or buy all the Man Utd merchandise they can. Meanwhile their local teams struggle to survive.

Man Utd were reasonably poor at the time, whilst the Town were just about at the peak of their form. But Man Utd, with their massive following, were able to influence all but the most unflappable referee (it's only natural, even if only subconsciously, referees want to please the crowd).

And Old Trafford, at the time, was the most intimidating ground I had been to (I understand it has changed now, to corporate entertainment and kids' painted faces). It was also, despite its impressive scale, an ugly stadium. Its three symmetrical sides making up an unattractive concrete bowl. The intimidation factor was brought about by the fact that the away section, for such a small following as Luton Town, was surrounded to the left, right and rear by home sections - filled with Man U's "have a go heroes". We were, on occasion, gobbed at by those behind us. Lovely.

I can't remember Utd's goal, only the weak passback that led to it. I don't recall whose fault it was, only that Sealey was screaming (as was his wont) for him not to pass it back, and that the mistake was picked up on by Ashley Grimes - later to become a Town hero during his short time at Kenilworth Road. However, the most memorable thing about the match was the penalty that threatened to get Luton a point at Old Trafford for the first time in 658 years. Can't remember what it was for. All I do recall is that, before Brian Stein stepped up to take it, some in the Luton end were going "sshhhhh" so that none of us would make a noise that might put Steiney off. In the deafening, piercing, pre-penalty noise in Old Trafford it seemed an astonishing act of futility. We stayed quiet and Steiney, unsurprisingly, missed by a couple of inches.

And so we were denied the lovely feeling of a tiny little away following going bananas, knowing that thousands of others in the ground are looking daggers at the post-goal tomfoolery. Instead, the loudest cheer of the day was secured by the miss and we, along with Brian, were served up thousands of "wanker" signs instead. (28/01/87).

Score: 1-0
Attendance: 39,927

19/10/85: Hitting Shilts for seven
Luton Town v Southampton

These are the matches that make it all worth while. Not against the big teams, the matches to which every Tom Dick and Harry turn up, but against Southampton - a match for which the major draw is that your strikers are up against **1985** *England's number one keeper. Despite being beaten seven times, Shilton had a good game. He saved loads of shots, but Luton (and his defence) gave him plenty of opportunity. Only 8876 inside Kenilworth Road, but we had a mighty fine time. Apart from the travelling support.*

Emeka Nwajiobi, the tank, hit the first on five minutes. Brian Stein got his first on 32 minutes. Ricky Hill on 35. Three up at half-time, so the result wasn't in question.

Steiney scored his second on 54 minutes, then little Preece got the fifth five minutes later. Ray Daniel scored on 88 minutes before Luton got a penalty and an opportunity for Stein to get his hat trick. Despite being the first choice penalty taker on occasion, a famous victory against Newcastle during the promotion season springs to mind (he scored two of three goals from the spot and the Hatters won 3-2 after being 2-0 down) his kicks were always a bit dodgy. Even in that game his penalties were a bit rubbish.

Mick Harford was the first choice penalty kicker, but obviously Stein was given his chance to score his third - a chance we were talking down on the terrace. There was, we'd decided, no way he'd beat the England keeper. And Steiney stepped up anyway and blasted possibly his best ever penalty into the back of the net; an emphatic way to round off a fantastic win. (9/11/85).

Score: 7-0. Town scorers - Nwajiobi, Brian Stein (3), Hill, Preece, Daniel

Attendance: 8,876

19/10/96: Luton Town v Peterborough United

A good, old fashioned, no-nonsense, emphatic win. Especially nice because our own favourite, Paul Showler, scores a couple of goals. Oh yes, we have our fun at Showler's expense - and our theory that he looks like a tramp. He's paid, as we maintain, in scraps for his dog with a win bonus of a roof over his head for the night, and another bottle for his brown paper bag. His kit sponsor, we reckon, is The Big Issue. Terrace humour eh? What about it?

Anyway, we reckon Showler is ace down the wing and bags a brace.......using his poaching instincts.....sorry. Steve Davis gets one too and we're all pretty pleased with ourselves thank you.

Score: 3-0. Town scorers – Davis, Showler (2)

Attendance 6,387

23/10/96: Coca-Cola Cup Third Round.
Wimbledon v Luton Town

I must be losing my religion. Everyone who knows I'm a Luton fan (and gives a toss) is asking if I'm going tonight - to the "big match". Apparently it's only me who can't see the glamour of an evening match at Selhurst Park against Wimbledon. Alright, so Wimbledon are the in-form Premiership side (they were second in the league at the time).....but it's still Wimbledon. And, with apologies to Crystal Palace fans, Selhurst Park has got to be one of the most uninspiring grounds in the league ("what about bloody Luton" I hear you cry - and with good cause). A hole in the ground, miles from anywhere.....South London's municipal ground for the homeless. I've been there quite a few times - I've seen Luton win against Palace and Charlton there (I've also seen them lose a fair few times too) but it has always seemed like more effort than it was worth. Last Boxing Day we traipsed across London in taxis and looking for non-existent train services only to find the match had been called off when we got there. Maybe when I said "never again" that time, I meant it. Above all, I suppose, there's the saving up we're currently doing to go to Prague.

Given the relative league positions, the result is quite an upset. But "the Crazy gang" wouldn't be crazy if they didn't do this sort of thing. Ceri Hughes scored the equaliser - obviously hoping there are a few scouts about. Of a crowd of just over 5000, as many as 2000 were apparently Town fans (I saw Michael and Chris at the train station - our reps) - who will have easily outshouted the Wimbledon fans. Up for the cup.... I shall, of course, go to the replay and try and get romantic for the Coca-Cola cup there.
Score: 1-1. Town scorer – Hughes
Attendance 5,043

Chelsea director Matthew Harding, and four others, die in a helicopter crash on their way back from watching Chelsea lose at Bolton the same night. Chelsea in particular, but football in general, are in mourning. Harding was a strange breed amongst football execs - a true supporter. Traditionally chairmen and directors put money into a club with an aim of making some more. Harding was a real supporter

- with a lot of cash, which he threw at Chelsea to help them rebuild Stamford Bridge and the team. He was a massive benefactor for Chelsea, and a contributor to Labour party funds. But the loss to football fans in general is that of the model credible director. Up in the directors' box wearing a replica top and cheering in the goals with the rest of the fans - instead of sitting stiff in a suit regarding football as corporate entertainment. A fan with millions and millions to spend on the Club - an embodiment of the "if I won a Double rollover lottery" dream for our own Clubs.

26/10/96: Luton Town v Bournemouth

Like the Peterborough game, this was a strangely subdued match. Again the Town didn't play particularly well - but again won at a canter. Michael was away on a foray to Glasgow for some obscure reason (probably to see his Scottish faves Raith Rovers - he carries his lucky Raith scarf to Town matches) so it wasn't quite the same in our seats - although it was good to have brother Andy come along. After scoring from a penalty (which was just a little dubious, although the Bournemouth fans were outraged) Tony Thorpe put his shirt over his head like Ravenelli to display a t-shirt with "1-0" written on the front. And when he scrambled in the second, from a horrid defensive mix-up, he took his shirt off altogether to reveal "2-0" on the t-shirt back. He's an arrogant swine - but it says something for the confidence of the team.

"It's good to be winning games when we're not playing well" is the cliché that Lennie trots out after the game.... Well, yes it is, but we're surely in for a barnstorming league performance before very long.......please let it be Tuesday. (*28/10/96*).
Score: 2-0. Town scorer - Thorpe (2, 1 pen)
Attendance: 6,086

27/10/87: We're supposed to be at home
Littlewoods Cup 3rd Round (at Filbert Street, Leicester)

1987 *I suppose it's good for a laugh, once in a while, to have a wildly unpredictable chairman. There is little doubt that David Evans did loads more harm than good for Luton Town FC. The away fan ban transformed the popular image of LTFC, from a team that the football world had a soft spot for, to the most hated club in the league. But, for his political aims, it was vital that his football club's unlikely league status was preserved - so he put some of his hard earned self made millions of pounds, into maintaining a squad to do the job with some style. When he finally caught on that, though he had turned LTFC into a model of the ghastly Tory vision of the future for football (circa 85), Margaret Thatcher wasn't going to come to Kenilworth Road on a date with him, he sold the ground to the council, made a tidy profit on the money that he and his directors had put in over the years (losing the club it's only real asset), and nicked off to pursue his little political career in Welwyn and Hatfield. However he was still, on occasion, a laugh at Luton - like when he told Arsenal they could offer £10M for Mick Harford and he wouldn't sell him, and when he carried out his promise to make us play away from home in the Littlewoods Cup to avoid inevitable away fan mayhem in Luton.*

To avert the angry hordes of Coventry City so-called supporters coming to town, Evans arranged for the Littlewoods Cup tie to be played at Filbert Street Leicester. Buses were put on to take the home support up to Leicester, those travelling only having to fork out just £1.50.

We went on the train, six of us, paying four times that amount even with children's tickets; drinking beer but not really upsetting anyone except a rather pedantic ticket inspector. When we got to Leicester we were met by around thirty policemen who were in turn amazed at the size of the Luton contingent coming off the train. They had expected to escort hundreds of fans to the ground, but ended up giving us a lift in the meat wagon instead.

The atmosphere inside the ground was very strange. Filbert Street was almost empty apart from the "away" end full of Coventry fans, obviously singing "You're supposed to be at home", a light sprinkling of Luton fans around the rest of the ground and a section in the corner for Leicester fans. We were in the main stand enclosure, the rain was coming down persistently, and we were getting soaked.

If anything the atmosphere and the rain only made for a more enjoyable night. We didn't expect to beat the current FA Cup Holders but, on the night, Luton never looked likely to lose. Micky Weir scored early on and, after Mick Harford made it 2-0, we were coasting. We sang in the rain and made a special point of trying to upset David Speedie, the feisty but aging ex-Chelsea striker playing for Coventry. Every time he came within earshot we'd shout "Speeeeeedieeeeeee" in a high pitched whine. My, how he must have hated that. If memory serves, he got so upset at our taking the rise that he got himself sent off and then did one of them Cantona flying kicks at us. Of course that never happened, he probably didn't even hear us, but it was funny at the time.

On a quagmire of a pitch Coventry pressed briefly in the second half, pulling a goal back to make the score 2-1, before Micky Harford caught them on the break to score Luton's third.

Score: 3-1.   Town scorers – Weir, Harford (2)
Attendance: 11,448

Looking at a train timetable at half time it came to light that, to catch the last train home, we'd have to get back to the station in a matter of a few minutes after the final whistle. We were at the exit when the ref blew up and then ran for the station, a lung busting run which was momentarily held up when we were jumped by a gang who sprang out of an alleyway. Thankfully one of our assailants was a schoolmate of the brother of one of the blokes we were with so, with a cry of "It's OK, we're Luton" we continued our breathless jog to the station.

At that time, and on that cup run in particular (up until the quarter final), we were going to matches with a couple of blokes from Slip End and a few of their mates from Dunstable. It was the nearest we ever got to being a gang, and although they were too young and weedy to even consider themselves as hooligans, it was clearly the sort of image they wanted to portray. Simon, Matth and Pete, and worst of all I (being a couple of years older than most of them), just tagged along like bloody sheep. (17/11/87).

28/10/96: I'm all tense and expectorant about tomorrow night. I had a bad dream last night about terrible trouble at a Luton v Sheffield Wednesday game staged in Luton's Stockwood Park. A Luton fan ran onto the pitch and head butted David Pleat, who was the ref (and of course the Wednesday manager). The choice of venue and referee for the match were surely terrible mistakes that the authorities should have foreseen. Anyway, after the head butting incident all hell broke loose.

I suppose I'm a little concerned about trouble at Watford. The Watford hooligan element is hardly notorious but they've been wound up lately. Meanwhile Luton has a larger hooligan following, who turn up to about two or three games a season and always seem to cause sporadic trouble in Watford. Of course the bravado amongst Town fans deems that we always wear colours at Watford (although I'll wear a jacket until I know how the land lies). And with Claire and Max going too this year, it's more of a bind than usual - we'll have to keep ourselves in check with our swearin' and a'bayin' and venom spewin'.

Most of all, I'm just wound up. I don't really enjoy these matches - the stakes are too high. A disastrous result tomorrow night could decimate confidence amongst the fans....this diary could easily fall into neglect as a result. Watford haven't beaten Luton for years and years, when we beat them it rubs it in even more but, unless we go up and they stay down (or, God forbid, vice versa), it's got to change one day. Not tomorrow please.............

In the evening it's another night of AC Meringue torture. Now I'm running at the gymnasium I feel quite a lot fitter and last the first 12 minute game without gasping desperately for air. Sadly, for the team rather than myself personally, I find that I am still hopelessly slow. And rubbish at football. When I used to play outdoors I could make up for it by finding enough space to compensate - indoors it's impossible. My team mates have caught on to my deficiencies in skill and speed and wisely never pass to me. The only service I provide to the team is that of bollard. I stand in front of an attacking player - he passes to an unmarked team mate - the opposition score. We lost 9-1 and 7-0 tonight. On the plus side, our new mate Paul isn't as obnoxious as last time, he keeps his mouth pretty much shut, I think he realises the knives are out.

29/10/96: Watford v Luton Town

Bastard. Luton score midway through the second half after hitting the post and the bar three times. Watford equalise in the last minute of injury time (which went on for ages, even though there were no injuries). The thousands of Luton fans (I reckon there were about 4000, but other estimates range between 5000 and a rather extravagant 8000) came home as dejected as if we'd lost.

We left at about 6.15pm but the Watford turnoff on the motorway was at a standstill and, when we eventually got parked, we had a long walk to the ground via the allotment path and the game had already started. Typically of Watford there were only three turnstiles open at the Luton end and hundreds of fans waiting outside to get in. We missed about 15 minutes of the game.

The atmosphere behind the goal was good - but not as good as last year when we stood along the side of the pitch (we still easily outsing the Watford end). Our group had the misfortune to be sitting/standing next to a group of young pissants who joined in the songs with gusto but, obviously one match a season supporters, didn't know the words too well. "You dirty Northern bastard" shouted one of them after a Watford player had fouled a Town man. Eventually they left to go up the back, where they could get help with the lyrics.

The match is the typical frenetic crap but, of course, when Showler scores the Town end goes crackers. There are little bits of trouble in the ground - a pocket of Town fans who seem more drunk than violent are led out of the main stand (thinking they are Watford fans the Town crowd shout "Scum" at them as they are apparently led away by the Police.....and in to join their fellow Luton supporters), there is a scuffle between Police and Watford toughs after Mitchell Thomas is spat at whilst waiting to take a throw in. When Watford equalise their fans go wild as well - with a mini pitch invasion up the other end. As with last year, when Watford equalised with a little more time to play, their fans can claim a moral victory. They were the ones smiling at the end of the match - but they've still not beaten us (except in the Anglo-Italian Cup) for ten years.

This is the sort of fact that provided us with cold comfort on Tuesday night. Facts that would, quite rightly, have earned the considered response of "Aaaaaaaaaaah" from Watford fans. But in the cold light of day, probably next Friday by the time they get off the high, they might think back that it wasn't a last minute winner that they had celebrated - merely the fact that Luton hadn't beaten them again.

Back in Luton the pub was like a morgue afterwards. We said "Shit" alot, made moaning noises like Chewbacca the wookie, and drank our way solemnly through two pints of the current, excellent, guest beer - Smiles.

Score: 1-1. Town scorer – Showler
Attendance: 14,109

Claire, working in St. Albans, goes back to work and to her colleague who went along to the match with his friends who are Watford fans. He and Claire have a good working relationship, which latterly involves their calling each other "scum" through their adopted allegiances. Simon is a nice bloke but, if he's not bullshitting, he's got some dodgy mates. He tells Claire that there was quite a bit of trouble in Watford - and of his mate who got a black eye and was arrested before the match only to be let go by kick off and rushing out at full time to go and "find some Hatters"....oh, well, *really.*

NOVEMBER

2/11/96: Plymouth Argyle v Luton Town

I've been to Plymouth only once, and that's enough I feel. However, today I could've done with an excuse to go out - stuck at home, bored to ribbons. Because we're saving, going to Plymouth wasn't an option, although, had we not been saving, I'd have found another excuse.

Claire's got work and got the car. I go into town in the morning and put on a bet; which we usually do as a group on home Saturdays (we always lose - mostly because of Michael's tendency to wrongly predict draws) but it seems a little sad going into a bookies on your own, although I do feel a sad sort of romance towards the life of people who sit in there all the time with their thin roll up fags and their fruitless systems – those who start conversations "I would've won with.....".

I return home and sit around waiting for something to happen. The football starts and Radio 5 announces that Luton are winning 1-0. I prepare a steak and kidney suet pudding and, when that's done, it's 1-1 on the Teletext. "Genevieve" is on the telly so I decide to have a pleasant afternoon watching that instead of worrying about the football. Whilst Wendy is faffing around deciding whether or not to go on the rally I look back at the Teletext. 2-1 to Luton.

I'm all tense now, can't really concentrate on the film. Kenneth Moore is wowed by his girl playing the trumpet but, when I switch over to text again, it's bleedin' 3-2 to Plymouth and Thomas has been sent off. I leave Genevieve to chug along at 15mph towards a happy ending whilst I'm off to listen to the radio, read WSC, and sulk. The final results come through and, great, we've equalised. Good old Tony Thorpe.

Score: 3-3. Town scorer - Thorpe (3)
Attendance 7,134

A fraught afternoon. Pictures on Anglia news on Monday show that the Town contingent got soaked on Plymouth's open terrace. It would also appear that the game was a rather bad tempered affair - there's a loyal supporter anecdote or two in there somewhere.

There is also an Amdram production at Luton's St. George's theatre which I'm reviewing for the paper. One of the thespians is a workmate of Simon and Michael and they, with other colleagues, turn up (including loudmouth Paul - hoorah!) - as does Simon's new girlfriend Katharine. Nice girl. The play is a reasonably poor but we go to The Firkin later (where we bump into Martin and his girlfriend Steph). Amongst other things we talk about the Wimbledon match, which Martin wants tickets for. Simon, eager to impress, asked Katharine if she had ever been to a "big" football match. She replied "Well, England v Scotland". Luckily for all concerned the club's stupid guest ticket arrangements priced all our would be guests out of contention. We had five interested parties - but at £15 per ticket for us and guests we chucked that idea out of the window

Martin said he'd like to play for AC Meringue. And asks "who's the idiot who reckons he can do it all?". Paul is there, trying to work out why no-one is up for the " monster drinking session" he rushed to the pub for (and apparently oblivious to Martin's question), I tell Furlow "oh....that's Tony" just in case. Gutless git. (*9/11/96*).

9/11/85: Jingle all the way.....
Tottenham Hotspur v Luton Town

There was a time, not so very long ago, when there was a "Big Five" group of clubs in the country - Man Utd, Liverpool, Everton, Arsenal and Spurs - the clubs which had all the money, the fans and the impressive grounds. These were the teams that everybody else wanted to beat. I mention

that because I rate the above game as the most glorious away win I've ever seen - even though Spurs' fall from grace over the past few years has been remarkable. White Hart Lane has seen redevelopments which have seen a great old ground look like a bigger version of the new industrial estate shoebox grounds in the lower leagues. Improved facilities, better views, no atmosphere, totally lacking in character. White Hart Lane in the mid-eighties was going through that transition. The old East stand, complete with the famous shelf terrace was still there, whilst the new West stand (complete with double-decker executive boxes) looked out of place......but very impressive. The away fans were given a terrace, and some seats, right of the goal - with a nice low roof so we could make plenty of noise. So much nicer than the open Clock end at Highbury.

The stature of the club, and the inspiring football they played, coupled with such a great ground, made Spurs the best London away game by far. The only problem with Tottenham is it's so far away from the tube.

Anyway, that didn't matter on my first visit because I went on the bus - although I can't remember who with. I'm pretty sure I wasn't with my brothers, so it must have been with some of Andrew's friends. I can't remember any of the game, it stands out because of the amazing result and for the fact that it was the debut for Luton's smart blue Adidas away kit. I can remember that there was no question of fluke in the result - we simply played Spurs off the park. The Tottenham fans, I read in the paper afterwards, were singing woefully about their lost stars of yesteryear (there's a Greaves/grief pun somewhere there, but I cannot be bothered). No matter, we had Micky Harford, Brian Stein and Ricky Hill....... oh, those were the days.

Anyway, at the time, those WERE the days; and we knew it. We heard none of the Spurs fans' singing the blues in the packed Luton end, it was joyous bedlam in there. Oh what fun it is to see Luton win away....(23/11/85).

Score: 1-3. Town scorers - Harford, Stein, Hill
Attendance: 19,163

9/11/96: Luton Town v Notts County

"You'd of been proud of me" says Michael on the way to the bookies prior to the Notts County match. "I was waiting for a bus the other day and when it came it was that bloody awful Watford bus". Due to a strongly suspected Hornet influence within the Luton & District bus company hierarchy, a double decker adorned in Watford colours often runs in and around Luton, whilst the rosette the company use in their colour adverts is yellow, black and red. "I refused to get on it and waited half an hour for the next one". And indeed we did feel proud - even if some of the laughter was at, as well as with, him.

Lutonian minibuses - resplendent in their white with orange and blue stripe livery - must be the preferred means of public transport for the discerning Town fan. Unfortunately they never seem to run on a route you ever actually need.

It's a cliché but there's a ring of truth around the idea that a team, which doesn't play well but still wins, will go far. The idea is that they will eventually wake up and beat all comers - but, with Luton, lucky wins are usually forebears of a longer run of ignominious defeat. But who knows? Maybe this year we really are going to come good. Not that this win was particularly lucky. Notts County didn't provide any opposition. Sad really. County were relegated to the First Division with the Town (they actually sent us down) and had always seemed like a proud little club, the oldest in the league. Apart from their keeper, who played out of his skin, the rest of the team seemed demoralised. Meanwhile the pitifully small away support (all old blokes and kids - very few fans in their 20's) despondently, quietly, called for the sacking of their manager Colin Murphy. "There's only one Colin Murphy" sang the Maple Corner, being irksome, with very little style. Notts County also sported one of the nastiest away kits ever seen - the lack of imagination in design (an oversized club crest on yellow shirt and shorts) only matched by that of the team playing in it.

Score: 2-0. Town scorers – Thorpe, Hughes
Attendance: 6,134

11/11/96: At last AC Meringue show the form and spirit which will surely, one of these weeks, see us win a game. Simon, with his mind on his new lass, fails to pick Martin and me up. Thinking he is stuck in traffic (or an amorous clinch) we rush to the leisure centre to make up the numbers - only to find them all there, and not too perturbed that we are late. Martin and I watch the first game, which ended 8-0 to the opposition. We play the second game and only lose 4-1 to a group of, admittedly inept, lads. In the final game it's 5-3 and everyone is up for next time. We're like the Allied team at half time in "Escape to Victory". Keen. Sadly I'll be coming back from Prague at the time which, quite unexpectedly, seems something of a swine now. Thurlow's appearance on the scene brings about more calls for Paul (who is getting less annoying as the weeks go by.....but is still a git) to be bought out. (*12/11/96*).

12/11/83: No to MK!
Luton Town v Birmingham City

1983 *It's pretty fair to say that, for much of the `80's, Luton Town fans had good reason to hate the board of the Club - and not because of a dereliction of duty in terms of keeping a good side. We knew the team was good. And we were holding onto our best players - Luton Town provided, albeit just for the one match, England's striking partnership (aka Brian Stein and Paul Walsh) away to European Champions France. It didn't seem fair that they should have been dropped after just one match, but the big clubs would never allow a team in Luton's position to hold on to such prolific players now. Goodness knows how much a player of Ricky Hill's calibre would make in the nineties.*

Such things were of secondary concern during the battle to save the club (see the chapter on the relocation quandary). The boardroom's insistence during the early-mid Eighties was that the council's planned relief road would make it impossible to stage games at Kenilworth Road (the road was built some years ago, nearest to the part of the ground where the club amazingly found just enough room for a new stand to be built).

Supporters were disgusted, and instantly alienated, when it was learnt that the board were looking towards relocating to Milton Keynes. The small Luton fanbase, so the argument went, simply didn't deserve a First Division club. I've never understood this theory. Surely the most deserving supporters are those from the smaller clubs who follow their local club through thick and thin. Why are Man Utd fans more deserving? Because they buy more replica shirts in the high street (of every town in the country) than any other set of fans?

An anti-MK rally was held in People's Park, about half a mile from the ground. The guest speakers included all the local MPs, and a couple of ex-LTFC employees, whose loyalty towards the town had cost them their jobs. It was a stirring occasion, attended by a good percentage of the crowd who then marched on to the ground.

Apart from the somewhat disappointing result, it was a great day - even if some of the marchers were gutted that, no, we (and more especially their mates) hadn't planned to boycott the match in protest.

There were other boycotts and demonstrations, and heckling of the directors' box. The then chairman Denis Mortimer eventually had enough and left, to be followed by David Evans who pursued the MK line until the council there chucked the proposal out. Evans went on to make a mark of his own but, for a little time, it seemed like the supporters had won.

Score: 1-1. Town scorer - Brian Stein
Attendance: 11,111

The most astonishing thing about the match, at least as far as the Editor of the programme (which, typically, didn't even mention the demo) was concerned, was that the crowd numbered 11,111 the score was 1-1 and the Birmingham equaliser was scored by number 11. (3/12/83).

12/11/96: Coca-Cola Cup Third Round Replay
Luton Town v Wimbledon

The Town versus "The Crazy Gang" and, like the song goes, it's a *crazy, crazy, crazy, crazy* night. Luton play really well in patches, but can only score through an own goal - a lead held until the equaliser in the second minute of injury time. "This is bloody worse than Watford" (same injury-time equaliser scenario) says Michael, and I spend the time between full and extra time arguing why he is wrong. By the end we're all left deflated, but taking it so philosophically that we're discussing why we're not really that pissed off. All I'm worried about is that the result will dent confidence, nobody reckons it will. Andy even says that he couldn't give a toss about the FA Cup this season either - a claim I quickly poo-poo.

But, hell, we're just putting on a brave face. Their equaliser was so late into the match that the bloody keeper had come up for corners (Feuer did the same at the end of extra-time - leading to the strange sight of two pairs of goalie gloves going for the ball). Worse still, Mick Harford, Luton's hero (currently at Wimbledon, surely set for another heroic return to Luton in the future), set the goal up. Luton had so many chances to seal the game beforehand. At the end of the match we filed past a young lad, head in hands, crying his eyes out. He'll learn.

I was saying before the match that Wimbledon fans seem to be inherently trainspotter/chess club types - I saw two such stereotypical "Nigels" on my way through town earlier that evening. However, I was horrified to see that some sad old buzzard had taken the big match scenario as an excuse to bring his big bass drum into the ground. Thankfully his monotonous thumping wasn't brilliantly received - but what the Dickens is going through people's minds these days? Sitting pretty in their allocated seats they've forgotten how to behave like a football crowd and are now looking to Football Italia for tips.

Score: 1-2. Town scorer - Blackwell (og). He Crazy
Attendance: 8,076.

16/11/96: FA Cup First Round.
Torquay United v Luton Town

So the Town didn't fall apart after the Wimbledon loss. Apparently the match was poor but, as Lennie Lawrence rightly said, it was "a potential banana-skin". Far too busy fretting about how I'm to finance our holiday to Prague to consider going to Devon - although it would've been nice, especially as we've got friends in Exeter we could've stayed with. Anyway Radio 5 report Hughes' goal just before half time, after which it's a case of no news being good news. (*17/11/96*).

Score: 0-1. Town scorer – Hughes
Attendance: 3 ,450.

17/11/87 Bladder pressure and Sealey under siege
Littlewoods Cup, 5th round. Ipswich Town v Luton Town

1987 *In the days, not too long past, when the gulf between clubs of the (then) First and Second Divisions wasn't huge it was pretty standard fare to see an aspiring Second Division team beating a midtable First Division side - especially when they were drawn at home. Great though they were when they happened, the hope of a Luton Town away win in the league seemed to hinge on the opposition either:-*

1) underestimating plucky little Luton or
2) being Watford.

Ipswich, with that Second Division chip on shoulder, would surely be wanting to make a point against Luton - proving themselves worthy of higher league status and going on another stage in the cup. We weren't going to win, but we were certainly going to be there.

This time the mode of transport was to be the supporters' bus; with the seasoned supporter veterans at the Dunstable pick up point joined (to their obvious and understandable embarrassment) by the unfamiliar faces of the little band from Slip End and the half dozen acne scarred mini-yobs from Dunstable. All swear words, chewing gum and Luton songs. And, to prove we were hard, cans of beer. Loads of them. Why, at a conservative estimate we must have boozed our way through two cans a'lager a man by the time we got on the bus. Ipswich is a long way away from Luton - going east is notoriously tedious for those used to using those lovely fast motorways. It was quickly obvious that we would be needing to make quite a few toilet stops before we got to Suffolk.

The bus driver was adamant. There would be no stops. Forget the mental pictures of coach doors opening with great falls of piss cascading onto the pavement followed by the ubiquitous hooligan element. It wasn't like that. Pretty soon the bravado of those who had partaken of beer was replaced by pained expressions once the bad news from the front of the bus was confirmed. The pain on the bladder was amazing; and as I looked around, there were others, staring with a look of terror in their eyes at the front of the bus; pleading for the driver's mercy. Eventually he did stop, though he wasn't happy about it. The relief was fantastic.........

The game was all about holding on too. Brian Stein scored on four minutes, which was just a couple of minutes after we got into the packed little section of terrace they'd given over to Luton fans. After that it was all Ipswich. They were all over us, wave after wave of Ipswich attacking, with Les Sealey in the Luton goal having one of the best games in his Town career.

At the end of the game, as if I can remember, we cheered heartily.

Score: 0-1. Town scorer - Brian Stein
Attendance: 15,643

The bus ride on the way home was made sadly memorable for the fact that Simon was accused of getting gum on a seat by our reactionary driver. He didn't do it - not that that matters much now. Even so our Dunstabilious "friends" had jumped on the side of Simon in the argument, if only as an excuse to hurl relentless abuse at the driver. However, there was more serious trouble to occupy the police's time on other Luton buses that night (thankfully, as the driver had attempted to get the police to arrest us all). A great night for the Town, an ignominious one for some of our travelling support. (19/01/88).

17/11/96: Don't really have enough spare time, or inclination, to watch Northampton v bloody Watford live on Sky TV. But Michael expresses an interest and comes round. Dire game - both teams have a hopeless style of hit and hope play. Northampton apparently score (to which Michael gets quite enthusiastic) only for the goal to be disallowed as offside - the magnificent Sky replays show the full horror of the linesman's wrong decision. Watford score a good goal in the second half and the match ends 1-0. Not nice to watch.

18/11/96: Claire and I fly out to Prague for a week away. The pilot keeps telling us that the weather in Prague is deteriorating as we circle around looking down on the fog. After one aborted descent, which was a little scary, we have to fly on to Vienna and on to a bus which trundles tortuously slowly towards the Czech Republic. Having only seen the tourist centre of Prague before, it is something of an eye opener to drive past a town like Brno where it looks like everybody lives in identical blocks of dreary flats built during the Communist regime - none of which appear to have curtains. Meanwhile, whilst McDonalds and KFC are in Prague, the rest of the country is obviously still frontier land to mass crass American commercialism. The Marlboro cowboy stands tall on the main road billboards selling the American dream and lung cancer to the, naturally delighted, Czechs. When he finally gets us to Prague, the driver decides he is stopping nowhere except the Hilton - which is good news for the suits but bad news for Claire and me; trudging through some pretty dodgy looking streets, suitcases in hand, totally foreign, looking for the nearest metro station. Eventually we get to the Flora metro, then onto Starometska station, and to our digs - two minutes walk from the Charles Bridge. A good holiday - it was suprisingly easy to forget all about the football.

Thereby...

19/11/96: Czech Ice Hockey League
Sparta Praha v Litvinov (& Preston North End v Luton Town)

We only ever watch Ice Hockey in Prague - because Claire fancies herself as a Sparta Prague fan. Meanwhile I plump for the away side.

The match pretty quickly becomes a walkover for Sparta, whose fans are loving it. When they score the noise isn't an English "Yehhhhhhh" but the European goal celebration inflection which sounds more like "Yohhhhh". In the crowd are certain identifiable groups; we sit near some well behaved but enthusiastic soldiers with acne. Behind the goals teenagers jump around on their seats, sing "here we go Sparda, here we go", and occasionally throw things onto the ice. To the side of them are a smaller group of older blokes who are a tad threatening and are into the old Hitler salute. Lovely. On the other side of the arena sit the small away following - only noticeable when they score, and the Sparta fans sat above start chucking stuff at them. The crowd is over 6000.

Strange how people can get so excited about a game played to a backdrop of booming muzak every time there is a stop in play. Queen rock anthems. The bloody birdy song. And, just to prove they're up to date with shite pop, The Spice Girls.

Score: 8-1

Walking out of the arena, before embarking on a journey on a number 17 tram - in the wrong direction - I remarked to Claire that the Town were probably just kicking off. Half an hour later I'd forgotten all about Preston North End and wondered which end of Prague the deserted tram terminal where we ended up was - luckily there was another number 17 about to go back the other way so we hopped on that.

It was Thursday before I saw the result via a day old Daily Express in Wenceslas Square. It's a small world, but I bet I was the only one there that morning to quietly pronounce "Shit" at the news of a Luton Town defeat coupled with a Watford last minute win. (*23/11/96*).

Score: 3-2. Town scorer - Davis (2)
Attendance: 7,004

23/11/85: The walking/hopping wounded
Watford v Luton Town

1985

A match which wins inclusion in this book for a few reasons, none of which particularly justify it. Firstly, the win was great because it was at Vicarage Road. Secondly, because Watford had an unbeaten home record beforehand. Thirdly, because my brother Simon had suffered an injury to his foot on the morning before the match.

The injury happened back in Luton, he's got a way of incurring injuries that make him look like he's been involved in or been the victim of hooligan activity (see 23/3/94). It quickly became apparent that he'd really hurt himself quite badly, which wasn't so bad on the bus but meant that he needed our support to hop up the winding path through the Vicarage Road allotments.

He was alright again once we'd managed to prop him up against a crowd barrier inside the ground, where we'd kindly positioned ourselves on the terrace running alongside the touchline - and not behind the goal where it was always packed.

The last few minutes of the game were exciting fayre. Watford equalised a first half goal by Mitchell Thomas with ten minutes left only for Steve Terry to turn the ball past Tony Coton with four minutes to go. The own goal was celebrated heartily..... but my main recollection of the aftermath is my brother hopping around like a mad thing - shouting "mind me foot, mind me foot, mind me foot" at everyone pogo-ing around him. (5/03/86).

Score: 1-2. Town scorers – Thomas, Terry (og)
Attendance: 16,197

23/11/96: Luton Town v Bristol Rovers

"I wonder how the Town are getting on" was on my mind in Prague - but it was quite easy to forget all about it on Saturday.

Score: 2-1. Town scorers – Marshall, Thorpe (pen)
Attendance: 5,791

24/11/96: Slavia Praha v Jablonec

What I really wanted to do during this, our second, stay in Prague, was to go and see Bohemians Praha play. They're my fave Prague team for several reasons. Apart from the cool name, there is also the story of their badge which features a kangaroo. Apparently, during a tour of Australia in the 1930's the Bohemians were so taken with the marsupials that they decided to take a couple back to Prague as club mascots. This they did and, rather than having to acclimatise to the bitter Eastern European weather, the kangaroos promptly died. And, last but certainly not least, they're really rubbish - stuck at the bottom of the Czech First Division.

Sadly, and apparently because at a last home game (against Jablonec) a 16 year old threw a firecracker at the opposition keeper - perforating his eardrum - they weren't allowed to play at home the week we were there. God knows where they played, I bought the sports papers - but they were unintelligible to me - meanwhile the tourist offices only seemed to be able to answer questions on opera or Mozart concerts.

So, we went to Slavia Prague - whom Paborski used to play for, helping them to win the Czech league last year and get into the European Cup. Their ground is amazingly old fashioned. An oval, with two open terraces on either end. An open stand - apparently made of meccano and put on top of the existing terrace on one side of the pitch and the main stand on the other - the best seats (priced at just over a quid - it's less than 50p on the terraces) are benches.

One fantastic thing was the bloke going around the stand selling "pivo" (beer). Normally I'm all for drinking beer at strange times. I will habitually drink a pint on a cross channel ferry if the bar is open at 5am. Just a pint. I never really want a drink at the time, but I enjoy the fact that I can. Normally it would be the same at a football match, but it was so cold.... the thought of having to take one's hands out of parka pockets to hold a plastic beaker of cold lager just wasn't that appealing. Perhaps the cold also had an effect on the fans' urge to applaud their team. Whatever, it's the quietest crowd I've ever been in - they only shout when they score and they didn't even applaud the team when they came on, although there were a couple of firecrackers going off after Slavia took the lead.

Being a bit of an anorak, I bought a Slavia Praha shirt - although the price tag of the equivalent of £31 was a little out of keeping. Very few fans were wearing it. The same price comparison between top price seats and replica shirt prices in England would mean that, with the best seats at Kenilworth Road at about £20, a shirt would cost £1240. Hopefully the price of football, as a percentage of the Czech weekly wage, is significantly cheaper than it is in England (though Adidas apparently don't give a toss). Even so that situation, and the state of the ground, only reinforce the financial gulf in modern football. UEFA seem to be doing all in their power, by way of preliminary rounds, to make sure that teams from poorer countries - and their crappy grounds - don't blight European competition for too long.

Score: 2-1.

Before we went to the football I rang Andy at home, to find out how the Town had got on. I had a dream that they had lost 3-0, so was delighted to hear they'd won. Sadly, for someone who had convinced themselves of almost indifference whilst away, I found myself asking such questions as "so, what end was the penalty at?".

30/11/96: Bournemouth v Luton Town

We get back from Prague and, of course, I'm hankering to see Luton play again. Make arrangements with Michael for a boozy train trip before, thankfully in hindsight, Simon offers to drive. He's late, as always, and has his Katharine with him - which is surprising. She nice girl. He gimp. And they're still deeply in love...which gets sickly, and a bit frightening when they're billing and cooing at 80mph on the M25.

Simon worked in Bournemouth for quite a while when he worked in kitchens (from which time he sometimes dines out on his "the time I brought dogshit into a posh hotel" anecdote) and so we follow him in the town for a good pub. It quickly becomes apparent that he's clueless and we end up in a pseudo Irish theme pub looking for alternatives to soddin' Kilkenny. One pint of Bass then to the ground - which is a good old fashioned dump.

Luton fall behind in the first half but class tells and by half-time we're 2-1 up. In the second half the Town's tactics change to all-out defence and, when that doesn't work, desperate defence. Suitably encouraged Bournemouth, who really are a dreadful team, score two goals in the last fifteen minutes.

A diabolical result. The only point of interest was a tramp, and his dog, tucked away in the corner of our terrace. "Showler's Dad" we said. It was quite touching, as we waited as close to the exit as possible to get out on the final whistle, to see that he'd put his coat over his shivering dog.

The loss meant that my lucky orange Kahuna watch (bought off QVC, the shopping channel, not great quality) had lost its touch regarding away league games - and that my lucky Bronx style hat was never lucky in the first place. (*3/12/96*).

Score: 3-2. Town scorer - Thorpe (2, 1 pen)
Attendance: 6,086

DECEMBER

3/12/83: Ruining Christmas
Luton Town v Coventry City

It's been the same in the top flight for over 20 years, whatever you do - don't go losing at home to Coventry. But Coventry, like Wimbledon (like Luton), are one of those teams that every

1983 *other team expects to beat and often doesn't*

By the '83/84 season we were going to all the home matches, walking there and back the couple of miles from Slip End to the ground. On the way we would meet up with young Stuart Kedge, walking to the ground from his home in Caddington.

We all used to queue up at the minors' turnstile to the middle section of the Oak Road and having paid £1.50 to get in a police constable would search everyone and a "child" with cigarettes would be told to pay the £2.50 adult entrance. Often was the time when Kedge would have a lit fag "hidden" in a cupped hand, clutching hold of the packet in the other, laughing his head off once safely inside that he had outwitted the coppers again.

On the way to the ground we would stock up with sweets from the sweetie shop in Maple Road, Cola Cubes mostly, sucked until the top of the mouth would bleed. And homeward we'd cancel out the beneficial effects of walking back up the hill by buying bags of chips. The walk home, through Whipperley Way, Stockwood Park and under the motorway bridge, was always filled with discussion, which would tend to get heated and eventually personal after a defeat. Anyway, after this game I told both my brothers what I'd got them for Christmas - and advised them as to what they could do with their presents.

Ruined Christmas for everybody. (2/01/84).

Score: 2-4. Town scorers - Pearce (og), Aylott
Attendance: 10,698

     ☙   ☙   ☙   ☙   ☙   ☙   ☙   ☙   ☙   ☙   ☙

3/12/96 Luton Town v York City

Tuesday night. Awful game. The goals came in the second half, the first as we were just about sitting down and getting cold. Those incredibly loyal York City fans who did turn up were quite impressive, following up "Shit ground no fans" (fair point, oh so predictable) with a special mention for the old Bobbers stand which is now a row of executive boxes (over half of them empty). "What the f***in' hell is that?" they shouted. Good point, well made. About five or six of them sang "Millwall" at us, somewhat oddly. Millwall fans famously rioted at Kenilworth Road eleven years ago....the wounds have healed somewhat since then (in fact, the night is of little more than anecdotal interest now for those of us who were there).

However, you've got to praise fans who travel over 300 miles on a Tuesday evening to see such a lousy team. We left the ground after the game and, as we waited to cross Dunstable Road, the York supporters' bus went by. I applauded the fans thereon, as much in respect as sarcasm, and, not unnaturally, was given a "wanker" sign in return.

Score: 2-0. Town scorers – Marshall, Thorpe
Attendance: 4,987

7/12/96 FA Cup Second Round.
Luton Town v Borehamwood

"What I'll be happy with" I said "is a nice easy win - a goal in the first few minutes just to shut them up". *Football Focus* had had a feature on Borehamwood, they're all bloody stockbrokers and looked quite unlikely to be able to play football. In the event the game was terrible. In the first half we had to sit in the upper bowels of the main stand. A terrible view, and with some strange case supporters, arguing amongst themselves and singing songs, with stamp foot accompaniment, way too slow. Borehamwood fans on the other hand were obviously in "big day out" mode. After they refused to be "outted" as Watford fans, the Town supporters didn't know how to handle them. So we let them get on with it.

By the second half we were back in our season ticket seats, blind to the fact that someone else might have bought the tickets (no-one apparently had). Borehamwood scored with about twenty minutes to go and, before Luton's equaliser, there was one of those periods of total gloom. We had showed, in the previous hour and ten minutes, an inability to score - and were surely going out of the FA Cup to a non-league side. I'd never seen it happen to Luton before although James Bowley, a friend of ours, told us that his Dad (who used to go to Town matches with my Dad) remembered the last non-league side to beat Luton in the cup in the sixties. Apparently it was Corby and, according to Bowley folklore, one of their players was wearing spectacles.

Reverting to Watford tactics, Feuer boots the ball up the field as far as he can. Two Borehamwood players muck up the clearance and Dwight Marshall equalises. The relief is tangible. Marshall scores again soon after and we win the game. We stay to applaud Borehamwood off the field - the emotion is complex - admiring, patronising and a feeling of "now piss off back to your day jobs and never darken our door again".

Score: 2-1. Town scorer - Marshall (2)
Attendance: 5,332

After the match Simon asked "Did you ever think, before the match, that we might get our biggest win ever?". No. He said he did. Stupid git. (*10/12/96*).

8/12/84 Preece and I make our debut.
Luton Town v Aston Villa

1984 *When David Pleat bought David Preece (skillful midfielder, fine passer, about four foot tall) no-one could have foreseen the many years of loyal service he would give the club. At the time he just seemed like another one of Pleat's bargain bucket pros of the like of Foster, Harford and Nicholas - perhaps a little younger; his youth evident with the bumfluff moustache he sported in the first pictures we saw of him wearing the colours of his old club Walsall.*

Thankfully he got rid of that before turning out for Luton. All we knew, in perfect faith of Pleat's skills, was that he'd fit in just fine......

I, on the other hand, wasn't so sure facing my debut for the club on the same day. A kid from school, called Adrian, who had no interest in football, had managed to get a job as a programme seller and would brag (as was his wont) about the free tickets and the small change scams which meant he was quids in every other Saturday. The free tickets were the draw for me, so I nagged him quite a bit that I'd like in if poss too. And so it came to pass that I turned up with Adrian one day to the programme seller's HQ.. The operation was run from a couple of terraced houses the club owned in Kenilworth Road, knocked together to form one big house - like The Beatles lived in in "Help!".... albeit with significantly less lighting and furniture. In fact, apart from the boarded up windows, the only attention to detail was the shelf running round the room where the programme sellers counted up their 50ps. There we met the organiser Cherry Newberry who, with her team of lads in this dingy den, resembled something of a Fagin figure. The interview, and I can remember it well, was "we'll give you a few games trial, see if you like us - and if we like you..."; then I picked up me programmes, and me bag, and out we went. I helped Adrian with his patch. We were in some quiet bit of the main stand and he explained that the Kenilworth Road (away) end was the most profitable, if a bit dodgy at times. He said that you could rip away fans off easier because, if it came to an argument, the police would tend to take the programme seller's side against the away fan.

In the meantime I was more worried about where my free seat would be.

When it came to cashing up, a little time before kick-off, my concern was to count up all my money before the match started; a frustrating proposition using my modest mathematical genius (soon be rated at CSE Grade 4 standard) under pressure.

I eventually finished cashing up and picked up my ticket to sit in the loftier parts of the main stand where the view is nothing if not badly obstructed. However it was a novelty for me, used to watching from the Oak Road terrace.

Preece marked his debut with a goal at the Oak Road end with a miss-hit shot. And so began an illustrious career with the Hatters that would run to a testimonial year. His benefit match, played before he had put pen to the new contract which he was "keen to sign", was against Man Utd. The ground was full - of plenty of screaming children and older Lutonian Reds. After the match Preece promptly went off to Derby County.

Score: 1-0. Town scorer – Preece
Attendance: 7,696

Still, Preece lasted longer employed at Luton Town than I did. At my second game, a midweek match against West Brom, I was still furiously cashing up at kick-off. After a few minutes we heard a dull roar from the ground. Everyone stopped for a second... "We've scored" said one of the regulars, and everyone carried on counting in silence (save for "wonder who got it" murmurs). I, however, was deeply pissed off with having missed a goal. Luton lost the match 2-1. I never sold another programme.

Apparently it was Steve Foster. (15/12/84).

10/12/96: Zenith Data Auto Windscreen Shield Round 1
Luton Town v Leyton Orient

The only attraction of this Little League Cup, according to Brian Swain in the Luton News, is £500,000 for winning - and "the glory" of playing at Wembley. The money would be good for the club, but they'd be better off winning it in a raffle. And the Wembley dream has been so thoroughly tarnished over the years, through crap competitions like this - and the play-offs - that surely no-one (save for fans of the dwindling number of clubs who still haven't been there....and they'll get their chance, soon enough), particularly Town fans who have been conned before, equates Wembley with glory anymore. The FA Cup still inspires dreams, the League Cup less so especially since selling out to Coca-Cola - but as a stadium it would be fair (and sadly accurate) to say that Old Trafford has more romantic allure these days than Wembley does.

So I missed the Orient match - as did thousands of others. The crowd, of just over 1500, was the lowest Luton Town attendance since 1933. Luton won, worse luck.

Score: 2-1. Town scorers – Davis, Grant
Attendance: 1,594

14/12/96: Luton Town v Crewe Alexandra

Now, this is the life. This is what we want. And it all started so quietly.....

Down the pub, as usual, I realise I've forgotten my season ticket and so have to run back home which (even accounting for my gymnasium exploits) isn't as easy as I'd expected. Perhaps it's because in the gym it's deemed acceptable to sweat like a pig - in the pub it's not encouraged. Anyway, upon my return Andy and Michael are talking to a Crewe fan and going over this season's games for clues as to how our teams will do. It's an interesting chat, which almost gets heated as our friendly Crewe fan tells how Watford have been the only team to outclass the Alex, and Michael relives the last minute Watford equaliser against the Town.... The other Crewe fans get increasingly noisy - singing songs about the railways and practising the Ravenelli shirt over the head thing that they tell us will follow a Crewe goal.

At the ground I buy a programme, for the first time in years, and whilst I am reading it Alexander scores Luton's first in about the third minute (obviously I looked up....a certain level of expectancy can be gauged in the tone of the crowd). From then on Luton play the best football they have for many a long day. The ref was a bit of a homer (we got a dodgy penalty and Crewe a man sent off as a result) but the Town were great. Three-nil at half-time, six-nil by the end - plenty of time for us to "do a Ravenelli". A Thorpe hat-trick and, after a disgraceful tackle on him, another Crewe player sent off (at which it was somewhat surprising to see Simon and Andy rush towards the tunnel to make sure he goes to the dressing room with "Scum" and "You wanker" ringing in his ears - I don't think they realised there was a copper stood right next to them). In all, apart from that, it was a fantastic day for Town supporters - we all went home, and out that night, smiling loads. (*15/12/96*).

Score: 6-0. Town scorers - Alexander, Thorpe (3, 1 pen), Showler, Oldfield
Attendance: 5,977

⊜　⊜　⊜　⊜　⊜　⊜　⊜　⊜　⊜　⊜　⊜　⊜

15/12/84: Mick Harford's debut/Dad's last stand.
Leicester City v Luton Town

1984 *One of those unlikely events that, in retrospect, seem more and more unlikely as the years go by. But Dad had decided to take my brothers, and our friends Matthew and Peter Bennie, to the match on the train. Perhaps it was because their Dad had, equally grudgingly, taken us to Alton Towers a few months before. I can't remember anything of the train trip, or 99.9% of the game. Luton, I think, went 1-0 up before going 2-1 down. So, we stood in the away section, getting abuse aplenty from the Leicester fans. Then, cometh the last minute, cometh the man... My only memory of the game is of Mick Harford, on his debut, rising above everyone to head home with seconds to spare. Looking back at an old copy of The Luton News I see that I've forgotten the Brian Stein opener, the Leicester equaliser and a missed Leicester penalty (that must've been good). The picture of Harford's goal is also inconsistent with my memory of it. Anyway, I know it was a last minute job and, my, how we celebrated. I don't know what my Dad must have thought but I can remember Matth, right up at the segregation fence, going*

*"apeshit" (now there's a term you don't hear too often these days)
and sticking his fingers up at the snarling Leicester fans....*
Score: 2-2. Town Scorers - Brian Stein, Harford
Attendance: 10,476

*The way back to the station must have clinched it for Dad, who has
only been to one or two home games since. We neither suffered nor
witnessed any acts of violence. But as we were led back to the station
at a snail's pace, walking with a large police escort behind a
constabulary meat wagon, our slow progress was tracked by a sinister
crowd in the shadows of the park adjacent. They seemingly made no
attempt to get at us - but it was a bit unnerving all the same.*

*To make matters worse for Dad, he found himself the target of
conversation from the man we call "Chief" (because of our great
teenage imagination - we thought he looked like an Indian chief).
Chieftain was always there, is still always there. He might be a great
bloke in everyday life, but as an LTFC fan he's a despicable, half-
drunk, half-wit - but he means no harm to other Town fans. In fact, if
you don't hide your colours he's likely to want to talk - and his tales
of alcohol and aggro are painfully dull.*

*Mick Harford, on the other hand, was just what the Town
needed. David Pleat's first wonderful First Division outfit played
football delightfully - but had something of a powder puff quality. We
had loads of flair but, apart from Basher Stephens, not enough
muscle. The signings of the defence-midfield-attack backbone of
(respectively) Steve Foster, Peter Nicholas and Mick Harford, coupled
with existing Second Division promotion veterans Mal Donaghy,
Ricky Hill and Brian Stein, saw Luton Town become a bone fide
topflight team.*

*This was the team which, for a few seasons, made Luton
capable of beating anyone at home (on plastic, I'll grant you) and
always likely to get a result away. It didn't last long, but at the time it
was really quite smart. (26/12/84).*

15/12/96: Bristol City 1 Bristol Rovers 1

Live on Sky! Sky have, in their wisdom, picked out a few local derbies in the second division as good for live broadcast. The Bristol derby is one, Luton/Watford in January another. The match ends with a last minute Rovers equaliser and subsequent mini-riot as City fans go to attack celebrating Rovers fans. The match is held up for five minutes and, at the final whistle, the Rovers players are chased off the pitch by a City mob. It's pretty depressing stuff. Unfortunately I see quite a bit of the same sort of hysteria surrounding our derby. Perhaps it has something to do with the fact that both sets of supporters know their clubs can't compete in the wider football world anymore - so the local rivalry takes on extra importance in the eye of the fans. I have, in recent years, (when we're doing nothing but slipping in the league) regarded the Watford games as the be all and end all of the season. And it is still overly important in my mind - as with, I reckon, most Luton and Watford fans.

18/12/96: Millwall v Luton Town

Went with Martin, and we met up with Mick, Neil and John (who shared a house with Mick while at college in Bradford a few years ago, so I know them from the Thrilled Skinny days). Mucking up the train times, as we tend to do in London, we got to the ground late - but remarkably ran into Michael inside. I haven't been to Millwall since the last Town match at Cold Blow Lane (which we lost). The new ground offers a fantastic view but seems somehow sterile. The crowd, all of 7000, never seemed particularly bothered as the game plodded on in the rain. Luton look good on the break but are let down by poor finishing and/or Bontcho (although James hit the post with a rasper). Millwall, on the other hand, have plenty of play but few ideas.

A creditable, boring 0-0 draw was on the cards until Ceri Hughes popped up in the very last minute with a shot from outside the area which went so slowly that I'd given up on it and was sitting back down. But the keeper's dive had, incredibly, been despairing and the slightest ripple of the net and my peers' cheering informed me that the ball had somehow crept in. And, incredibly, Luton Town were top of a league for the first time since 1982. It's a good feeling - but the reaction of some Town fans is doltish to say the least. Games like this often bring out an element who, though they don't appear to cause trouble - they'd like us (and the other fans) to think they would. And they aren't the wittiest orators - one prat in particular, sitting a good few rows behind and to the right of me, shouted for much of the game about the "Paki" referee (I still can't remember if the ref was Asian, he was probably just tanned). And, when Luton scored, Mr Bigot comforted himself by getting in a rage - endorsing the "Luton's going up" song by screaming "We're going up as f***in' Champions". I have, in previous years, fallen into a trap of believing that Town supporters are the wittiest fans in the world - people like this, sadly, belie that myth. I wish they'd leave us alone.

Score: 0-1. Town scorer – Hughes
Attendance: 7,077

Outside the ground we hid colours away and tried to blend in with the sombre atmosphere at the station (something I never find too hard to do in South London). Back at London Bridge we found a pub and had a couple more pints o'beer.

21/12/96: Brentford 0 Preston North End 0.

And Brentford, who've played one game more than Luton but scored less goals, go back on top of the Second Division.

24/12/91: The nightmare before Christmas

1991 *Being "into football" sat, by and large, pretty well with the Thrilled Skinny lifestyle. Football was slowly becoming fashionable but there were still plenty in the Indie Pop kid peer groups with which we mixed who couldn't really take in the idea that a football fan could be anything other than a moron. Nationally the scene was changing fast, football fandom was quickly getting downright trendy – but on a local level we were still viewed with a certain amount of incomprehension when we talked Luton*

Town FC. *Of course, at first, we delighted that such quirkiness had once again set us apart – within months our interest in football saw our little clique open up to those in the Indie set who felt free to admit a past or present concern for the goings on at Kenilworth Road.*

There must have been some anti-football, or at least anti-Luton, feeling in the pub that year though; because, on my seventh or eighth visit to the gents that night, I saw that some swine had thrown a Luton scarf in the urinal. A scarf which had, in due course, become sodden.

It has to be remembered that, being the biggest night out of the year, I was quite drunk at the time.

Ordinarily, I don't know, I would have gingerly kicked it out and left it in a quiet corner to die peacefully – but that night I decided to pick the scarf out, with the tips of my fingers, and wash it out. In the clean flushing water of the toilet bowl.

Sadly, in hindsight inevitably, my tentative grip on the scarf gave way. Before I knew it the powerful current took hold, I gazed in horror as the end fringes disappeared from the bowl on their way through the u-bend. And the so the scarf, and a notable additional Christmas gift for one of my brothers ("why is this scarf damp?" they would have asked), was gone.

I washed my hands, I tried to laugh it off, but the pain remains. To this day I can't believe it; but I know its true, I flushed a Town scarf down the loo.

25/12/96:

Christmas! Hoorah! Got a nice sweater....M&S polo neck, a couple of videos - Shooting Stars and On the Buses, a new Fred Perry, one of them "Polo" shirts - a fake from Abu Dhabi (where Father goes on business), a little cash, satsuma, loads of foodstuffs. (*26/12/96*).

26/12/84: Close encounter with the Luton Strikers.
Luton Town v Coventry City

1984 *By the mid-eighties it seemed as if every club was attempting to beat the hooligan threat by spouting the "traditional family values" line about football. Apparently, back in the good old days, the whole family would go to the match together. It might've happened. My Mum remembers, as a child, being passed down the terrace to sit at the front - though I rather think that this measure, apart from allowing the little darlings to see, also helped their Dads (and Mums?) to swear and drink without fearing that they might be passing on their bad habits; though this is of course conjecture.*

What is for sure is that Luton Town was one of the original, if not the first, clubs to have its own Junior Club. The Junior Hatters, which we all joined because they gave you quite a smart metal badge when you did. Watford took the Junior Club theme further than anyone. Many mature Watford fans, having suffered Aled Jones syndrome, still go in for castration so they can join in the songs and hit the high notes. I'm being regionalist of course.

Anyway, Luton in the mid-eighties supposedly "bringing the family back" into football. Women, you'd think, included. So, the brand new half-time entertainment they brought in was "The Luton Strikers" - an all girl dance team, similar to the American cheerleaders which died a death years before, gyrating to some dreadful disco shite in their leotards with pom-poms, on the centre circle.

More often than not a solitary, doubtless pissed, away fan would climb over the barrier and join the girls, only to be carted away by the police/stewards. The most popular part of the Strikers routine was when they bent over, to the obvious delight of the lads on the terrace. Oh yes, they were sex symbols alright. At a distance. For, on that cold Boxing Day of 84, the ladies had a treat in store for the Town fans in the Oak Road. Why, their routine would be performed right at the fences in front of the terrace. Beauties they were not......

Remember the scene in The Shining where Jack Nicholson is snogging that gorgeous young lady who, all of a sudden, is revealed to be a haggard old crone? It was that sort of realisation.

There were girls in the crowd that day, there are probably quite a few more regulars now. These days, thank god, the Club don't make life so cringingly awful for them. (2/03/85).
**Score: 2-0. Town scorers - Brian Stein, Daniel
Attendance: 9,237**

26/12/96: Gillingham v Luton Town

Gillingham doesn't know this, but the area is close to my heart. Bands from the Medway Delta provided some of the soundtrack to my late-teens and early 20's. My favourite band ever, The Prisoners, come from Chatham where there was once a thriving music scene spearheaded by renowned musician, poet and author Sir William Childish. I still try and see The Prisoners (reunion gigs), The JTQ and occasionally Thee Headcoats (though I don't like them much) when they play - and can still remember driving all the way from Luton to see the first gig by The Prime Movers in some little pub.

A 12 o'clock kickoff, which meant getting up at 8.30am. Accompanied by Simon, Katherine and, once we'd picked him up in London, Andrew. Obviously Gillingham is a little club, small ramshackle ground, and a section of fans near the away end who are experts in derision. However, their style of play is despicable - always on the hoof. Their team is made up of massive defenders, dwarflike midfielders and massive attackers. Their game is made up of running, winning balls in midfield and hoping to score through the scramble that follows a ball being hoofed or thrown into the six-yard box. Not pretty to watch, not easy to play against.

But the Town, although nowhere near top form, did alright. Thorpe scored in the first-half, followed by a scrambled equaliser. In the second half Thorpe scored brilliantly again and the rest of the game saw Luton pinned back, though we should have scored from at least two clear opportunities on the break. It was all looking just a little too much like Bournemouth for comfort - although, somehow, the Town defence remained solid. It was no surprise then when the ref decided, on ninety minutes, to take a hand in proceedings and award Gillingham a penalty. It was all too predictable.

What couldn't be predicted was the inspired save which Feuer pulled off, low in the corner, to win Luton the match.....I came so close to doing that stupid "I'm not worthy" thing. The match ended seconds later with the Gillingham players, nasty pieces of work, deciding to scuffle with the Town players. No such bother outside the ground as we went home, grinning like Cheshire cats and looking forward to the second Christmas dinner of the year.

Score: 1-2. Town scorer - Thorpe (2)
Attendance: 8,491

Later that day........ Plymouth 1 Brentford 4.... and so we're knocked off top spot again. I don't mind Brentford winning as much as their doing so by such a margin. I thought Plymouth were supposed to be hard to beat.

JANUARY

1/1/97: Luton Town v Bury
(Postponed. Pools panel verdict - home win).

Quite a big match, on our small scale, as Bury are third in the table - a Town win would have really opened up quite a gap (currently 5 points) between themselves, Brentford, and the chasing pack. Predictably, though we were blinded by optimism and bought tickets (Andy and I for our brothers, in the area for Christmas, and for our girlfriends), the match is called off early on New Years Eve.

Later in the evening, drinking out 1996 in the pub, we wonder with Ian when we'll get to see another game. Christmas has had a frightening effect on my bank balance, so Blackpool on the 11th was out of the question, although even if I had tons of money, I'd have to think hard about a trip to Blackpool in January, even though it's my favourite seaside town apart from Brighton. Apart from that, Ian tells us, there was the match at Northampton on the 7th in the Auto Windscreen Thing. A certain non-starter for me but Ian says that there might be a good crowd because Northampton have been looking to play Luton for years. Well really. Hopefully they'll beat us and take as much pleasure out of it as Reading took from winning the Simod Cup. (*2/1/97*).

2/1/84: Emeka
Luton Town v Nottingham Forest

 Chukwuemeka Nwajiobi came to Luton from Nigeria via Dulwich Hamlet and training to be a fully qualified pharmacist. In his debut, against Nottingham Forest, he made **1984** *an immediate impression. The man was a striker/human tank. He would get the ball and run with it, with no particular speed, defenders would rush in to dispossess him - and Emeka would simply run through them. Opposition players would simply bounce off him. He had massive, tree trunk, legs and was so damned strong it was amazing*

Emeka scored on his debut, a shot which he hit so hard on the turn that he ended up on his arse (arms in the air) in the middle of the Oak Road penalty area.

As a team Forest were far too strong for Luton that day, but their defence was heavily outgunned by Emeka.

Emeka was at Luton for a good few years, a charming man who always frightened defences. He also scored some good goals, presented another attacking option and always made for some laughs as we read the programme at away games to see how they misspelled his name. (14/01/84).

Score: 2-3. Town scorers – Walsh, Nwajiobi
Attendance 12,126

2/1/97: The long running saga of our trying to get England tickets reaches a typically frustrating conclusion. When I first rang the box office, about a month before the World Cup qualifying campaign started, I was told I was too early. Next time I rang I was too late - and was given a number to call on the 2nd Jan at 10am for remaining England v Italy tickets. Not suprisingly the line was permanently engaged....

4/1/97: Luton Town v Wycombe Wanderers (Postponed. Pools panel verdict - home win)

Very little chance of this game going ahead. Too skint to even go out in the evening, which is a swine......spend day "fart-arsing" around at home.

11/1/97: FA Cup 3rd Round. Luton Town v Bolton Wanderers (Postponed. Pools panel verdict - score draw).
It's getting predictable now. I make plans to do a Mystery Motorist marking for work (checking up on sales assistants.....a weasley way to spend time, but the money is handy) before the pitch inspection on Friday. So, instead of Kenilworth Road, we go to petrol sites in Buckinghamshire. Including, as a matter of interest, one that is very near to Wycombe Wanderers ground - I point out to Claire where we walked to get to the ground, where we put a bet (that very nearly came in) on, the pub which had the "Home fans only" sign up, the chippy we considered and the place where we parked....couldn't park there now - it's a building site. I even offered to drive Claire up the road to have a look at the ground. She didn't even feign interest.

We listen to Radio 5's coverage of the games that beat the freeze. The Wrexham manager belies the romance of the cup ideal by eagerly telling of the windfall that can be earned with an away match at a Premiership side. That he'd love to beat West Ham at home - but the hardnosed financial fact is that a replay would be the best result. There are few shocks. Reading beat Southampton 3-1. Wrexham earn a replay at West Ham.

12/1/97: The FA Cup 3rd round continues. Charlton earn a replay at Newcastle - *ca-ching* - and prepubescent football fans around the country give a high pitched cheer as Man Utd beat Spurs. Then the 4th round draw. With so few matches decided it's obviously a farce - but Graham Kelly and cohorts don't rest on their laurels, they make damned sure it's an embarrassing spectacle. Tony Gubba introduces the special guests - Peter Shilton ("who, after 115 years as a pro, hasn't yet been a Cup winner" - "There's still time Tony" says Peter, tongue in cheek, to the amusement of the selected audience of FA officials, the Reading manager and kids/blokes in replica tops who missed out on "Fantasy Football League" tickets) and Jim Montgomery, the keeper who played in the 2nd Division Sunderland side of 1972 who amazingly beat Leeds. He played a blinder that day but, maybe because he's not as famous a figure as Shilton now, Gubba hasn't as much time for chat "So Jim do you think a lower division side could still win the cup as you did back in '72?". "No, not these days". "Thank you". It's pretty lame stuff. They might do better to get Brucie in next time.... "So, Jim, tell us about your honeymoon". But it's over to Graham Kelly, looking characteristically uneasy, to mention the sponsors and explain the bleedin' obvious. Peter is to pick out the home sides.....make sure all the balls are out of the velvet bag (with FA insignia) and into the mechanical goldfish bowl which turns them at the push of a button. The button is pushed. The balls move around. And, after a few seconds as we admire the technology, the balls are picked out and the draw is made. Luton or Bolton get a potentially enthralling home tie against Chesterfield or someone else. The permutations make the draw almost as significant as a Mystic Meg prediction but, realising it's all going too smoothly, Graham intercedes close to the end of the draw with "give the button a push would you David". David sheepishly complies and the nine or so remaining balls (minus the one that Peter has in his hand) revolve round again. The suspense throughout is non-existent.

7/1/97: Autowindscreenshield round 2.

Northampton Town v Luton Town (postponed). Damn!
With any luck they'll decide the tie with the toss of a coin. And if Luton win, we should ask to make it best of three.

8/1/97: Kevin Keegan shocks the world, and Newcastle in particular, by resigning as manager. Stunned Geordies ask why, but the man is out of the country and all that is issued is a statement saying he felt he had done "all he could" for the club. Later on the word is that he had wanted to leave at the end of last season, had been talked out of it and had made it clear he intended to leave at the end of this season instead. However, due to the forthcoming floatation of the Club on the stockmarket and the implications of making that decision public, he had decided to go immediately. It's a pity. Keegan seemed a great bloke - even if, at times, it seemed he surely wasn't cut out for football management. He simply cared too much - the loss of the Championship last season obviously hurt him deeply. Danny Baker vilified Keegan for quitting on his Radio 5 show in the evening - saying he'd let all Newcastle fans down. He might be right, but I doubt it. It seems to me that the mental strains of a job, albeit at least partly self-imposed, meant that he had to give the job up - the apparent bad timing of the decision due more to the new financial pressures of Premiership football than weakness on Keegan's part.

11/1/97: Blackpool v Luton Town (Postponed. Pools panel verdict - scoring draw)
Something of a surprise - I really thought this one would be on. Oh well. Wouldn't have gone anyway. The pools panel gives us a score draw, which isn't bad, but with Brentford beating York 4-2 away (come on rest of the league - give us a hand) we really needed a win.

On Friday night it seems that everyone has developed a talent at meteorology, with particular reference to the chances of the Bolton FA Cup match taking place. Our milkman, picking up his cheque, reckons there is little chance - as he's the man who is up with the frost, I go with his theory. I half hope he's right. It's Andy's birthday on Tuesday night and, if the match is on, there'll be a ticklish situation as I miss going out for a Thai meal for the football. Andy will be OK about it (he's a wet blanket for not changing the date of the meal in the first place) but Max, and Claire (who'll miss out too), will scowl. So I make the most of "it won't be on anyway" excuses when I'm drawn and become fixtures expert instead. The game, I tell Ian at the bar, will be rescheduled for 25/1/97, the day of the 4th round ties.

13/1/97: Very mild day - there seems no reason why tomorrow's match would be called off. At work I sit next to the bosses' secretary. Sue. Nice woman. Today she is calling round dealers to ask whether they want to join Steve to see England v Italy. As usual most of the dealers (we deal petrol, nothing sexy like crack cocaine) have no idea who England are playing, or even where the game is being played. It'll be Wembley or Twickers. They only used to go to the rugby, but seem to have enjoyed Euro96.

I used to be bitter about it, but the FA are obviously so much more interested in courting corporate entertainment than they are in catering for "the fans". And I can't complain. For one thing it sounds pathetic when I do, and for another my boss (not a bad bloke really, realises which one of us is the real football fan, but regards such fixtures as no more or less than good business) gave me his England v Netherlands programme. Sue tells me that I might be lucky one day and get a ticket due to a last minute cancellation by a (double booked) dealer. That'll be nice, stuck in Wembley with a bunch of drunken corporate suits.

14/1/84: Close Shave
Luton Town v Arsenal

1984 *It must have been terribly disheartening for anyone with a social conscience in the mid-80's to hear little brats merrily joining in with the crowd during the latest rendition of the "You're gonna get../you're going home..." threat medley. The chants were aimed at the away support right up at the other end of the pitch, and the intended implication was that those bastards stood up there were damn lucky that the police and stewards and fences were protecting them from us – 'cause we're so bloody hard. The reality of course was a little different. The other end of the football pitch was as near to the away fans, and their own (equally empty) threats, as we really wanted to be.*

Those Lutonian toughs who wanted a fight were in the "Maple triangle" nearest the away section. The usual turn of events was that a small group would be in the away end, have a scuffle, and then attempt to avoid arrest (and a kick-in) by jumping back in with their pals. "Luton aggro, Luton aggro, Luton aggro" we would all dutifully shout from the safety of the Oak Road terrace. It was, on occasion, nastier than that; but thankfully it was almost always at a distance.

The Oak Road terrace had had its own battles, but most of them must have been in the 70's or very early 80's because we only really suffered one "major" (i.e. too close for comfort) disturbance when we stood there.

It was particularly bad because it was so unexpected. Groups of dodgy looking strangers could usually be seen, and moved away from, reasonably easily. They would normally be led out by the police after the resident Oak Road "big blokes from the back" had enjoyed a slanging match and thrown a punch or two at them. One such bout of dramatic posturing occurred before the Arsenal match, leading to two or three Gunner 'ooligans being led around the front of the terrace, swearing to the jeering Town fans as they went, by the police. All pretty run of the mill stuff for a match against a London team.

Then, just as we were settling down to watching the game instead, a bloke a few feet behind us shouted something unintelligible to us and "it kicked off" (as they say in the hooliebooks). A guy a couple of steps in front of us began laying into people in his immediate vicinity while his mates right behind us did likewise; meanwhile we did our best to get as far away from them as possible – which wasn't at all easy. The big gaps that used to appear on the terraces when fighting erupted, weren't made to provide a schoolyard arena for those fans not wishing to partake with a good view whilst they chanted "Fight Fight Fight Fight"; they were created by people clamouring to get out of the way. The outer fringes of the ring was no place to be – for there you'd likely get duffed in.

Another thing that made the attack alarming, apart from the fact that it was so near us, was that it was in a part of the terrace where nobody was really up for the fighting lark. What toughs there were in the Oak Road end stood at the back and were unable to rush to our aid – because all the traffic was coming the other way. It was pretty scary in there for a little while. Its not just that we didn't want to be hit and/or kicked (though that threat would have been more than enough for us to want to give the area a wide berth) but, for all we knew, these people might have been carrying knives.

Andrew, the heroic older brother, took charge of the situation and wisely decided that we'd better stick together and get to the front of the terrace until the police had sorted the trouble out. Good plan. So, we struggled to the front only to find that that was where the Arsenal fans themselves were congregating for a final flurry of fisticuffs before the police chucked them out. We saw what was happening, just in time, and ran off again.

The police eventually got them out to the sound of "You'll never take the Oak Road" and we, bravado restored, defiantly joined in. If there was any justice in the world the Town would have won that game – just to show them cockney swine. There wasn't. We lost.

Score 1-2. Town scorer – Kay (og).
Attendance 16,320.

At school the following Monday the football violence intelligence service, those whose interest in the game involved "supporting Liverpool" and knowing all about aggro (and "firms" and all that hard stuff), had a theory on Saturday's trouble at Luton. It was caused, they informed us, not by Arsenal fans at all – but West Ham hooligans who had got off the train at Luton after their match had been called off. It seemed feasible enough until one of them told me how you could tell a bone fide West Ham thug in a crowd. Apparently, he told me authoritatively, they all wore flat caps and had beards. I told him yes, that was right, them was the ones what did it.

Of course, his self-appointed status as expert in the field had been shattered by a failure to distinguish between two cockney institutions of the time – the ICF and Chas 'n' Dave, but I wasn't going to tell him.

"You'll never take the Oak Road" wasn't an oft heard chant at Luton at the time becase, as I've said, not too many tried. When Chelsea came to Kenilworth Road in September '84 the Town fans at the back had chanted "Chelsea, where are you?" In the middle of the terrace it was glaringly obvious, even before they started singing back, that there were strange faces everywhere. When they did start singing it was immediately obvious that the Chelsea fans were, very much, in the Luton end. In most cases it took an incident on the pitch, traditionally a goal, to trigger off a fight. The match on that day, mercifully, was a bland 0-0 draw. If ever a match seemed settled on police advice then that was it. Inside the ground at least, there was no major incident that day. (21/04/84)

14/1/97: FA Cup Third Round.
Luton Town v Bolton Wanderers (postponed).

Phoned up the club in the morning, the match is definitely on. At lunchtime I buy these ace desert wellies, really nice ones which had been reduced down from £95 to £49.95 to £45 to £33.75. Benchmade bargain with a fine finish (I really wanted a pair of Clarks originals, down to £18.75, but they didn't have my size), they should last quite a while longer than your usual common or garden £10 dessie.

Wore my new boots to drop Andy off his card and then to the pub prior to the match where the scene is pleasantly familiar. Keith and the fanzine boys are there, the latest edition of "Mad as a Hatter" has been out since the new year but they haven't had a chance to sell it yet. The sales team run like a well-oiled, certainly well lubricated, machine. They all know their pitches, the only question for most of them is whether they can down another pint before making a move. Keith has another question for me - whether I'd like to be part of a Hatters panel for some TV programme a week on Sunday. I tell him I don't know, we're busy on Sundays. And anyway, I'm under no illusions that my flirtation with the media is smooth outside print - I've been on the radio a couple of times and been a nervous wreck. People who suffer from vertigo (and I do, to a minimal extent) fear that, on the top of a high building, they might feel compelled to throw themselves off. When I've been live on BBC Three Counties radio I've felt the same sort of fear that, without warning, I'm going to say "f***". Apart from that, I was so bloody nervous last time I was on the radio, it was painful. It's self fulfilling prophecy which gets worse as the interview goes on. Whatever the case, as a media star, I tend to sound better in print.

Keith Hayward on the other hand is a natural on the telly and a good orator ("media whore" as I called him once, and the swine didn't realise I was pulling his leg). It's a pros and cons thing.... The info is sketchy, Keith seems a bit miffed that I didn't jump at the chance and doesn't give many details. Jez says it's in a pub, free booze for three hours, with Watford, Spurs and Arsenal fans (an opportunity to join hands and sing "We are the world" before the local derbies?). I tell him I'll tell him on Friday. He goes off, with his pals, to sell his wares.

Michael, accompanied by a girl, and Chris come in and a little bit later Simon walks in with the news that the match has been called off. It's a poor joke, but such is terrace humour - we tell him to shut up. He maintains he's not joking, it's been on the radio, and we spend the next minute or so calling him a bloody liar - but his face doesn't crack into a smile. So, we're the first in the pub to know - and do the bad news round. Eventually the fanzine boys come back too - all slagging the club off for not calling the match off earlier. And so I get to spend an extra couple of hours and drink an extra couple of pints down the pub - and get a bit drunk. Everyone is pissed off - but news that Watford's match was called off one minute before kick-off puts us in a happier frame of mind.

My voice starts getting slurred and I start forgetting people's names, so decide to go home via the kebabery.

17/1/97: My brother Andrew rings me up at work to ask about the Notts County away match which is, like, weeks away. "Will we need tickets?". "Wha?". I dunno, probably not. He's got a mate at work in the smoke who's "curious" about football, so he's taking him to see Luton away. Good choice. The two of them are following up that excursion by going to see England v Italy. The lucky swine. He's never shown any interest in England matches before. In a jealous rage I swear at him down the phone for a bit, but probably need to shout at him - an inch away from his face - in the guise of the hard done by "real fan" for optimum effect. Balls. Oh well, fair play to him. Spawny get.

18/1/97: Luton Town v Wrexham

It's just one of those things, you wait so long for the resumption of normal service and it's invariably a let down. Andy is ill after his birthday Thai meal - which serves him right for not putting it off to fit in with my plans (the bloke is so selfish). So he doesn't come down the pub pre-match.

Simon is late down the pub (well, he doesn't get there) having been "held up" in St. Albans. Finding he has a huge appetite, he decides to pop out of the ground during the game to nip off down the chippy. The bloke on the gate obliges and he comes back having bought me a bag too. He's a good boy. It's a great thing to be able to do too - I bet you can't do that at Man Utd or Spurs.

Luton v Wrexham was the first game I ever saw back in 1980. The Town won 2-0 but all I can remember of the game is Luton streaming away from a Wrexham corner only to be caught offside. I remember it from a vantage point right at the back of the Oak Road, where I couldn't possibly have been.....unless I was on Dad's shoulders...oh, might've happened. Such thoughts are the only interest this afternoon. Luton look "rusty". Simon recognises, during the Town fans' rendition of "You fat bastard" to ubiquitous mouthy fat bloke in the away end (performing the time honoured response of holding out stomach, patting it, putting arms in the air), that terrace humour has all but died. "Who ate all the pies?" the fans in the corner go on, automatically, proving the point.

Immediately after the match Claire and I shoot off to Cheltenham to see Steve (prior to doing service station markings on Sunday). Steve is in his element at college there. He's so damn popular, especially with the young ladies, it's unbelievable. Good luck to the blighter, like he needs it. (*20/1/97*).

Score: 0-0
Attendance: 6,167

19/1/88: Did you say "a cat"?
Littlewoods Cup, Quarter Final. Luton Town v Bradford City

1988 *There was no way that Luton were going to lose this one. By now, and given the favourable draw, we very much fancied our chances of doing something big in the cup. Even so, Luton managed to make very heavy weather of beating Bradford. It even seemed, as the minutes of the second half ticked away, that there might have to be a replay up north - where the chance of an upset (i.e. as in "my being") would be greatly increased.*

Their keeper made a daft mistake, picking the ball up again having dropped it and dribbled it in and then out of his area or summat, and Luton scored from the free kick. Time, amidst the cheering, for a big sigh of relief, loss of pressure and eventually a second goal. "WEM-BER-LEE" we sang, "WEM-BER-LEE" we continued, "WE'RE THE FAMOUS LUTON TOWN AND WE'RE GUN T'WEM-BER-LEE" then we started again with "WEM-BER-LEE". It's a song that these days we sing in sarcasm.

The Bradford fans in the terrace next to us, our being separated by a fence and line of stewards, weren't as happy and started lobbing coins and tiny bits of terrace at us. It didn't bother us unduly until someone misheard the word "coin" for "cat" - which meant we left the ground laughing quite a lot at the thought of a terrified moggy, claws and teeth ready, landing amongst the Luton fans. Blood and fur carnage on the terraces.

Score: 2-0. Town scorers – Foster, Harford
Attendance: 11,022

On the Hoppanstopper back to Slip End our aspiring hooligan pals were particularly obnoxious to the driver and other passengers. Worse than their actions was the fact that, embarrassed though we were by their f***witted antics, we could only sit back and let them carry on.

Anyway, that was the last time we went to a match with that crowd. Perhaps they've grown up a little now, in any case we never see them at matches these days.

Even so, at the time, having decided to chuck that lot - we had a League Cup Semi-Final to look forward to! The semi-final draw was kind to us (as we all thought the FA Cup semi-final draw was later). Arsenal had to play two legs against Everton whilst our semi, against Oxford, would provide the Final's underdog. We were also pleased that the first leg was away. (10/02/88).

20/1/97: A night of mixed fortunes for AC Meringue. We lose both our games of course but the way we achieve the results differs. In the first game we're 1-0 and then 2-1 up in the first half before Martin comes on, and with cavalier abandon leaves the defensive post for forays forward, leaving me at the back alone most of the time. We lose 3-2. Paul gives away a penalty, by keeping outside his area and shouts "No f***ing way" at the good old boy ref. Tosspot. In the second game I suss out a bright new way of rotating duties with the half time substitution whereby the fresh legged sub goes up front whilst the knackered first half forward goes back to defend. The plan depends on keeping position, concentration and guile. Unfortunately our opponents are young sporty types who quickly suss that we're not very good and start taking the piss - passing the ball about, drawing the opposition (which is especially humiliating) and scoring apparently at will. We lose 5-0. However, their sub on the sidelines tells Steve Nash that we're a lot better than the first team they played. It was us! We are improving! One win this season will do for us.

21/1/97: FA Cup 3rd Round.
Luton Town v Bolton Wanderers

"It's off" says a wag in the pub - and in just about every pub in Luton tonight before the game. Ho ho. Rather than tonight's match, the talk in the pub is of the Watford match on Monday night. The plan is apparently "down the pub early". Then there's all the usual talk of the likelihood of trouble. These blokes (the fanzine boys) aren't trouble makers by any means, but such talk is always likely. Fans seem to feed off the reflected adrenaline. Although, if and when trouble happens, the first thought is to keep out of it - there will still be interest about how, where and when incidents occurred. There will obviously be some trouble; there has been a sinister rise since the rivalry was re-established when we got relegated from the old First Division. Hopefully that rise (which I think peaked when some Watford idiots leafleted Luton pubs, with "we're gonna duff you up" type literature, before the corresponding fixture last year) has now been checked. However, the latest edition of a Watford fanzine apparently urges fans not to go to Luton - avoiding giving money to us, and the perilous journey to and from the ground. The game is live on Sky, but it will still be interesting to see how many fans Watford take away. Pundits would say that a big derby atmosphere is great, and I'd agree, but where do you draw the line given that most of the atmosphere is born out of deep mutual loathing. The media love drawling over the unique atmosphere of the Glasgow derby - the same feeling that creates it is also known to kill a kid who wears the wrong scarf in the wrong part of the city.

Anyway, the fact is that nobody is really thinking Cup football this year. With regard to tonight's match some are of the opinion that it might be best to be knocked out. I see their point, but don't really agree. FA Cup runs are nice. The Autowindscreenshield is a different story.

The match is good. Bolton are an extremely good footballing side. We've seen it before, they go up to the Premiership, lose two or three of their best players, are relegated and start again. They're top of the First Division now - they'll probably be there again this time in 1999. Luton also play like they know there are scouts afoot - Thorpe particularly plays a blinder. But after Bolton take the lead it never looks very likely that the Town are going to score.

We're sat in the middle of a block in the Kenilworth stand - which affords a much better view than our season ticket seats in the antiquated main stand. However, it isn't nearly as useful for the amenities and in the second half I really need the toilet, increasingly badly. I don't know where the ref gets all the added time from at the end but, as luck would have it, Bolton get the same injury time jitters as Luton have had a couple of times this season. Feuer goes up for a corner and in the ensuing melee Marvellous Marvin scores. The Town fans go, rather surprisingly, WILD. The ref blows time soon after, I dash for a lash running past some twonk doing a solo of "You're not singing anymore" at the Bolton fans. Two queries. Firstly, they were never singing much anyway. Secondly, does he really think they can hear him - his voice cracking up from 90 minutes of similar abuse - right at the other end of the pitch?

Score: 1-1. Town scorer - Johnson
Attendance 7,414

We walk home and decide that, well, we might just hold out and win on penalties at Bolton.

25/1/97: FA Cup 3rd Round Replay
Bolton Wanderers v Luton Town

And then again we might lose in normal time. In fact we lost in the second half.

Because I was busy sanding and varnishing shelves, I was allowed to watch Sky's Super Saturday scores service for fans who "can't get to the match this week" (i.e. 99.9% of Manchester Utd fans). And what a great service it is - with goal flashes up every time the ball goes in the net anywhere. Luton go 1-0 down. Then, wow!, 1-1.......the score service computer doesn't know whether it's Thorpe or Marshall that has scored....No, they both have! 2-1 to the Town.

And so it stays until half time where the reporter is talking about a possible upset.

Damn. Bolton equalise soon after the second half begins and I start to worry at the detrimental effect extra time might have so soon before the Watford match....but not for long. The screen flashes 3-2 to Bolton and we go live to the reporter who tells us about it - while he's talking over goal 3, goal number 4 is scored. Perhaps it's not a totally bad thing, we're best out of the cup really. It'd be nice if the Town could get another consolation goal.... "GOAL Bolton 5 Luton 2".

The full time scores start coming through and are well underway before "GOAL Bolton 6 Luton 2" flashes up to show that play/cruelty hasn't stopped everywhere.

It's a bit of a stuffing..... and the futile cup dream is over for another season.

Score: 6-2. Town scorers – Marshall, Thorpe
Attendance: 9,713

27/1/97: Luton Town v Watford

"The Luton bank holiday" we were told, a few of the fanzine boys having apparently decided to spend all day in the pub. Most of us go to work as normal, under the usual pre-derby stress, but Andy and I go to the pub early anyway. Claire and Max stay behind, with wine, to watch the match (and the almost perverse pre-match programme - which informs viewers that a cheeseburger at Kenilworth Road costs £1.80, Bovril 70p) on Sky.

The atmosphere in the pub is tense though there's no hint of violence, no hint of a Watford fan. The all day drinkers are in the back of the bar cheering the video of the 4-2 win at Watford a few years ago (the last time the match wasn't drawn). Nick Gazeley (of the fanzine, affable bloke) comes in with the girl, Helen, who co-hosts the Sky Saturday/Sunday morning football filler - aimed at supporters under the age of four. It's a rubbish programme - I sometimes watch it whilst getting dressed because, apart from the subject matter, Helen and pals are marginally less annoying than Zoe Ball. Anyway, it's pretty sickly to see how some of the lads are fawning over her.

The walk to the ground was memorable, if only for its uneasy nature and the amount of police on duty near the ground. There seem to be quite a few self-acclaimed aggro merchants about but there's no trouble on show - just plenty of "We hate Watford". And plenty in the ground too. Watford have a pitifully small following but manage to make themselves heard. Most of our songs are the anti-Watford standards we know and love but, as if to prove that quite a few aren't enchanted by hatred for the ragged band of deadbeats and sixth formers to our left, the pro-Luton songs are sung by more people. We join in just about everything, swearing like heroes when called upon to do so.

There are a few stereotype skinheads about - but the haircut is surely a bit of a giveaway. Maybe they're here to show they follow the 70's, football aggro/neo nazi, code rather than that of gay icon. Maybe news will surface at the weekend about scuffles and pubs "done over"; I somehow doubt there'll be much to talk about.

The match, probably because of the importance the fans place on it, is crap. Watford, typically, play horrible football and manage to bring the Town down to their own despicably low level. How the (potentially) massive live TV audience must have felt.... On Sunday Newcastle 1 Notts Forest 2, Chelsea 4 Liverpool 2 - Monday Luton 0 Watford 0. (*1/2/97*).

Score: 0-0
Attendance 7,977

28/1/87: Kenny Dalglish, the man they seldom called Mr Magnanimous. FA Cup Third Round Second Replay.
Luton Town v Liverpool

1987 *One theory that Match of the Day commentators John Motson and Barry Davis never tired of trotting out in the 80's was Liverpool were never more dangerous than when they're a goal behind. They would find solace in the line when Liverpool went a goal down and echo the words triumphantly when the apparently inevitable equaliser was scored (usually followed by more delighted whooping at the Liverpool winner).*

Liverpool were undeniably the team of the 80's but, when Luton had a plastic pitch, and if incessant moaning (primarily by Kenny Dalglish) is anything to go by, they hated coming to Kenilworth Road more than any other club. In their previous match on our plastic a few month earlier (see 25/10/86) they had been beaten 4-1 - by the pitch, obviously, not by Luton.

The controversy of the 1987 FA Cup meeting was the nadir of the relationship between the two clubs and, even though (and likely because) Liverpool took the moral highground, it was Luton fans who were left with the smirks.

Liverpool's dislike of Luton's pitch was well documented before the Cup draw. They weren't very keen on the away fan ban either. That had already meant LTFC's exclusion from The Littlewoods Cup that year but the FA had (gutlessly) decided to invite Luton Town into their competition. Anyway, the controversy surrounding the game caused enough interest to get the BBC up to cover the match live. The game was a poor advert for plastic pitches in ominously poor weather and ended 0-0. Liverpool had the chances to win but clearly saw the opportunity to get Luton Town back at Anfield - on a proper pitch, in a proper atmosphere etc - as a moral victory. The consensus of opinion (which, in our quieter moments, we couldn't disagree with) was that precocious little Luton would suffer the mighty wrath of Liverpool come the night of the replay.....

But, come the night of the replay, the weather was decidedly dodgy throughout the country. Not that that affected Anfield unduly - its wonderful undersoil heating meant its wonderful sacred turf was as lush, and green, and playable as ever. But at Heathrow the plane that was chartered to take Luton Town up to Merseyside was stuck on the icy tarmac, going nowhere. It became obvious that the Luton team weren't going to make it, and the game would have to be called off - or cancelled. Seemingly preferring the latter, Liverpool took it upon themselves to invite the FA to throw Luton out of the cup, whilst Kenny Dalglish made a point of welcoming (in full view of the press corps) the small band of Hatters fans and Brian Swain of The Luton News who had managed to get up to Anfield. The FA, on weighing up the evidence - including Luton Town's own sob story - decided not to throw the Town out...... but, we feared all the more, the Liverpool backlash would be mightier still....

When the rearranged match finally did go ahead we sat around the radio at home, fearing the worst. As the game went on without any score it became increasingly difficult to sit and listen to the commentary of the siege of the Luton goal. An Ian Rush goal was even reported, followed (eventually) by a retraction - it had only hit the side netting. Pete was round so we went out instead, so he could have a fag, wandering around Slip End talking up the "shame, but we've done well to get this far" line. We came in again, wincing, ready to hear the result, then out again when we heard the match was going to extra time. Suffice to say that we were very happy with the draw, and the moral victory. It wasn't so much a two fingered salute to Liverpool FC, more a moony in the direction of Kenny Dalglish.

These days of course the match would have gone to penalties (which would have meant at least five penalties against Liverpool in one night - more than the Anfield season ticket holder sees there in five years) but, this being "the good old days", it was second replay time. Liverpool offered to play the game on a neutral ground (presumably not Loftus Road) but Luton, obviously now enjoying their role as "Giant nose tweakers", declined the offer. And won the toss. Back to plastic.

Despite our original fears that, having done so much, the Town were still just as likely to lose, the match was bleedin' marvellous. Luton played Liverpool off the carpet. A famous victory - made all the sweeter because, uh oh, Kenny didn't take it too well....

Score: 3-0. Town scorers - Brian Stein, Harford, Newell
Attendance: 14,687

With Liverpool beaten, the way was set for a historic cup run. The fourth round tie was against QPR. No trouble. However, they did manage to hold us to a draw at Kenilworth Road. Then they beat us 2-1 in the replay at Loftus Road.....which, looking back, kind of mucked up our chances of FA Cup glory totally. (6/10/87).

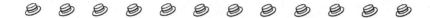

FEBRUARY

1/2/97: Notts County v Luton Town

The match which my brother Andrew has been going on about for months as he and his mate Paul (who turns out to be a Liverpool fan) drive up from London via Luton to pick up Michael and me. It appears that my brother's interest in the fortunes of the Town has been encouraged by his workmates "in the smoke", plenty of whom are also exiled fans of some no good team or other. And Paul, strangely enough, is interested in seeing Luton. It takes all sorts.

The journey up is painless. Paul seems a good bloke and he drives fast without being frightening. It's also nice to hear more of the second Beatles anthology album - although driving through Nottingham's suburbs listening to "Across the Universe" seemed a little odd....nothing's gonna change John's world, but my own sad little version is going to be affected by the outcome of a football match. Despite my brother's useless directions we eventually find the ground, park up and find a pub.

Notts County's ground is smart but they appear to have no fans - which is sad. Saturday Night and Sunday Morning started in the Notts County social club; Arthur Seaton may well be drinking on his own if he still frequents the bar. Even so in the strange atmosphere, which is only disturbed when the sizeable Town following sporadically organises a unified chant or two (and Luton fans are well used to giving up on a chant which isn't gaining any momentum), Luton don't make any inroads. Notts County's football, even at home, is the despicable hit and hope style so prevalent in this league.

A poor first half is only marked by some of the lads in our end who, hysterically, are waving about a blow up doll. That causes a bit of excitement amongst their peers - and by holding fists in the air they proudly show off their lovers too.

A sloppy first half is followed by a dire second in which Notts County score a sloppy goal on the break. Luton seem unlikely to do anything about it, and are quickly reverting to pot shots. Then, amazingly, one such effort - a thirty yard effort by Hughes fools the goalie (there might have been a bobble or a divot.....or a crap keeper) and the ball bounces under his stretching armpit and into the net. Wahey!

Then, with just a couple of minutes to go Graham Alexander pops up to volley a winner in front of us, causing a mass celebration - not least from Alexander himself. "Ooh-aah-Alexand-araa" the Luton fans sing up until the final whistle.

It's a good away win, a rubbish game.

Score: 1-2. Town scorers – Hughes, Alexander
Attendance: 4,866

4/2/97: Windscreencup or whatever it's called
Northampton Town v Luton Town

Wahey! We're out of the Mickey Mouse! I've been slagging the competition off quite a bit in the paper recently and Brian Swain's (Luton News/Town's press guru) said that everyone connected with the club wanted a win. The reasons for getting a good run in this competition were listed variously as; the chance to get to Wembley, the chance to win £50 000, another game in the competition would have meant Ceri Hughes would have to miss one less league match through suspension. Such is the magic of the cup.

Score: 1-0
Attendance: 4,201

8/2/97: Luton Town v Plymouth Argyle

Because of recent dismal failure we never go to matches these days expecting to win - but you do get the feeling at games like this that the players would want to get back to promotion form as quickly as possible - and against a team who had just lost their manager it surely looked on the cards.

It's a poor turnout from our lot at the match. Michael has gone to visit his sister in Adelaide, Chris is.....dunno where (mysterious character that he is) and Simon, even more mysteriously, is nowhere to be seen. It turns out he was in Leeds visiting Katherine's sister. With Katherine. Max has borrowed Michael's season ticket and Claire has turned down the opportunity to use Chris's - and here's me trying to paint South Bedfordshire as a hotbed of footballing passion.....in the North East fans would queue up overnight for the chance just to see a season ticket.

Mind you the footballing fayre on offer in this neck of the woods is of such a standard that, if it wasn't for the social side, buying a season ticket would seem a very dodgy decision. Division 2 might as well be named the Nationwide Airborne Division as team after team pay homage to the game according to Graham Taylor. Luton stupidly, but predictably, are bullied into fighting like with like in the first half - booting the ball towards massive Plymouth defenders hoping that little Dwight Marshall will rise above them. Plymouth get a penalty. Feuer saves it to great applause - and that embarrassing bowing thing which the Plymouth fans, quite rightly, sarcastically mimic every time Feuer kicks a little dodgily. In the Plymouth goal is Bruce Grobbelar, currently fighting pretty damned serious match fixing allegations. We taunt him, quite well I thought, with "He's going down, he's going down, he's going - Brucie's going down". But Bruce is a class act - instead of pretending he can't hear, he dances along to it (which is a crowd pleaser – though his pretending to play the guitar in accompaniment looks a bit silly).

The second half brings the goals. This season we have been spoilt to some extent by the fact that when Luton score, we usually win. Thorpe scores and he appears to be looking straight at me as he runs toward the crowd. I react with the usual standing on seat, shaking me arms about and shouting out summat like "Come On! Let's beat these bastards!". The bloke sat next to me, it turns out when they equalise, is a Plymouth fan. Thorpe scores again, with a looping header and then bloody Plymouth equalise again........what's going on? The match ends 2-2. We stay behind to applaud Feuer,

Thorpe, shout "Sort it out Lennie" and listen out for the no-lose Brentford v Watford game which ends, not surprisingly, in a 1-1 draw.

In the evening the pub is still playing host to about a dozen Plymouth fans displaying their shirts. This year's kit - green and white stripes (remember Pacers?) is quite smart. Meanwhile those wearing the obviously old strip, green and white....regions and lots of piddling flashes, look stupid.

Score: 2-2. Town scorer - Thorpe (2)
Attendance: 6,827

We stop for one before getting home to watch the pay per view Naseem v Johnson fight on Sky. I feel quite bad having gone against my principles by paying for this.....but that Naz is bloody ace. It may be that pretty soon all major sporting events will be on pay per view TV. Man Utd will make a fortune as will Rupert Murdoch - normal Sky will probably only have Division 1 rights, and I'll get rid. (*12/2/97*).

10/2/88: Littlewoods Cup semi-final first leg.
Oxford United v Luton Town

1988

The worst grounds in the league, in my experience, are Selhurst Park and the Manor Ground at Oxford. The away terrace at Upton Park used to be awful too - it's improved a lot now apparently.

The Manor Ground might seem a charming collection of strange little stands and terraces, but there always seemed much to dislike about the place. First and foremost they had the biggest crowd control/view obstruction fences of any ground I've been to. At most grounds, you didn't have to move up the terraces too far before the fences at the front no longer obscured the view of the pitch. On Oxford's nasty little open away end the wire mesh fence was as high as the terrace so, no matter where you stood, you were watching some of the play through fence mesh. Also, perhaps more tellingly, I don't think I've ever seen Luton win at Oxford - they won 5-2 earlier in the season, but I wasn't there. More astonishingly, on the Saturday before the first leg, the Town had beaten Oxford 7-4 at Kenilworth Road. Seven-four! I went to that match, it was one of the worst I'd ever been to - both defences were rubbish.

This game, on a freezing Tuesday night, was bound to be different. I'd driven Simon and Matth and Pete up in my first car. My green Ford Fiesta, scarves out the window of course.

On the pitch, covered by a light covering of snow, Luton took early control of the match and Brian Stein scored before the break. It's not difficult for an away following to fill the terrace at the Manor Ground - but the reaction in our end to the goal seemed particularly frenzied. Oxford came into the match in the second half, which was somewhat against the plot, and scored an equaliser. And then, after a disgraceful dive in the area, were awarded a penalty.

The semi-final penalty hero was Les Sealey. He saved it. Cue more feverish animation on the Luton terrace.

I can't remember the rest of the game. On the way back, crawling through the post match traffic, I was talked to by a traffic policeman for creeping, rather than running, a red light, my car just adding to the congestion on the junction. "I'm sure it was amber" I told the policeman. "No it was red" he said. I apologised, still feigning innocence, and drove on. Oh yes, me and my green Ford Fiesta, we was like Luke Duke and the General Lee when it came to trouble with the law. (28/02/88).

Score: 1-1. Town scorer - Brian Stein
Attendance: 12,943

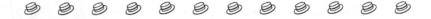

12/2/97: England v Italy
D'oh! Watched it at home. Andy and Max came round to watch the telly and listen to me swearing.
Score: 0-1

15/2/97: Bristol Rovers v Luton Town

As promised Claire and I visit Northampton to see her brother. Compared to Northampton, Luton is a bit of a dump. This view can be blamed in part on the inherent, commercially destructive, Lutonian self-depreciation. We're all well adept at nodding pseudo-gleefully as people from all around the country tell us what a hole we live in. When we toured with Thrilled Skinny we only put up with a few months of that before we went on a pro-Luton crusade telling people, lying if needs be, that Luton was indeed a beautiful place. The fact is that we lived, worked and socialised in the town. We loved it. It was home.

But there's no doubt that Northampton is a good place with a big open market square, a thriving pedestrian high street and lots of good pubs. And their shopping centre has a Virgin Megastore - to which we headed to purchase Claire's Mum a copy of the "Evita" soundtrack. On the way, and although I had mercifully not spent the day preoccupied with events on a muddy field a few hundred miles away, I was struggling to convince myself that the vibes I was getting from Bristol were of a Town win. It was about 4.35 and as we walked through the shopping centre I was waylaid by the television sets in Radio Rentals as the videprinter started.

Alone at first as the last goal flashes came in, I was soon surprised to see the density of the crowd and the density of the people who made it. Pictures of the scenes following an FA Cup shock - Chesterfield 1 Notts Forest 0 - raised a few eyebrows and at one boorish voice behind me "I can't believe it - Notts Forest lost at Chesterfield"...... the sound was turned down on the massed ranks of tellies, Steve Ryder's reaction could not be heard, he obviously thought his expert opinion was warranted.... More results came through and within a minute or so the Chesterfield result was confirmed as was the quote from matey "I can't believe it - Notts Forest lost at Chesterfield". Maybe he had a goldfish like memory - or maybe he really couldn't believe it.....

Northampton is a student town and the crowd was a pretty cosmopolitan bunch (and Man Utd weren't playing). The compulsory home town fan made himself known by sitting down cross legged on the floor and hopping up immediately after Northampton's score came through - the dramatic effect was lost slightly by the fact that his team had earned a 1-1 draw away from home, robbing us of the chance of a bit of animated reaction. Luton's score eventually appeared. Lost 3-2. Balls.

I stormed into Virgin, heading for Rock and Pop "D" where I hoped to find the reissue of Dexy's last album and avoid Claire and her brother whilst I indulged in a few minutes sulking. Claire catches me a bit early, she asks me where she might find The Stone Roses and I sarcastically snap "I dunno, try 'S'" at her....

I can't find "Don't stand me down" (I've been looking everywhere, I can't find them anywhere, where have they hidden them?). And my mood gently improves as we shop for tea (the meal, not the beverage) at Sainsburys. The grim overview of the game, through Teletext, has to be performed - and at least it wasn't a grotesque loss (like losing a two goal lead with ten minutes to go), 1-0 up, 3-1 down... it happens.... all too often for Luton fans..... during relegation campaigns. Relegation isn't on the cards - but neither, as yet, is the confidence needed to be promoted.

Nice evening in a good pub, The Fish, selling some good ale - better and cheaper than Firkin Luton (hey, that Firkin/F***ing pun is great for pseudo-writers and brewers alike isn't it just?)
Score: 3-2. Town scorers - Thorpe (pen), Waddock
Attendance: 5,612

17/2/97: The penultimate AC Meringue set of matches - three of them and, as we're depleted in numbers, Paul is there and we're all playing every match. In the first we draw level before getting knackered in the second half and the floodgates open. In the second game (against the second from bottom team) we're 1-0 up in the first half which includes the longest period in which I've been on the ball - time wasting in the corner. In the second half we let in two sloppy goals and lose. Between matches we talk about joining a lower quality league - an under 12 league or something. In the final game I suffer the indignity of going in goal (which I quite fancied beforehand) in the first half and letting in two own goals - the first of which was really pathetic - through my legs from a pass back from my brother. The second was by Tony and seemed to me to be placed in the corner. We lose the game...by loads. I don't know. One doesn't strive for sporting ineptitude - it just seems to sit comfortably on my shoulders. My last great hope is that I may be.....well, I'm almost certain I am...an undiscovered spin bowling genius. But the bloody class structure in English cricket means one only gets to test out this theory on scrunched up bits of paper at work. Why should this be when England need me? WHY? (*22/2/97*)

20/2/94: A different time in another country...
FA Cup 5th Round, Cardiff City v Luton Town

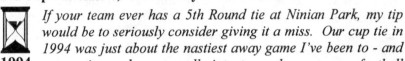

1994 *If your team ever has a 5th Round tie at Ninian Park, my tip would be to seriously consider giving it a miss. Our cup tie in 1994 was just about the nastiest away game I've been to - and at a time when, to all intents and purposes, football hooliganism was at its most unfashionable. Though not, apparently, in South Wales.*

The tickets for the open end terrace cost a disgraceful £14 and, for that, Luton Town fans were meted out some appalling treatment by the fans and officials of Cardiff City FC.

A group of us (apart from my brother, Michael and Chris I didn't know any of the others) went west in a mini-bus. We managed to park quite near the ground and, having heard about the Neanderthal reputation of some of the Cardiff following, made a point of keeping our heads down and walking quickly to the away end. Inside the ground we heard stories of dodgy situations from the fanzine boys (who came on the train) and Andy and Max who drove.

Luton had a fair following that day, including a small number of idiots who lorded about like they were part of an invading army; embarrassing us in their three lion emblazoned shirts and baseball caps, and despicably making a show of tearing down a Welsh LTFC flag, even though a couple of our best players come from Wales. When the going got frightening, the nationalists merged in with the rest of the crowd.

The game was tight but Johnny Hartson (who was barracked throughout the match for being a "Swansea Jack") gave Luton the lead in the first half. Our celebrations were tempered by Ian's pronouncement "we're dead".

Of course he was exaggerating, but the problem of how we would get out of the ground safely at the end of the match loomed larger as the minutes ticked by.

In the second half Cardiff equalised, before Preece scored Luton's second - a goal that had more than a touch of offside about it. After Preece's (rather frantic) goal celebrations at our end of the ground a Cardiff fan got onto the pitch before the restart to "have a word" with him. He was walking on the pitch, not running, pointing his finger at Preece. Even so it seemed ages before he was challenged and taken away.

Elsewhere in the ground it was obvious that the atmosphere was getting increasingly ugly, with the police and stewards lining the home terraces to stop a pitch invasion as the Cardiff fans pushed against the safety gate.

And, at the end of the game, there was a full-scale pitch invasion. Luckily the police managed to keep the Cardiff fans a decent distance away from the away end. Elsewhere in the ground there were Cardiff fans ripping out the seats..... in their own ground. Then as they left and walked past the back end of the away terrace they chucked anything they could get their hands on over the wall and onto the Town fans.

Scary stuff, whilst we waited for the gates to open. We stood waiting for quite a while, whilst it quietened down outside. But the aggro wasn't over as a gang of Cardiff stewards started laying into a group of Luton fans.

When we eventually got out, there were still too many people milling about for comfort, and we saw that the Shoreys Travel Bobbers' bus had had some of its windows put through. Heads down, walk on - trying to hold Michael up a bit. He seemed oblivious to the menacing atmosphere and was happily striding forward towards the industrial estate where the minibus was parked, whilst we tried to keep pace with the police.

When we got to the minibus, we found a couple of the tyres had been let down. As we perused the situation, and read the calling card (scrawled on the back of a fag packet), a transit van screamed round the corner and blocked off our bus's exit. With it having already been singled out, I honestly expected the van to have been full of thugs, ready to do us over - or have a rumble - or whatever hooligans do. It was really bloody scary.

Thankfully, it was just some bloke taking down lamp post adverts for "Big match reports" in the Mail on Sunday. He trundled off as quickly as he arrived and we split the scene, on our flat tyres, to find a service station in a safer vicinity.

After the match Rick Wright, Cardiff's chairman, astoundingly blasted the hooligan behaviour of Luton fans adding, with particular reference to the beating meted out by his stewards, that anyone coming to Cardiff City, looking for trouble, would get "more than they deserved". His words caused outrage back in Luton but, true to form, he totally ignored the hundreds of letters of protest he received. (23/03/94).

Score: 1-2. Town scorers – Hartson, Preece
Attendance: 17,296

22/2/97: Luton Town v Preston North End

Michael is back from Australia and is as eager to offer exciting Antipodean anecdotes as a stone is interested in giving up blood. All we really got to know was that it was hot - but he didn't stay out long enough to get a tan, he stayed with his sister and he rang his Mum to find out how the Town got on. Still, it was good to have him back. In the pub we're met once again by Andy's workmate who "helps" us with the quizzer. Trouble is, he's too bloody good. If he doesn't know an answer he works it out - like one of them Raptors on Jurassic Park. He invariably steams in to correctly answer a "no-hope" question, so that quite soon no-one else wants to press a button and soon after that the game gets very dull indeed.

The same cannot be said of the match. In the first half David Oldfield scores a hattrick and Paul Showler is back in the team and making loads of difference. I like Bontcho, he seems a really nice bloke, he's also an (ex) Bulgarian international. He played in the '94

World Cup semi-final for gawd's sake. He's shown flashes of class, last season. He's so.......rubbish.

Anyway, Oldfield scores a hattrick. For the first goal both Simon and I were in the process of having a wee - I'd made an excursion to the tea trolley to see if they sold gum (they didn't, but my nails didn't suffer too much anyway) and, hearing the crowd, managed to get back in the ground to see Oldfield on the floor and the ball go in the net. I caught up with Slim, pissing it up the wall, and told him we'd scored. He'd guessed. The "we've scored" crowd noise is pretty distinctive.

The rest of the half goes by in a blur. Luton, like Monkey, are irrepressible - Oldfield completes a great hattrick and then sets up Waddock for his second goal in as many games (2).

The second half was never going to be as good, and wasn't. Preston scored early on to give their fans hope of "doing a QPR" (who drew 4-4 at Port Vale a month or two ago having been 4-0 down at halftime). But it was never going to be. The Preston fans kept us mildly amused with "We're going to win 5-4" before they're taunted by the all new dimwit Luton song to the tune of "Knees up Mother Brown". It starts, simplistically but quite nicely, with a verse of "You're not very good", carries on with "You are worse than that" before the last (idiot) line "You are f***ing shit". Terrace humour eh? Simon and I bemoan the almost total lack of wit these days and turn to Michael, who hasn't heard the new song before. He's laughing.

Mitchell Thomas scores another for the Town with about twenty minutes left after which the match is pretty uneventful. Great game though. An excellent performance. But Simon strangely decides that 5-1 isn't a proper scoreline, 4-0 he suggests would have been a good win, 6-0 a rout but 5-1 is apparently neither one way or t'other. I feel like slapping his stupid long face. (*1/3/97*).

Score: 5-1. Town scorers - Oldfield (3), Waddock, Thomas
Attendance: 6,896

28/2/88: Les, be friends.
Littlewoods Cup semi-final second leg. Luton Town v Oxford Utd

1988 *This match was chosen for live coverage on the BBC, because Arsenal had beaten Everton at Goodison in the first leg of their semi and at 1-1 this looked like more of a match. Luton were firm favourites but Jim Smith was one of the pundits in the commentary box who stood by the thought that Oxford would win through. Nobody, save for a few optimists in the Oxford section, would have agreed (indeed, it looked as if Jim himself had been put up to backing his old team). I had marked the occasion by marking my replica Town top with the message "Going to Wembley"; it looked quite smart in my mind's eye, awful in reality...... I'd totally ruined it.*

Luton won the match in the first half. First from a free kick from Ashley Grimes and then a goal by Steiney. The second half was just about holding on to the lead, not letting Oxford back into it and, in the crowd, singing our way to Wembley and preparing for the inevitable pitch invasion. Simon was a little bit keen to get down the front in preparation. There would seem to be little need for this, unless you really wanted to catch up with a player and give their sweaty back a slap of encouragement. I'd done this a few years earlier, congratulating Ricky Hill after some match or other, I didn't expect the experience to be quite so wet.

Simon was there, right at the front, and when the final few minutes were being played there were quite a number of fans on the edge of the pitch behind Les Sealey's goal. John Motson made the stupid, sensationalist, comment "Oh, and I'm sorry to report, that there are people on the pitch", when those at the edges were doing their best to stay off, despite the pressure behind them.

Of course when the final whistle went Simon was in a great position to congratulate Les Sealey. However Les was having none of it, he ran from his penalty area to tunnel, letting Town fans know in no uncertain terms that he didn't want them to get in his way.

Apart from Les getting angry, it was a joyful time for the rest of us as we streamed onto the bouncy plastic surface. On our tour of the ground we took a minute to go into the home dugout and view the pitch from the manager's viewpoint (it's not the best view). Some kid found the PA microphone and asked us to say a few words. We sang the "ole ole ole ole, we are the Town" song which was popular at the time. Apparently, before a club official cut the line, our song was broadcast across the ground (not that we could tell, the noise was so great anyway).

A great result with the prize, Luton's first Cup Final since 1959, fantastic. I'd never been to Wembley before. Unfortunately the Town managed to get into the Simod Cup Final as well, so my first visit to Wembley was for a Mickey Mouse competition. (27/03/88).

Score: 2-0.   Town scorers - Brian Stein, Grimes

Attendance: 13,010

MARCH

1/3/97: York City v Luton Town

Whilst Luton Town are battling away up in Yorkshire, we're down in the smoke enjoying the hospitality of Mick and Julie on the occasion of Julie's birthday. And a fine time we have too. Them guys (Mick, Mally, Martin and Keiron) can all put their drinks away - which I'm well up for. Drinking all through the afternoon and into the evening. In such sparkling company it's not hard to forget all about bloody football but, at videprinter time, I prop up the bar and crane my neck to see the scores go by. Andy, and to a lesser extent Mick, are mildly interested by my interjections into their conversations.......Brentford drew......Watford drew again.......Crewe won.....Bury lost.

Eventually the 1-1 scoreline comes through and I rejoin the party - wishing we had a league table to pore over. Pretty quickly after that I couldn't care a stuff as the booze flowed freely - we went to a few other pubs, got drunk and met friends and brother (and his new girlfriend - nice girl - name of "Ange") that we'd not seen for quite a time. (*3/3/97*).

Score: 1-1. Town scorer – Davis
Attendance: 3,788

2/3/85: Never a dull moment.
Luton Town v Sunderland

1985

A game which only sticks in my memory for the fact that, on the final whistle, I remember saying "Now, that wasn't a game which will stick in the memory long". We won, but in those days we were bloody FAB, as fans we'd become blasé about such victories - Sunderland.....should've beaten them 4-0. And being so disinterested in a run of the mill win (when two or three years earlier I'd have been over the moon for having actually been there to see Luton win), proved that by now we were regulars on the Oak Road terrace. There was a little group of us who stood in a regular spot - a third of the way up the terrace, to the right of centre in the middle cage. There were my brother's mates from school, and a few of their mates from Dunstable or Caddington. I'm not sure I even knew them all by name.... I remember there were a couple of teenage girls (friends of Andrew's friends) who always wore boaters and were capable of unwitting thrill distribution in the crush of a big crowd. We knew the songs, the faces and the woman who stood a few yards in front of us who wore woolly Birdseye gloves.

At half time our revolutionary electronic scoreboard carried a marriage proposal from a bloke in the main stand enclosure. The melee in the crowd in that area, caused by the "That's Life" team cameras, pinpointed the couple and (against our advice) Babs said yes. "Match of the Day", "Sportsnight", "That's Life" - LTFC were on the telly all the time in those days. And, thanks to Millwall fans, the ground was soon to feature on the national news broadcasts too. (9/03/85).

Score: 2-1.   Town scorers – Harford, Hill
Attendance: 8,019

3/3/97: The final AC Meringue games. Ever. It's noticeable that those of us who see Luton - Simon, Michael and myself - are the only ones who have remained quite enthusiastic about playing (and losing every game). Our reaction to defeat (after defeat after defeat) is along the lines of "it's a laugh though innit?". The others, by the end, are more convinced by the idea of abject humiliation. Spotty little oiks, with some football skill, have been laughing at us. Sadly some in our team have found that they *do* give a toss.

I don't. I think it's great, even if I am quite probably the worst of a bad bunch of players (I blame Michael, my partner in defence, for just about everything).

Disinterest has meant that, for our finale, we only have four players until I manage to persuade Andy out of knee joint injury retirement. Both our final games are against teams with only four players. We're soundly beaten in both, although Andy manages to score in one. The git. I've played for weeks and barely had a shot on target..... he comes in for one week and gets all the glory.

And so it ends. In ignominy. One point in a couple of dozen matches. Apart from that famous draw (a game in which, perhaps crucially, I didn't play), our best results were the mandatory 3-0 defeats on the nights when we didn't turn up.

It's a shame, t'was a cool name.

4/3/97: Chesterfield v Luton Town

I was thinking about going to this game, for a couple of minutes, before finding out that I had already arranged to see the Dunstable Amateur Operatic Society production of "Me and my Girl" that night (read my review in The Luton News/Dunstable Gazette back issue - copy on microfilm at Luton International Library). Apparently it was so foggy that night that, when the Town got their penalty equaliser, the Luton fans at the other end didn't know a thing about it. Reports shouted from fans in the main stand confirmed rumours that a penalty was given, and the fact that it had been converted was deduced by the lack of noise from the home crowd following the kick (the ball being kicked strangely appears to have been heard by all) before the sight of Town players running back toward the centre circle confirmed a goal had been scored. To find out who had taken the penalty, one of the blokes on the terrace phoned his wife back in Luton on a mobile phone and asked her to look it up on Teletext.

Andy's Mum, Mary, was also at the Queensway Hall to see the show - and we met Bob, Andy's Dad and our old landlord, in the foyer on the way out. I asked him how the Town had got on. He didn't know they were playing.

Score: 1-1. Town scorer - Thorpe (pen)
Attendance: 3,731

5/3/86: Really hitting the big time
FA Cup, 5th Round, 2nd Replay. Luton Town v Arsenal

1986 *I loved this game. Another 2nd replay. The first match was a 2-2 draw at Kenilworth Road (it was particularly packed in the Oak Road that afternoon if I remember) followed by a 0-0 draw at Highbury. The first replay was noteworthy for a couple of reasons. Firstly, and personally, because although I had a coach ticket my Mum flatly refused to let me go; which was unheard of. Apparently Dad, who had jetted off to Italy or the States on business, had left the explicit instruction "don't let the boy go to Arsenal". The git. I moaned and whined and sulked until, eventually, Mum relented. But I'd lost the bloody coach ticket. Cue more sulking.*

Meanwhile at Highbury, with the pitch rock hard with ice, the Town were under the cosh for the whole of the match (I read later), including extra time. With very little to cheer on the pitch, the Luton fans created their own entertainment, chucking a football about the Clock end...... it was dead good apparently.

Luton won the toss at the end and the 2nd replay appeared to me to be the consummate Luton Town performance. The Oak Road was packed out again and, on the pitch, Luton simply played Arsenal off the field. Foster scored the first after 23 minutes, but the star was undoubtedly little Mark Stein. He was everywhere and on 52 minutes he managed to hassle David O'Leary into turning the ball past Lukic in goal. On 79 minutes he got the third himself, and ended up being carried shoulder high off the pitch.

What made the match so great was that, apart from an FA Cup quarter final against Everton, it bode so well for the future.

Brian Stein was injured, Mick Newell cup tied, but with little Mark Stein playing a blinder we had, it seemed, strength in depth in the squad. Arguing whether or not Mark was potentially as good as or better than his brother.....those were the days.

The match was the highlight of the 1986 FA Cup run. In the quarter final, at Luton, Mark Stein put us 2-0 up against Everton. We were sure, at that moment, of another FA Cup semi-final. Sadly, as at the semi-final the year before, we couldn't hold on. Everton came back to draw 2-2 before beating us 1-0 back up at Goodison. Andy and Steve went to that match. It forms the backdrop to their chilling "being chased all over Liverpool" anecdote. (6/04/86).

Score: 3-0. Town scorers - Foster, O'Leary (og), Mark Stein
Attendance: 13,251

8/3/97 Youth Team Match.
Luton Town v Wycombe Wanderers

A bit sad I know, but fuelled with the potential feel-good factor that a win over Millwall in the afternoon would lift our hearts with, and having heard good things about our ace young striker Liam George, the beer had talked on Friday night and decided that we go and see the lads. The youth team play at Luton rugby club - a nice new building behind which a narrow strip of land twixt road and motorway squeezes in one football and two rugby pitches. There is quite a steep bank between the pitches, the top of which affords an excellent view - better than most, and especially our view at Kenilworth Road. But the motorway, behind a fence and down another bank, still looks within hoofing distance. The background noise of the motorway is deafening, and what's more the pitch is right underneath the flightpath of incoming jets at Luton airport. These kids must long to play for the first team if only for the peace and quiet.

Score: 2-1

Later, that very same day - Luton Town v Millwall

So, what is it with Millwall fans? Going down the pub before the match has been fine for years now, since I've been going anyway, no trouble with rival fans. We've even had Millwall down since 1985 and they've been fine. But there's something about Millwall and big matches which brings the lowlife out of the woodwork - and this match was a big top of the table clash.

In this situation there are a number - an unacceptable number - of Millwall fans who decide that the best course of action is to prove that they're harder than the opposition supporters. It's the Neanderthal mentality which went out of fashion years ago. It's almost embarrassing thinking about it but at the time, well done lads, it's intimidating. The atmosphere in the pub was terrible - and only because of Millwall fans, sat at the back, being obnoxious. They looked like stereotype hooligans - short hair, vacant expressions, one even had gulf war style combat trousers on. The fact that there wasn't trouble in the pub was down to the fact that the Luton fans didn't rise to the bait..... and if that was because we were scared - well done to the Millwall boys - one of whom made it known he was a local from Caddington "there, that's shut you up" he shouted at the Town fans, all doing our best to ignore him. God, how we miss him at Kenilworth Road.

The atmosphere was equally nasty in the ground - quite a few of the old fighting chants getting an airing, crowd scuffles and Millwall fans chucking coins (hitting at least one small child in the face).

As for the game - Julian James was sent off early for two dodgy tackles. But Luton had much of the play, hit bar and post a few times, playing brilliantly in the circumstances. The ref had as much of a hand as anyone in both Millwall's goals - having a direct free-kick retaken after encroachment and letting a blatant off-side go. This sounds like sour-grapes but, as far as the game goes there were more highpoints than low. But the afternoon had already been soured.

It'd be nice to blame all the bad feeling on a large minority of fans in the Millwall end but, sadly, the fixture attracted the smaller but equally nasty Luton contingent who were involved in clashes after the game. Hooliganism isn't as deep rooted in Luton as it obviously is at Millwall but it's sadly naive to believe that Heysel and Hillsborough have made football related violence intolerable for all fans. It's deeply unfashionable now and, at most clubs not stuck in the dark ages, hooligans have been alienated by other real fans - but the kind of disaffected idiot who wants to cause trouble at a football match doesn't give a toss about fellow fans, opposition fans, the image of the town and the implications for the club blighted by their "patronage". (*12/3/97*)

Score: 0-2

Attendance: 9,109

9/3/85: NOT TURNER!

FA Cup 5th Round, Second Replay. Luton Town 1 Watford 0

1985

So, at Luton in 1985 we had flair players and we had hard players. We had very few dodgy players, but one who certainly fell into that category was Wayne Turner. However, it's important to put that theory into context; if he was a Luton Town player today his dogged determination would make him the fans' favourite. Back in `85 the announcement that he was in the team would be greeted with a groan.

Meeting Watford in the 5th round of the FA Cup in 1985 gave Luton the chance to avenge the defeat in the 3rd round the previous year, but it proved to be just as difficult. The first game, a tense 0-0 draw at Kenilworth Road, was memorable for the Monday night crowd it attracted. Everyone was trying to get into the ground at the same time and there was a great crush outside. The garden wall of a house next door to our section of the Oak Road terrace collapsed and, post Heysel, that sort of scenario is the stuff of nightmares, but at the time it was funny (except for the owner of the house). Inside the ground we had no chance of getting to our regular spot, so stood near the back of the terrace swaying and surging wherever the current took us.

We didn't go to the replay (although we went to quite a lot of away games by that time, evening kick-offs were a different kettle of fish in Dad's eyes.....we probably didn't even sulk). By early in the second half Luton were 2-0 behind before Nwajiobi and Hill made the score 2-2. No goals in extra time. Chiltern Radio had live commentary of the match provided by their respective Luton and Watford experts Brain Swain and Mike Vince. Their summing up of the match (I was too nervous to listen live) was typically biased - Vince "....but a hint of offside about Nwajiobi's goal Brian?", Swain "Not at all - a brilliant goal".

The second replay was set back at Kenilworth Road. Again, the terrace was fantastically packed and again we couldn't get near our regular spot. This time we were near the front, right in the centre. And again, the game was tight; finally turning from the most unlikely of sources.

Because Peter Nicholas and David Preece were cup-tied that year, Wayne Turner's appearances in the cup run were just about assured. Something of a utility player - he could play dodgy defence or slot in midfield to break up, through his own participation, promising Town moves. Wherever he played he was, for Luton, a natural Achilles' heel. But, he's a Luton boy, a tryer, a battler...... the Luton crowd liked him, he was a loveable character, but we all held our breath whenever he got the ball. Yes, we had a soft spot for Wayne, but that spot wouldn't be on the team sheet if we had our way.

So, the third match was another tense affair - with good chances few and far between. So when Paul Parker made the pass of the match to split the Watford defence, I really wanted it to be Brian Stein or Ricky Hill running onto it. It all went so quickly, I remember looking to see which Luton player it was, running onto the pass. I remember shouting "NOT TURNER!" and, the next moment, jumping up and down like a mad thing after he'd successfully slid the ball into the net.

It still amazes me. I'm sitting here looking at the picture of the goal. Turner coolly putting the ball past the despairing tackle by Simms and Coton in goal. Such things simply weren't in Wayne's limited repertoire. It was Wayne's 24th birthday, he was suffering from flu, my only theory is that at the time he was suffering some sort of delirium.

Wayne Turner was carried off the pitch that day - and was never booed (very loudly) again.

Score: 1-0. Town scorer - Turner
Attendance: 15,586

A few years ago there was a post-season open day at the ground, including a five-a-side tournament. I managed, through quite a bit of crawling, to play on the Kenilworth Road pitch as sub for the Mad as a Hatter team. I had half expected that playing on the hallowed turf would miraculously turn me into a fantastic player (in a "Billy's boots" kind of way). It didn't. Even in a dodgy team I stood out, in a Turner-esque way, as by far the worst player.

Meanwhile Wayne, playing for the LTFC works team, was on an adjoining pitch turning on the style with other ex-Town pros. Thankfully the Mad as a Hatter team were knocked out of the competition before coming up against them. Being run rings around by a player I made such fun of, ten years before, would have been awful. Instead I was just happy to gawp in admiration, for the second time (but perhaps not so flabbergasted this time). Wayne was Reserve Team Coach at the time, and later Lennie Lawrence's first team assistant until he was relieved of his duties, and left the club during the `97/98 season. The club, quite touchingly I thought given the pressure for Turner's sacking from some of the fans, invited him to stay on in some other capacity. He turned them down. The club wished him well - and so, I know, do a great many of the fans. (13/03/85).

12/3/83: Scouts
Nottingham Forest v Luton Town

Slip End Cub Scout group was the jewel in the crown of the local community back in the early 80's. Membership was at about 98% of eligible youngsters. We looked smart in our uniforms and sang sweetly when doing the carol rounds at Christmas - all money collected to charity, of course.

1983

The Scout Troop was a different story altogether, blighted by acne, teen angst and virtually no discipline. The leaders wore uniform, but Scouts refused to. Quite a lot of the kids didn't go through to the Scouts but, as Andrew was already there, and had told me that "the induction" (i.e. being chucked, fully clothed, into a lake at camp) wasn't really anything to worry about, I had no qualms about joining up.

Although we had great fun, the troop was a rabble, and an obvious embarrassment to the South Luton & District Scouting hierarchy. After a particularly rowdy night hike competition against Caddington (our deadly next village rivals - though we also had time on the way to find, and burn, a Watford bobble hat), the troop was taken over by Ron "Popeye" Pridmore who had previously run a Sea Scout troop, and his wife Daphne.

Most of the older kids left immediately, in favour of the pub. Ron and Daffers, Scout names "Skipper" and "Skip", were a comedy double act in themselves - and were joined by Sid, a postal worker who looked like he was 108 years old. But, credit where credit's due, they managed to change Slip End Scouts into a highly disciplined unit - although a few (but only a very few) of us managed to make sufficient fun at the expense of our leaders to make it all worthwhile.

Most of the troop were square (working, oh so stiffly, for their flippin' Queen's Scout Award), but an even higher percentage were fans of Luton Town. And, when Skipper generously let us listen to Final Score, taking a break from hours of tying bloody knots, at camp one Saturday, there was uproar as the highly unlikely victory at Nottingham Forest was read out by James Alexander Gordon. We were "camped" in a hut in Phasels wood and the news caused us all to jump in the air, run around, and make lots of noise.

Skipper eventually shouted us down and gave us a stern lecture, accusing us (typically idiotically) of hooliganism.

Score: 0-1. Town scorer – Hill
Attendance: 14,387

Andrew eventually left the Scouts, as a patrol leader, having had an argument with one of the leaders. He had planned to tear off his stripes in disgust but, because Mum had sewed them on so well, the drama of the situation was rather lost as he took an inordinate amount of time nibbling the badge off, gerbil fashion, with his teeth.

Pete and I became the first Slip End Scouts to be officially thrown out. A fully uniformed Scout disciplinary squad, including Popeye and Daffers, came round to both sets of parents to tell them why they'd come to their decision. Afterwards Dad, barely suppressing his laughter, asked me not to derive some sort of perverse pride from being chucked out. So I didn't. Much. Mainly because the eventual cause of our downfall, involving a thanksgiving parade, a bus and an emergency meeting of the patrol leaders' council, and an official verdict of "disgracing the Scout uniform", isn't worth telling anyway. (14/5/83).

12/3/97: Wrexham v Luton Town

I had planned to go to one "stupid" (a long way, midweek, match) away game this season, but drumming up support to avoid driving up on my own is difficult. Even so, I was off work all week and Martin had said he was "definitely up for it". By Wednesday, typically, he's skint. There's always the Bobbers bus..... but no, I'm not that committed these days - and the fact that I even consider going all the way to Wales on my own on the supporters' bus is a bit sad.

Anyway, it's a night in with the Teletext, cheering the fact that Luton had scored through Davis and then damning the loss.

The day after Claire and I went to Leicester to check up on petrol stations. Leicester had won a place in the League Cup on Tuesday and I felt the need, for the first time this season, to take the Luton Town scarf (one of them little car window affairs - held up by, and bought by, suckers) out of my back window.

Our games in hand gone, and little or nothing gained, the season didn't look all that hopeful anymore. (*15/3/97*).

Score: 2-1. Town scorer – Davis
Attendance: 3,392

13/3/85: Millwall Memories.
FA Cup 6th Round. Luton Town v Millwall

1985

Football grounds always look different on the telly to how they look in real life. I remember watching Sportsnight on the night of the Millwall riot at Kenilworth Road and, when looking at the pictures from the end of the match (and after we'd made our escape) when the thugs were on the pitch chucking orange seats at the police, it took a couple of seconds to register that that was Luton's ground being ripped up.

"We'll laugh about this one day," we said inside the ground on that night as the scenes got increasingly ugly in all parts of the ground save, for our amazing good fortune, in the Oak Road end. We did laugh, but only nervously on the night. Because of where we were, and our route back home, we were saved much of the violence that fell on the rest of the town that night. But we weren't to know that at the time. It was, and remains, the scariest night I've had to endure at a football match.

But it always looked on the cards after Leicester failed to beat Millwall in the previous round of the cup. In view of Millwall fans' fearsome reputation, Luton Town and the police seemed staggeringly ill prepared for the night ahead. Despite the opposition and the fact that the match was an FA Cup Quarter Final, it was not deemed important enough to make all-ticket, whilst the police later stated that they had decided on a "softly softly" approach to the invading hordes. The fans knew there would be trouble; it was just a question of how much. We were all shocked at the result as hooligans from all over London came to Kenilworth Road with the sole purpose of wreaking havoc.

We were pretty excited on the walk into town in anticipation of the first cup quarterfinal we had ever seen, but that mood was displaced with tension as we got nearer the ground. We didn't used to walk in via the town centre (where the thugs had been drinking since early afternoon) but the mood amongst the Town fans was clearly subdued as they hurriedly headed for the comparative safety of the ground. But somehow the mood of a moment is lost with some people. Matthew decided he wanted to make his regular pre-match stop at the shop for Cola-cubes; we tried to explain that maybe it wasn't a good idea this time, but in he went leaving us waiting. Whilst Matth' was in the shop, blissfully making his sweetie selection, our nerves jangled outside. Suddenly a hired minibus, windows all smashed, screeched round the corner - full of Millwall fans singing the "eee-eye-oh" song (a chant which sounds silly now but, as a warcry that night, was pretty scary). It stopped near the shop, from where we quickly snatched Matth' and insisted that he come with us. Right now.

It was early but there was already a small, nervous queue outside the Oak Road entrance. A bloke, whom we often saw down the ground at the time, told us that he had a fiver on the Millwall fans bringing down the scoreboard at the Kenilworth (away) end. Very good.

Once we were, thankfully, inside the ground the atmosphere was very eerie. They hadn't brought the scoreboard down but they were lighting bonfires on the Kenilworth Road terrace. Some were also climbing up the TV gantry on the terrace; the PA requested they stop in the name of safety - and so more of them climbed on. As the minutes ticked by, the Kenilworth Road end filled out dramatically whilst the Oak Road remained half-empty. Apparently, thank god, the gates had been shut with many London thugs still trying to get inside.

As far as I can remember, the biggest pitch invasion was before the start of the game. The Millwall fans came towards the Oak Road end and then started throwing coins at us. Kedge got hit on the head by an empty half bottle of whisky and was cut above the eye. Everyone went as far up the terrace as possible to try and avoid being hit, although there was one young lad scrambling around on the floor at the foot of the Oak Road, out of sight of the hooligans. As the coins bounced back (off Luton fans' heads) and down the terrace he was pocketing them. He must have made a few quid that night.

They seemed to be there for ages, though amazingly didn't attempt to "take" the end. I can remember the songs of defiance from a few Town fans being quickly hushed out by everyone else in the Oak Road for fear that it would incite those on the pitch. Meanwhile the plea of "get the rabble off the pitch" could just be heard from those few Millwall fans at the other end who had turned up to watch their team and not the London Utd hooligan invasion of Luton. Those on the pitch eventually got off, and into other parts of the ground where they harassed, hit out at, and generally menaced the Town fans throughout the match. Kedge meanwhile heroically declined St John's ambulance attention (it was only a titchy cut) but was shaking so much that he could hardly light his fags.

The match, interrupted by another pitch invasion, didn't really matter much. I can remember Stein's excellent goal - which was followed by possibly the most muted reception ever to follow a Town goal at Kenilworth Road. We couldn't look forward to the semi-final until we knew how the Millwall fans would react to their team going behind.

After much wise pestering from Simon and Matth' (who had caught up with events by this time) we left about five minutes early. Andrew and Kedge stayed to the bitter end and were chased down Maple Road for their pains. We all managed to get away without much trouble, but we were very lucky.

Score: 1-0. Town scorer - Brian Stein
Attendance: 17,470

At school the next day we were treated like war veterans. Teachers asked us "were we there?" as if it was the prelude to trauma counselling. To be honest, we were overjoyed at having got to the semi-final. But other Town fans, and Luton in general, suffered badly that night. I found that out a couple of years later when I told the ladies at Whitbread (where I was a YTS kid) about the events at the ground, only to find that they had suffered far more at the hands of the Millwall hooligans at lunch and home time that day.

The aftermath of the Millwall riot, and the Heysel disaster, was harsh for ordinary fans. The Conservative Government regarded football supporters as scum. The social worth of the football fan, perceived to be and treated like an animal, was instrumental in the policies that would go on to cause the Hillsborough disaster.

In Luton Town's case the "cure" did more harm to the club than the problem itself. David Evans (who could, if he wanted, have made the Millwall match all ticket) used the violence to condone his "no away fan" policies which, along with our plastic pitch, made Luton Town the most unpopular club in the country.

Post Heysel, we also suffered from the ban on English clubs in Europe. We should have qualified for Europe in 1988, but weren't allowed to. Luton Town are unlikely to qualify again in the near future for anything but another EuroDisney Cup like the Anglo-

Italian. It's a selfish point, but I must admit not wanting to hear and watch the BBCs gushing "Liverpool in Europe" programme when they eventually got back into European competition. Liverpool have a long and prestigious European record - Luton fans were robbed, by hooligans in Liverpool colours, of our chance to see a few games abroad. So I was pleased when Bruce Grobbelar almost single-handedly ended their European cup campaigns... but these days I wish them the best in European competition, along with every other English team (with the occasional exception of Man Utd). (13/04/85).

15/3/97: Crewe Alexandra v Luton Town

After not going to Wrexham I was determined to go to Crewe and Michael at least was up for it. So I drove, and drove, and drove. Once past Fort Dunlop (or whatever they want us to call it now), searching out Villa Park and strangely missing Walsall's ground, the M6 is a pretty dull motorway. Meanwhile the long journey, and the petrol used, means that Michael and I are having an expensive day (Michael pays up OK - he's never been allowed to forget giving a measly £2 for a trip to Peterborough a couple of seasons ago).

Gresty Road - the home of my trainspotting brother's second team. Crewe Alexandra were fourth division stalwarts in the early 80's when Luton were on the up... How times have changed... Still, there are sadder indications of our decline from grace.

Crewe seem a distinctly likeable club. Small, neat ground. Decent fans. The team try their best to play football, and they provided us with our win of the season.

The Crewe crowd are possibly the quietest I've heard - they have a small set of fans near the away end, stood up and singing. They seem a friendly bunch though. When the Town contingent (which include our embarrassing quota of idiots) were up in arms over a dodgy decision by the ref, they smartly rebuke us with "sit down and behave yourselves". The Lutonian wits hit back, quite well given our usual standard, with "Where's your anorak" (Crewe fans being identified with trainspotters). We were later treated with derision, quite rightly, when our boys churned out the embarrassing "you're not very good" song.

The game was always going to be difficult, both teams pushing for promotion, and in the end it was a dirge - though Luton arguably had the better chances. The result did little good for either club, but the other results went for us again.

Score: 0-0
Attendance 4,474

21/3/97: Luton Town v Brentford

Big, big match - covered live on Sky on Friday night. Second v Top in the league. It's a little bit odd in the pub beforehand, being a Friday. It's also a little odd that Michael has decided to ask his new girlfriend, Helen, along. Thankfully she doesn't have to witness Michael in "football match" mode - she's off to see her mates in Chicago's later and is just having a quick bottle of Hooch.... She's 20 apparently... she looks younger.

On the way to the ground we see the Hale Bopp comet - which is pretty impressive really.

Inside the ground the atmosphere is a bit tense. After all these years of grim relegation battles Luton fans seem to have forgotten how to enjoy themselves properly.

Brentford have the best of the first half, which doesn't help the mood of the crowd. It never even looked like getting nasty, but there is a distinct feeling of *angst* in the air as we scream wholeheartedly at every referee's decision against the Town. As the game goes on, the Town get more into it and in the second half Tony Thorpe scores what proves to be the winning goal. We go bananas - on the seats - and cheering - and hugging - and that. I stupidly believe that there are only seconds of the game left, having persuaded myself that the game kicked off at 7.30, not 7.45. But the game goes on, the crowd doesn't whistle at the ref, and reality starts to dawn on me.

When the game does end, and Luton go top of the league, it's pretty joyous at Kenilworth Road. There is a bit of a crush on the way out of the ground as the exit is blocked by the queue to the ticket

office on one side and the Sky vans on the other: still we're in high spirits and go back to the pub to celebrate. *(24/3/97).*
Score: 1-0. Town scorer - Thorpe
Attendance: 8,680

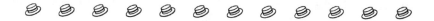

23/3/94: The enigma of Scotty Oakes
FA Cup QuarterFinal: Luton Town v West Ham Utd

1994 *Have I ever mentioned that I hate West Ham? No? Well, that would be because it simply isn't true. Despite what Hammers fans might feel towards Luton Town (there's a West Ham fan book entitled "An irrational hatred of Luton") all I see is that plucky little East London team that Alf Garnett supports. The one that Trevor Brooking and Billy Bonds used to play for. Gor blimey Guv'nor - and they won us the World Cup in `66 you know..... that Julian Dicks is a bit of a hothead in't he eh? And, who can forget, "there's aaaaonly waan Stoo'aht Slate-aaaa". The only time I felt anything close to hatred for the Hammers was when my brother Simon came back from the 1989 Littlewoods Cup Semi-Final, West Ham 0 Luton Town 3 (would you Adam 'n Eve it?), with his shirt covered in blood. Turns out he was punched in the nose by accident during the good old fashioned cockney knees up which followed Harford's opening goal.*

The 1994 Quarter Final replay, after a 0-0 draw (which we had to watch in the sweltering backroom of the pub because the tickets sold out) was remarkable only because it marked probably the last great night on the terraces at Luton Town. By then the whole ground was seated, save for the upper tier of the Kenilworth Road end. We thoroughly enjoyed the Newcastle replay in the third round (2-0) and, in the end, the West Ham match too.

The match was also the greatest night (to date.......?) in the career of Scotty Oakes. A player with occasionally amazing talent he was, until then, more famous for the fact that he was the son of one of Showaddywaddy. But that night he scored a hat trick, was on the back page of every newspaper the following morning, and suddenly had a £2,000,000 price tag.

There used to be a big digital display in China, in Peking probably, which counted down the seconds to the time when Hong Kong was re-patriated (there's one in Greenwich now, counting down to the Millenium). There might have been the same sort of clock counting down Scotty Oakes' worth, down from two million quid, set off the day after his West Ham hat trick. Having shown how talented he could be, Scotty Oakes' apparent laissez-faire during boring old run-of-the-mill league games quickly lost him favour in the eyes of the Town fans and, apparently, Premiership Scouts.

Before David Pleat took him away to Sheffield Wednesday, Scotty Oakes, our supposed star player, was being booed by Luton supporters. Pleat paid less than a million for Oakes, but few were too upset. We'd been ripped off of course, nothing new there, but the general consensus was that this time it was by Oakes and not Pleat. (9/04/96).

Score: 3-2. Town scorer - Oakes (3)
Attendance: 13,166

24/3/97: FA Youth Cup Quarter Final
Luton Town v Watford

Strange night. The pub is empty pre-match but the two sides of the ground that are open are reasonably full, particularly the main stand. Watford bring nearly as many away as they did for the league game. For some reason Watford play in their red second kit (why they need a second kit now they're not playing Norwich I don't know). It's good to see that the banter between the fans is comparatively good natured - of course when they're calling each other "scum" it's not going to be exactly friendly - but the vehemence of recent league derbies isn't there. The other strange thing about the match is that it is Watford who look like winning, our starlet striker Liam George having been injured and being out for the rest of the season and the Town Youngsters don't seem to have much chance up front. Meanwhile the

Watford kids were thwarted, on more than one occasion, in goalmouth scrambles as they tried to bundle the ball into the net - admirably taking on the nature of their first team mentors.
Score: 0-0

A week (or maybe two) later the "Kids from Town" beat Watford Youth on penalties after a 1-1 draw at Vicarage Road. So, we did beat Watford this season after all. In the semi-final against Leeds, Luton lost 1-0 at home and 2-1 away. Still, admirable stuff. *(29/03/97)*.

27/3/88: Whoring the Wembley Dream
Simod Cup Final. Reading v Luton Town

Before 1988 I had never seen a match at Wembley. Once or twice I had been tempted to go and see England play, but I had made up my mind that the first time that I would go would be **1988** *to see Luton Town play. Opportunities were therefore slim, the FA Cup and League Cup finals, so I largely kept this secret to myself.*

After the 1985 FA Cup semi-final Watford Pete, whom I sat next to in Sociology on Monday mornings (he was always the first or last person I'd want to speak to on Mondays to go over the weekend's football), put on a sickeningly credible show of sympathy before telling me how fantastic Wembley was - Watford having got there in the 1984 Cup Final, and how we cheered Andy Gray's dubious goal.

Wembley was football's Camelot. The magic of the big cup competitions was that the final was played at Wembley. The prize, up until the final, is to get to go to Wembley.

When animal rights protesters burned down Luton Arndale's Debenhams for some reason (fur coats it would've been, or eye make-up tested on rabbits), in the summer of `87, I took the opportunity to take their free courtesy bus into Debenhams in some suburb of North London and, from there, get the tube to go to Mercs and Shellys and The Virgin Megastore. Ben Sherman shirt and Viz (you couldn't get it *in Luton in those days - and it was funny then) bought, I trundled back via Wembley Park where I got off the train and made my way up to Wembley stadium. At the end of Olympic Way, in front of the twin towers, I said a silent prayer that I might return in the not too distant future to see Luton Town play here.....*

And, what would you know, my prayer bore fruit - although God has had a lasting laugh at my expense. Following a brilliant cup run Luton Town reached The Littlewoods (League) Cup Final in 1988. However they had also contrived to get to the final of the piddling Mickey Mouse Simod Cup Final - and it was this, rather than the illustrious Littlewoods Cup final, which would see my supporting debut at Wembley.

And what a waste of time..... Wearing my "Road to Wembley 1988 - Littlewoods Cup Final" t-shirt (to make it clear that this certainly wasn't our big day) I joined the other 13 000 bored Town fans sitting about at the tunnel end of Wembley whilst about 40 000 Reading fans (regaled in their Simod Cup memorabilia) had a whale of a time at the other end.

Mick Harford scored the first goal for Luton, and then Reading scored four - including a penalty for a foul which was clearly outside the area....but whatever. Of course there was the necessity to appear not to be bothered by Reading fans' taunts (which was a bit of a lie at the time although, as recently as `95/96, it was amusing that the Reading fans continued in attempting to rile us with Simod chants), but there was clearly a feeling of "what the blazes are we doing here?" amongst the Town supporters. Had we won (as we were clear favourites to do), it might have been different. But not that much.

Score: 4-1. Town scorer – Harford
Attendance: 61,740

The Simod Cup, like just about every other competition Wembley puts the final on for these days, was surplus to requirements. I've been to Wembley to see Luton four times. Two Littlewoods Cup Finals which were great (although winning is quite a lot better than losing); the Simod Cup Final, which would have been a non-event even if we'd won; and the 1994 FA Cup Semi-Final against Chelsea where Luton didn't perform. But it was the venue that irritated me because, as a spectator, it would have been much better in a neutral venue: Highbury, for example, and a chance to watch my team from the famous North Bank.

Having said that, my ticket for the 1988 Semi at Spurs wasn't for the East stand shelf (where many of the Luton fans were, and I'd have liked to have been), but in the flippin' away end from where I'd seen the Hatters before and since.

In `94 it cost £20 at Wembley for a seat high in the upper tier, with a view obstructed by the new corporate entertainment led Olympic Gallery.

And so one's Wembley ambition has been tarnished by the fact that, when it had once seemed impossible, it is now rather probable for just about every Club in the League.

So, Port Vale, Crewe and Bury fan, please don't delude yourself into reading cup glory into outings to North London to see your favourites play in the Auto-Windscreen Shield or Play-off Finals. When you take up the seat that your massively overpriced ticket has bought you in a half empty stadium, you might realise that Wembley has become the country's premier events whore - ready to stage any two-bit competition final in order to cash in on the small club supporter's Wembley dream. (24/04/88).

29/3/97: Burnley v Luton Town

Quite possibly the result of the season. It was brilliant.... The result that is - as for the game... I dunno. It's my Grandmother's 80th birthday so the family get together to surprise her. It's rare enough for the four "kids" in my family to gèt together (I don't see that much of my sister, Emma, these days) so that's nice. Katherine comes too, but Claire is at her cousin's wedding. Meanwhile we all fret in the car on the way to Dorset about meeting with our cousins and uncles. However, it turns out (as it always does) to be a good day - they're all good folk and so, deep deep down, are we. And Nanna Belle was delighted.

My brothers think I'm lying when I tell them that I've heard on the radio that Luton are winning 1-0. They're probably confused by my lack of enthusiasm - but I've seen 1-0 leads overturned too often. But it's a pretty happy car when we hear the result.

Another good result is that Andrew is staying in town, and Steve is up from Chelmsford too - so we have a good night out. We play a few games of pool in the local then wander down to the pub. The fanzine boys are there - but we're the only ones smiling.

Apparently the match was very grim - away wins can be like that. Defending a 2-0 halftime lead, against a big and loud home support, was obviously not easy to watch when the feeling is that if one goal is let in then the team would crumble. But Burnley didn't score did they?! Even so, they look like veterans of some sort of military campaign in the pub - the effect of their being pissed up on booze probably has as much to do with their mood as the memory of Burnley's onslaught, but they're still very dour faced. We're the only ones grinning.

Score: 0-2. Town scorer – Thorpe (2)
Attendance: 15,490

APRIL

1/4/97: Luton Town v Bristol City

April Fools Day - Steve is back from Cheltenham and has procured Michael's season ticket. It looks as if Luton are really going places, but Bristol City nearly spoil the day completely.

In the pre-match first goal sweep stake in the pub I pick out B10,and within four minutes City get a penalty (a clear decision, but we scream "cheat" at the ref and the player who went down) and my man steps up to take it. My £20 is on the line - so, dear reader, do I want B10 to score? Feuer saves the penalty and I cheer as loudly as anyone. B10 follows up to score. We all stop cheering. I'm gutted but, hey, it's not as bad for me as your common or garden going 1-0 down - I won £20.

And I'd offered to swap my B10 with Keith's niece who had L10, Tony Thorpe. Luton go 2-0 down on 40 minutes, but Davis pulls one back before half-time. Thorpe gets his goal to equalise in the second half and then the match is all set up for a Town winner. It doesn't come and in the end we're lucky not to get beaten as Bristol break away.

The result is a bit of a bugger - but it's all my fault, well, Michael and I. Firstly Michael wasn't about, having been talked into taking Helen on a romantic meal (though one wonders just how romantic Michael gets when he's preoccupied with LTFC). That means his lucky Raith Rovers scarf isn't in the ground. The scarf's luck is good for home games only. Meanwhile I forgot to wear my gaudy orange "Kahuna" watch which I bought from QVC (The

Shopping Channel) - good for home league matches whilst the Town still have eleven men on the pitch. (*6/04/97*).

Score: 2-2. Town scorers – Davis, Thorpe
Attendance: 7,550

@ @ @ @ @ @ @ @ @ @ @ @

6/4/86: John Bond and Razzmatazz
Birmingham City v Luton Town

1986 *A strange match in that it was played at 11.30am on a Sunday morning. St Andrews wasn't a happy place during the latter stages of the '85/86 season with the Blues second bottom of the league and relegation looming large. The gloom was almost tangible, but not inside the cover of the programme. On the inside of the cover there were two pages for the manager's message. John Bond's words, six paragraphs in large print were on one page; one of these paragraphs read "At Forest last Monday we were slaughtered! Nothing less!", which must have been a morale booster. The other page is entirely taken up with a big picture of John Bond, grin from ear to ear, with a big cigar in his right hand. Obviously the format was decided, and the picture taken, before the start of the season - but nothing remotely said grim determination. The picture provided a bit of pre-match entertainment in the bleary eyed and yawning Luton end.*

The Town won the match, typically professionally 2-0, with Harford scoring at the beginning and the end of the second half. Birmingham were looking for the equaliser, but never really looked like getting it. Mr Bond hadn't seemed to convey the relegation dogfight message to his players (or the fans). The match ended, we applauded. And then went back home to South Beds.

Score: 0-2. Town scorer - Harford (2)
Attendance: 8,836

Arriving back at Kenilworth Road in the late afternoon we saw that The Luton Flyers American football team were playing. Hoorah for the plastic pitch! The bloke on the gate, seeing that we had come from the Birmingham match, let Simon and me in for free (the game was already in the second quarter....or something). The crowd was comparable to a well attended reserve game, with quite a few fans (likely friends and family of the Flyers) doing their best to razzmatazz. I'd been quite interested in American football since Dad bought me back some Pittsburgh Steelers gear from the US in the late 70's. I'd avidly watched the highlights on the TV since - in which the action was condensed and the gaps for time-outs (and commercials) weren't included. It took a cold Sunday afternoon at Kenilworth Road to show me just how excruciatingly boring American football is. (6/09/86).

6/4/97: Rotherham United v Luton Town

I was going to go. HONEST. Michael had it planned - BR (or whatever they're called now) apparently have a £30 for four people deal if booked in advance. Michael, Chris and I are up for it but in the end Michael can't get the ticket. However, the post match atmosphere in the pub is markedly different from after the Burnley game. In they all come, grins all over their faces - happy to share their thoughts on the game and their green 'uns - and slagging me off for not going. They're all very happy - and very pissed.

Results went for us this week. Bury lost away. Brentford drew 0-0 at home and Watford lost 1-0 at home to Crewe. Wa-hey! Poring over the green'un table in the pub, we worked out that - given that we still have Bury and Stockport to play at home- the Championship is within our grasp, although as alcohol took effect it got tougher to work out the permutations. The rest of the evening passed in a happy, boozy blur.

Score: 0-3. Town scorer – Thorpe (3)
Attendance: 2,609

8/4/97: Luton Town v Wycombe Wanderers

A copy of last week's matches - great away result followed by disappointing home draw. Wycombe, deep in relegation trouble, have more to play for than Bristol City, their league position meaning that prior to the game everyone is confident.

The game, to put it mildly, wasn't good. Wycombe had obviously only come to Luton to grind out a draw whilst Luton end up wanting for ideas on how to get round the 11 man defence. Having said that, both teams had their chances and, if it wasn't for more abysmal refereeing, both teams could have had penalties. Town had two clear appeals - the first was a blatant handball in the area whilst we couldn't see the other one, but the fans up the Kenilworth end certainly had a good shout. After that, and almost certainly because of it, Wycombe were denied a penalty as James handled a cross inside the area. After the two Luton shouts were denied the ref, and certainly the linesman, bottled making the decision. Had Luton scored from the penalty they rightly should have had then Wycombe would have had to come out and try to play. Because nothing was given, they were allowed to shut up shop, waste time and play defensively throughout. Some of the abuse that Town fans near the tunnel have dished out to referees recently has been a bit much - but, wrong though it is, a vociferous crowd does affect the decisions of ref and linesmen. But the standard of officials in this league is very poor. The ref and linesman succeeded in ruining this match. (*12/04/97*).

Score: 0-0

Attendance: 8,117

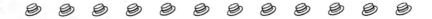

9/4/89: Big Game Glory Hunting
Littlewoods Cup Final. Nottingham Forest v Luton Town

When Luton get to Wembley, the majority of our support is made up of glory hunters. People from Luton who might never consider going to see a match at Kenilworth Road, but are

1989 *prepared to plonk a straw boater on their heads and walk up Wembley Way when called upon to do so. I've nothing against these people really, at a club like Luton there's never really the suggestion that they are taking tickets away from the "real fans", because the real fans are well provided for too. Some die-hards will obviously turn their noses up at them but, when it comes down to it, the glory* *hunters are coming along to subscribe to the feeling of community spirit and civic pride that major Cup Finals provide.*

But they also miss quite a lot.

Having made my momentous decision to stop supporting the Town after the glorious Final of '88, I didn't need too much persuading to trot along to Wembley as a glory hunter the next year. I went along with Mick, Mally and Thurlow and we set about (in the Assembly Rooms in Kentish Town for some reason) getting pissed. And so we did. Going to the pub, especially prior to a big match, is grand - but getting drunk beforehand only means you miss out. That, and the feeling that we had this year just come along for the ride, detracted greatly from our enjoyment of the match. Wembley had also changed for the worse. The year previously we had been standing on the upper tier terraces. Now the upper tier had been seated over, we were in the lower tier behind the goal, the only terraces left at Wembley. The view there didn't compare with that of the upper tier. There was also the small point that we lost the bloody match, which didn't help our enjoyment of the day either.

It had all started so well - with a Mick Hartford goal to put us 1-0 up at half time. Perhaps it was a bad omen. Big Mick is a Town hero, but his big match goals have always been preludes to defeat - Harford scored to put us 1-0 up against Wimbledon in the semi-final of the FA Cup last year (lost 2-1) and against Reading in the Simod (lost 4-1).

In the second half Forest were all over us, like Arsenal were the year before, but managing to score too. They scored an equaliser before Les Sealey made his mark. With his bad omen new hairstyle to go with his '85 semi-final perm, Lees had a self-made opportunity to recreate Dibble's penalty save of the previous year; having rather rashly brought Nigel Clough down in the area. Clough himself took the penalty and, possibly failing to see the historic and ironic significance of the kick, scored

Hopes that Forest would rest on their 2-1 laurels were dashed when they went and scored a third.

A right swine that was. Being glory hunters, our work was done on the final whistle as we trudged, cussing and cursing, out of Wembley. The true fans stayed behind to applaud the players' valiant efforts and having got to the Final for a second year running.

We caught the first train out of Wembley Park that afternoon having succeeded, not for the first time that afternoon, in missing the point. (15/04/89).

Score: 3-1.   Town scorer – Harford
Attendance: 76,130

9/4/96: Late vintage Flaherty
Luton Town v Stoke City

1996

Michael Flaherty, Aussie Mike (as he's never known) from Adelaide. He's lived in Luton for so long that, as I like to tell him (to wind him up more than anything), he's an Englishman now.   Understandably, he has none of it but, although his accent has a twang which would be picked up by an elocution expert, he accepts that he has in many ways become a Brit.

It hasn't always been the case, especially on the Kenilworth Road terrace - and not very long ago either.   We used to stand near Michael on the terrace, not because he was a colleague of my brother and on nodding terms with the rest of us; but because he was entertaining.   Totally committed and involved.   And loud.   With the ability to sing the songs with slightly dodgy inflection and, even better, to passionately shout out really strange things.   Our feeling at the time was, no matter how wide of the mark anything we shouted was, Michael would do worse.   It's hard to remember many of his cries off the cuff - other than his classic "WHAT COLOUR GLASSES ARE YOU WEARING REFEREE!?".

Great stuff.   Unfortunately osmosis set in over the months, he started to get the songs right and the shouted abuse was soon as bland as that from the rest of us.

Even so, he's still capable of a gem or two if he doesn't try.

The latter stages of the '95/96 season were dire.   Under Terry "top six side" Westley the Town had succeeded in proving their potential as relegation rather than promotion candidates.   Westley was sacked just before Christmas and Lennie Lawrence took over. The team put a spurt on but after a disastrous run in March (five games, one draw, four defeats) another relegation looked almost inevitable. We started losing games at home too, which is never a good sign. In the Stoke game, the Town played well enough to earn a draw at least, although we really needed a win, only to be beaten by an injury time winner.

Ultimately then, the match was a swine. Still, in its early stages, it provided perhaps the greatest Flaherty quote. The ref, one Uriah Rennie from Sheffield, is a big bald black gentleman. Referee baiting is Michael's forte and when Mr Rennie was in perceived earshot Michael, somewhat amazingly, shouted "YOU PROMISED ME A MIRACLE REFEREE". Odd. A Simple Minds lyric surely.... what was going on in Michael's own simple mind?

And then I sussed. The referee looked (in so far as his being big, bald and black) like Erroll Brown from Hot Chocolate. Excellent. After the rather muted, and understandably quizzical, reaction to his first shout I knew that he'd have to have another stab at it. I whispered to Andy and Simon to get themselves ready for the inevitable.

And yes, the next time Mr Rennie wandered over to our corner of the ground Michael was ready "COME ON REFEREE - YOU SEXY THING". It was a great moment. Actually, it was possibly the highlight of the season.

Sorry to anyone who perceives this tale as in any way racist. Certainly the fact that Mr Rennie is black was vital to Michael's describing him as sexy. And granted, nobody taunts bald, white refs with Elton John quotes. But no, he isn't a racist - and neither are the vast majority of the rest of the Luton Town crowd. Most of our best players in the past few years have been black. Far from having a large racist element, a popular chant in the early eighties was "We're black, we're white, we're f***in' dynamite. Luton Town. Luton Town". They don't chant them like they used to.

Mr Uriah Rennie from Sheffield is now a Premiership referee. Michael Flaherty is still supporting Luton Town in the Second Division.

Score: 1-2. Town scorer - Grant
Attendance: 7,689

12/4/97: Walsall v Luton Town

Lennie Lawrence says that we need at least four points from the following two away games to stand a chance of winning the second division title. So, we go and bloody lose the first of them.

And it started out as such a nice day. Michael had been talked into driving, for the first time on the motorway and, once he got used to it, was soon midlane driving like a gimp. I didn't want to push the lad too much, I asked what he was planning to overtake once or twice, only for him to point out a lorry in the far distance. Someone has daubed "Luton Shit on Watford" on a bridge, which is funny - and a bit embarrassing, hopefully someone will cover that up once Luton fans have had their fun and Watford fans been mildly riled.

Walsall's shoebox ground is right on the M6, on a soulless place next to a retail park, the nearest pub looks a good mile away. However, it's warm, there are tons of Luton fans and when we get in the ground there is a distinct air of *laissez faire* from the Walsall fans - who are supposedly cheering their team into a playoff place. The Hatters' fans meanwhile make noise aplenty from our end.

The first half is pretty dire, with Luton's defence unable to cope with Walsall's tricky number 11 whose cross eventually leads to Walsall's opener. "Can't we stop that f***ing number 11!" shouts Michael - a concern quickly endorsed by the bloke sat next to me, who becomes an increasing pain in the arse as the game goes on. He's sat, sweater clad, with his equally wrapped up wife - loudly telling her what is wrong with the Town's play, hoping that one or more of the blokes around will take the bait and join in his line of qualified condemnation. Nobody takes up the offer.

Luton are lucky to be only one down at half time but, at the start of the second half they seem to be far better playing toward the massed (and quite loud) Town support. Our new loan signing Andy Kiwomya responding with an equaliser from a free kick, then Steve Davis puts us into the lead with a header. Michael puts it down to his wearing his lucky (away) scarf which I had been wearing during the first half - as shirt sleeve sunshine outside wasn't getting through in the ground and it was a mite chilly.

The feel good factor didn't last long. Slack marking led to Walsall's equaliser and eventually to their third. Jubilation, not for tenth time this season, was turned to despair. Matey next door, snug in his sweater, drowned out minutes before, is audible again - and nearing his zenith. As an over intricate Town midfield move is about to break down he complains, quietly at first, that the players are "fiddling, fiddling, fiddling"; Walsall tackles start coming in and he gets louder to the point where, when possession is inevitably conceded, he's screaming "Y'FIDDLING, FIDDLING, FIDDLING". There was no way back - either for Mr Sweater or Luton Town.

For a new ground, the Bescot stadium hasn't got the parking sussed - we're stuck in the car park for ages, listening to the radio and trying to draw some encouragement from the fact that Bury have lost as well.

Score: 3-2. Town scorers – Kiwomya, Davis
Attendance: 5,415

At the pub later the beer, and its spokesmen Andy and Steve, appear to be talking up plans to go to Blackpool on Tuesday night. An unlikely scenario - especially coming from these folk. I take the "well, I'm up for it - but you won't be" line - and try to cajole Steve into coming even though he has to be back at college in Cheltenham the day before. The following day, once the alcohol had worn off, Andy is still up for it. But no-one else is. So, I take a half day off work (Andy has Tuesday and Wednesday off).......(*15/04/97*).

13/4/85: FA Cup semi-final, Everton v Luton Town

1985 *The football supporter, though he or she knows the team better than most, maybe isn't the best critic. While my head tells me, without a shadow of a doubt, that the Luton Town I've been watching recently are ....compared to the teams that I grew up watching...rubbish, my heart and my habit cling on to every crumb of comfort and hope available - saving them up for those quiet minutes of reflection when good sense launches an excellent case for chucking it all in.*

In hindsight however every fan of more than a few years' standing has some opinion as to the best team they've ever seen. I never saw Joe Payne, Gordon Turner, Bob Morton, Graham French or Malcolm MacDonald play for Luton. But I did see Ricky Hill, on a regular basis. The FA Cup semi-final team of 1985 wasn't the best Luton side I've ever seen - but it came as close as it got for a big game. The team which Pleat took into the First Division was a flair side - made even flairier by the acquisition of Paul Walsh from Charlton. The Walsh and Stein "partnership" (I regarded Walsh as a bit of a hogger, Stein the composite team man) was even picked by Bobby Robson to front England for a 1984 match at Euro Champions' France - a small club coup which the big clubs would never allow to happen these days. That team scored lots, but let in more; so Pleat went on to build a team bigger on strength than flair. The players he bought in would quickly become Luton Town heroes - Steve Foster, Mick Harford, David Preece, Emeka Nwajiobi and (the dark sheep of the family since he went on to play for Watford) Peter Nicholas.

But throughout Pleat's first glorious reign at Kenilworth Road, the team was built around Ricky Hill, the most skillful player I've seen play for Luton. Hill, capped by England quite a few times, was one of those players who, according to the pundits, would have been better off at "a more fashionable club". But Hill stayed at Luton, and we loved him.

The 1985 Semi-final against Everton at Villa Park wasn't necessarily Hill's best match (I'm no analyst), but whenever I think of him I see the picture in which he's just taken the shot to put Luton into the lead that day.

In fact, my recollection of the actual day is through snapshot memory. I can remember better the feeling of exuberance preceding the match. Fans who were getting over the trauma of the night Millwall came to town realised that, by winning the football match that broke out sporadically during the violence, we had a big day to enjoy. I remember our going to the ground and queuing up for the £4 tickets (which was an astonishing price at the time) for the Holte end. We saw Ricky Hill going into the players' entrance. Most of us were awe struck, whilst Hill looked a little bit embarrassed at the gawps he was getting - and nodding, with a fixed smile, to those who offered the question "y'alright Ricky?". On the walk home we sat at the top of the Dallow Road hill; looking down at the town, and onto our tickets, romanticising about the Cup and little Luton's heroic part in the competition....and catching our breath. It's a bloody knackering climb.

The Northbound carriageway up to Birmingham that day was a sea of orange, white and blue. Inside the ground it was the same (although the orange obviously wasn't too much in evidence in the Everton stands). Straw boaters everywhere and loads of people you never saw near the football ground before, who had dug out the scarf and/or replica top from the last time they bothered. But there was no "loyal fan snobbery" about the day - everyone from Luton was just there to enjoy themselves. We didn't expect to win....... the crushing disappointment was that we came so close to doing it.

Luton played brilliantly against the League Champions and the first half saw Hill's goal at the Holte end - a moment I can remember from the picture of Hill, and the sight from our position as the ball hit the post and went in as Southall, rooted to the spot, just stared.

I honestly can't remember too much more of the match other than, when Everton were awarded the free kick with four minutes to go, my supporter's intuition told me that despite (and possibly because) Sheedy having scored from a near identical situation in their quarter final against Ipswich, he was never going to score this time. It just wasn't going to happen.

It did. Sheedy hit the ball unconvincingly but it somehow went in past the newly permed and sprawling Les Sealey.

Everton overran an emotionally shattered Town team during extra time, and Derek Mountfield eventually scored a winner (minutes from a replay - but the damage had already been done) whilst their fans wouldn't even let us sing "You'll never walk alone" without trying to drown it out with their parochial catcalls.

They were more gracious outside Villa Park, swapping scarves and letting us know how lucky their team had been. As if we cared.

Score: 2-1. Town scorer – Hill
Attendance: 45,289

Of all the Luton Town matches over the years - this is the one I look back to as the most shattering. Why couldn't we have held out? How could the ref (the infamous John Alton from Hants) allow "play on" instead of awarding a free kick for Luton? Everton promptly took the ball away and embarked on the move that ended up with his awarding Sheedy's free kick. The TV pictures of a stinging shot by Hill, in the second half, which Southall saved, play over and over in my mind.... if only Stein had stuck out a boot to divert it into the middle of the goal instead of jumping over it....

Such feelings, thankfully, don't happen all that often to the football supporter. I felt worse before the penalty during the '88 Littlewoods Cup Final but, apart from that, I don't believe I've been so shattered. With the other "all-time downers", the other lost Semi-Finals and relegation battles, there always seemed time during the match, without giving up all hope, to at least reconcile oneself to defeat..... Perhaps it was my age too in '85, my youthful belief that this was really it - I was going to see Luton Town play in the FA Cup Final. Stupid isn't it? It's still a painful memory all these years later.

We came close again in the 1988 FA Cup Semi-Final, when ragged little Wimbledon muscled us out in the second half after Harford had given us the lead. Maybe it was because we had the Littlewoods Cup Final to look forward to. Maybe, because of that, and because we were favourites - there was a feeling of arrogance out of character with a Luton following. It's better to be an underdog. Whatever the case, we lost that match, we deserved to lose, it never really seemed like the end of the world. In the 1994 semi-final, which was made into a non-event by being staged at Wembley, Luton were totally outclassed by Chelsea.

So, I've been to three of the four Luton Town FA Cup semi-finals (the three we lost). It's supposed to be the cruellest stage at which to be knocked out of the competition. Even so 1985 seemed to be much crueler than the others. (17/08/85).

15/4/89: Hillsborough

 I was pretty pissed off with football after the `89 Littlewoods Cup Final anyway; an occasion which left me with the feeling that, after a year away, I simply didn't belong anymore. I **1989** *thought I'd have been more emotionally drawn back towards the Town. Maybe if we'd won.*

There was still the Saturday afternoon void to fill if we weren't on tour with the band. Steve and I would go to Hitchin Town sometimes. This Saturday, whilst Luton were at home to Coventry, we were in a field watching Caddington play. Notts Forest, like Luton the year before, had done well in both cup competitions and had an FA Cup semi-final against Liverpool at Hillsborough to play after winning the Littlewoods Cup less than a week before.

Everyone knows what happened at Hillsborough. Most will remember where they were when it happened. It was sickening. The pictures of those people pinned up against the bars of the cages designed to keep the hooligans off the pitch. It was pathetic. The contempt in which the authorities held the football supporter, epitomised by Luton's own away fan ban, had at last been the cause of the death of 96 otherwise innocent people.

Like the Kings Cross underground disaster (I had been there, earlier that day, Christmas shopping) there was the feeling of "there, but for the grace of God, go I". I'd been on the Leppings Lane terrace before. Rubbish view from the side sections (allocated for small away followings like Luton's), better off in the seats above or, as on the Oak Road terrace, the centre section if it's available. Apart from the pitifully inept crowd control outside, it was the push towards the best view which ultimately ended in so many fatalities.

Bill Shankly once famously said "Football isn't a matter of life or death, it's much more important than that". He was, on that occasion, talking bollocks. It isn't. Football means a lot, more than it should, to a lot of people. It's not worth dying for.

After the news, the pictures, the personal accounts and the grief, I was further appalled by the eventual outcome. It was decided to continue with the FA Cup competition anyway. "The fans would've wanted it". So, no doubt, would the bank manager. Another Merseyside Cup Final, the fences taken down at Wembley, and still there were fans invading the pitch when the goals went in. There were even fans, Liverpool fans, on the pitch at the end trying to get in on their team's muted celebrations. My abiding, sickening, memory of the final is of one such scumbag being fought to the floor by an obviously appalled Bruce Grobbelar.

The result of the Hillsborough tragedy? The Taylor Report meant we all had to sit down (and pay more). More importantly, as football is the be-all and end-all of life on this earth, Liverpool beat Everton 3-2 in the Final at Wembley. Hoorah.

I hated football then, more than I ever thought I could. It took me quite a time to get over that anger. Thankfully, other football supporters were more grown up (and felt less alienated by the sport they loved) and set about changing things for the better. In the end it was that same feel-good factor, orchestrated by the fans and their fanzines rather than the clubs or the FA or the police, that made football fashionable and made me feel like I wanted to go along again. (21/04/90).

15/4/97: Blackpool v Luton Town

The stupid midweek away game. I'm amazed that Andy is still keen. We set off at 1.30pm.

It's funny but, whilst I thought Crewe was a long way on the M6, once you know you've got to go a lot further on the motorway you get resigned to the fact - and then realise that, once out of dull Cheshire, the scenery is quite nice.

We see the tower first, then the rollercoaster - which looks fantastic.... We park up near the Pleasure Beach and get to the gates only to find the buggers are shutting it up - whilst the last few rides are still being run. They only open the park at 2pm - and shut it at five - I ask ye! That was a swine. There are small groups of football fans, mainly Celtic who have a friendly at Man Utd (currently crying over their fixture congestion), as we wander aimlessly around looking for rock for people at work and to spend a few quid on arcade games that are a few years out of date now. I was once an expert on that Japanese football simulation, circa 1992, I'm not that good now. I also enthuse about the old Star Wars game - only to find that it is decidedly low tech now, although the sound of Obi Wan telling me "the force will be with you. Always" still sends a shiver down the spine. About an hour before the match we find a big, empty, out of season pub near the seafront. One dodgy pint of Thwaites later we wander towards the ground.

The prehistoric open Spion Kop where we stood (two, maybe three, hundred Town fans) is an archaic shambles; weeds growing in the cracks in the concrete and half the terrace closed down in the distant past (along with most of the gates and a toilet). It reminded us of how far stadium design has come – as richer clubs move to large, comfortable, sterile football grounds. Memories of the terraces are usually based on the important matches when one was part of a big surging, singing mass of people. In reality quite a few games were viewed in conditions like Blackpool on a Tuesday night. I'd forgotten how liberating terraces can be. We found a place to stand, half way up the terrace and to the left, with a good view. We ended up being talked to by some weirdo, picking up on every comment we made. So when he went to the lav we moved up the terrace, acquiring an even better view. At all seater grounds, you could well be unlucky enough to be stuck with a nutter all season before you can move seats.

There's also room, on a terrace, to show emotions. In a frustrating night like a 0-0 draw at Blackpool there was room aplenty to turn away from the play momentarily after a lucky miss by the opposition. Room to step nervously up and down the terrace steps. Room to do the full "can't believe we've missed" routine - starting in a near ecstatic jump before going down, head in hands, to near the floor. Stuck like sardines in Kenilworth Road, and most other grounds these days, there simply isn't room to react.

But in Blackpool on that mild Tuesday evening, there is room and opportunity aplenty for such elaborate displays of frustration. Blackpool and Luton play to their strengths, but being as both teams are so strong in ineptitude, they cancel each other out.

Score: 0-0
Attendance: 4,382

Stage Two of the stupid away trip was the journey back and the decision that I had made, since we were "up North", to revisit our old haunt, The Kashmir curry house in Bradford (from the Thrilled Skinny days when we stayed in Mick's student hovels in the city).

Bradford, as becomes increasingly obvious, is miles away from Blackpool. We go on the motorway route, past a UFO which has landed to become Bolton's new stadium, and finally on to Bradford. The Kashmir hasn't changed much. The neon light display wasn't there seven years ago, and the place had had a lick of paint. But the Formica tables are still the same, the free chapattis, the same lovely cheap food. S'lovely.

However, the journey back down the M1 is tortuous, I don't know how I stayed awake. We listen to the late night Five Live chat show on which they've decided, for some unexplained reason, to talk about the sixties again - with an expert (and ex-celebrity) panel consisting of "Diddy" David Hamilton, some designer and the woman who made the Thunderbirds puppets. All seemed well prepared to trot out the most popular post-sixties clichés, and tell how they personally made London swing, although their knowledge of the decade in question seemed limited. At one point Diddy David, talking about The Beatles ("who heavily influence Oasis.....but are Oasis as good? I don't think so"), talks about "All you need is love" being recorded live on TV whilst John Lennon was on honeymoon with Yoko Ono. No-one in the studio is able to put him right. That discussion goes on for two tedious hours.

Andy, gawd bless him, stays awake in solidarity up until about junction 14 - after which he must have decided I could be trusted to stay awake as well to get us safely to Junction 11 and home. We get back, completely knackered, at 2.30am.

17/4/97: Meeting the Chairman.

Having written a piece for the fanzine about the possibility of fans having a say about the style of the new LTFC kits next season I'm invited, through Keith, to go to the club to meet chairman David Kohler.

Kohler's relationship with the fans hasn't always been easy. Cries of "Kohler Out" have rung round Kenilworth Road quite a few times since he came to Luton. They haven't been heard too much recently, but in the past he's been at odds with the fans for a number of reasons viz.: Not putting significant money into the club; his part in the sacking of popular manager Jimmy Ryan (after he'd kept us in the old First Division) in favour of David Pleat (who promptly took us down); his complaining of anti-Semitic abuse (which was news to most supporters) and his talking up the possibilities of moving the club to Milton Keynes if planning approval wasn't given to his Junction 10 plans.

Give him his dues though, he's never been shy in meeting his critics face to face. I first met him a few years ago after I slagged him off in the Luton News - I can't remember the occasion, or what he'd done/not done to justify my criticism. It threatened to be quite a tetchy meeting; I'd invited a few friends along, he had a few pro-Kohler Luton Town stalwarts and legal representation. He was obviously not happy about the stick he'd been getting from the fans (including death threats). In the end, and although we were not convinced by all his arguments, we were impressed albeit grudgingly (getting on with the chairman wasn't fashionable at the time) with the time, and the beer, he had for us.

I've also met him (along with Keith and some of the other fanzine bods) on the eve of his officially announcing his incredible, egocentric, "Kohlerdome" proposals. There seemed more than a touch of "pie in the sky" about his dreams, but the impressive nature of the stadium and (more importantly) the proposed site meant that, evil mastermind though he still might be, the plans were well worth supporting.

This latest meeting was the most low key of the lot. Keith was there, along with Jez, and John Pyper the Supporters Club guru is there with a pal. John seems to be on first name terms with everyone at the club. He tells me that Brian Swain, Luton News football correspondent for donkeys years, is resigning, which is a shock.

On the boardroom table there are a couple of kits laid out but, before we can get a good look at them, Kohler herds us into his office to show us an amazing new internet site on his computer. You can, quite literally, talk to dull Americans from all over the world. It's very high tech, Kohler obviously has a top range computer, and very boring.

The kits on the other hand look quite smart. There's a v-neck and a "normal" collared (excuse my ignorance of collar types here) shirt. I like the v-neck but the others like the other - and Kohler tells us all that the players have turned down the v-neck too. We've obviously not been asked to the boardroom to take part in any discussions, merely to give approval to a kit design which the club already know is OK. So, home kit is quite nice but the main '97/98 away kit is going to be the yellow abomination that is our third kit this year (as if we ever needed one). I tell Kohler, and Peter Landau the club shop bloke (an extremely helpful man) that playing in Watford colours is unacceptable. Sadly, the others don't really take up the cause. They take the point in one ear, through a gently nodding head, and out of the other.

We talk on a range of subjects - the two million quid loss; Tony Thorpe's future (he'll likely stay if Luton go up, off if we're not); season tickets up by 5% if we stay down, 7% if we go up and hoping that Labour win the election in view of the new stadium public inquiry. And we talk recent results, I take personal pride in being able to talk with authority with the others on the Blackpool match. We're in the boardroom for a couple of hours before Kohler tells us he wants to go home and chucks us out. He's got more time than most Football Chairmen for the fans but, at the very end of the day, he's got better things to do. The post chairman meeting, which has previously led to pints and heated conversation down the pub, is condensed to a mere five minutes in the car park.

19/4/97: Luton Town v Shrewsbury Town

Pre-match I have no line on this game other than it is potentially the most important match of the season. My reckoning is that, given that we've managed to muck up the last few home games, losing two points too many times, it's vital that we win today. This makes me something of a Jeremiah down the pub as I pedantically refuse to look towards Tuesday's match against Bury, having taken a win today for granted. My mood is improved by picking out L10, Tony Thorpe, in the sweep.

Inside the ground the atmosphere is as free of tension as my pals down the pub apparently are, and the lack of tension from the stands seems to have filtered into the minds of the players. It's a stroll. Shrewsbury are rubbish. The Town are awarded a penalty at the Oak Road end of the ground and, ca-ching, twenty pounds flashes up in my mind's eye. Thorpe startles me with a silly shimmy in his run (the sort of thing that makes you think perhaps there's a lack of confidence there) but ends up scoring.

In the second half Marshall, who we're all hoping recaptures the form he had last season before breaking his leg (he's never had the same pace since he's come back), back-flicks a shot going nowhere into the net.

The result is better than the match, which is pretty forgettable other than for the fact that I won the sweepstake again. (*22/04/97*).

Score: 2-0. Town scorers Thorpe (pen), Marshall
Attendance: 7,501

21/4/85: Mick Harford, media icon.
Luton Town v Manchester Utd

Oh, we had some fine games against the giants back in the old First Division days; although we never seemed to beat Man Utd too often. We stopped them getting the record for most **1985** *wins at the start of the season once - which was as good as a win, but most of our memorable "big five" giant killings were against the goliaths of North London and Merseyside.*

Anyway, the inclusion of this match is basically to show that it did happen. Micky Harford scoring a couple of goals, live on telly, the second of which was right at the death. The season previously United had beaten Luton 5-0 at Kenilworth Road - a match which was also live on the box.

I remember the second goal, a powerful header which hit the ground then looped up and into the net, which was excellent at the time. It was also entertaining to review later at home on video. For, after both of his goals, Mick Harford sought out the camera filming the aftermath - and looked straight into it, wielding his celebratory fist. What a poseur. What a man. Maradona did the same sort of thing, with bucketfuls less style during the World Cup in '94. But then, there's only one Micky Harford. (08/12/84)

Score: 2-1.   Town scorer - Harford (2, 1 pen)
Attendance: 10,320

Battling the Glory Guys in the schools and on the High Street.
Luton Town v Manchester Utd 1997

Admittedly the "deep seated hatred" of Man Utd felt by fans of just about every club (which, in reality, means little more malice wise than hoping they lose every match), is based on downright jealousy. Most teams in Britain would love to have even a fraction of the money that Man Utd make every year. But the biggest bugbear, locally, is that Man Utd's millions are being made on the high streets of places like Luton; through merchandise worn by kids who might have once become supporters of their own local sides. I've little doubt now that kids in schools in Luton who support Luton Town, at Kenilworth Road, get teased by their classmates - who support Man Utd by the medium of parents' credit cards. Those kids will grow up, with an interest in football that will seldom see them venture into a football ground, justifying their loyalty with the line "no (I'm not a glory hunter), I've been supporting them since the days of Cantona" like the last generation used "since Best"; the one before "since Munich".

When I was a kid the popular "glory" support was for Liverpool, but since Man Utd's enduring "not winning the Championship" joke died, there has been a wholesale shift in the market to them - they're obviously geared up better to exploit their success than Liverpool were. Even so, the Liverpool to Man Utd landslide shows that glory hunting is not a totally new concept in allegiance forming. I reckon it's got quite a lot to do with the rise of the nuclear over the extended family in Britain. These days there are plenty of folk who don't even know who their next door neighbours are - what are the chances of these people's kids supporting the local team? Is the support of a side, just because it's successful, a way of manipulating kids towards the career rat race of later life? Discuss.

Maybe because of the other options there is a mutual respect amongst traditional, particularly lower league, supporters. Luton supporters know that their peers could, if they so desired, follow the North London clubs (after the last Arsenal v Luton match at Highbury, there were noticeably more replica Arsenal shirts than Luton getting off the train at Luton station); or decide their loyalty lies with Manchester United - supporting via Sky TV, Match of the Day and glossy mags in the newsagents.

What the average Man Utd fan (who rarely, if ever, goes to see his/her team play), and every other "exiled" supporter, misses out on, is the sense of community spirit - the same spirit from which every local team was born in the first place (even if Manchester United have become the Harlem Globetrotters of football). When Luton Town do something special (rare though that is) then Luton town centre becomes an exciting, joyful place to be. When the club won the Littlewoods Cup in 1988 the atmosphere around the place was amazing as the whole town celebrated. Before a big match and especially afterwards - if it went well - the feeling of regionalised well being is contagious and electric. It's exactly the same feeling felt around the country when England do well. Trying to remember the last such occasion is difficult but, if memory serves, the concentrated nature of regionalised celebration makes it even better.

Lutonian Reds (like Cockney Reds, Eastbourne Reds, Tiverton Reds, Slip End Reds and Watford Reds) surely can't do the same when "their" team wins. On the face of it the Manchester United fan has more to celebrate than any other fan at the moment....but that celebration must, in all but a handful of cases, be muted by the fact that they made the decision to alienate themselves from their local community. When Man Utd win the Cup, Luton doesn't celebrate (and neither does London, Eastbourne, Tiverton, Slip End or Watford).

Of course the feeling of despondency when the local team loses is something we have to live with as well (quite a bit in Luton), and there we don't have the advantages of the contemporary Man Utd supporter. For, heaven forbid, when the going gets tough for Manchester United - the high street sport shops will be delighted to kit the glory gluttons out in the colours of Liverpool, Newcastle or Arsenal.

21/4/90: Missing a decent cup of tea and LTFC.
Luton Town v Arsenal

1990 *This isn't the place (I've been reliably informed) to write up the Thrilled Skinny story, which personally I find a shame - great days....great days. Anyway we toured all over the place, for months at a time for four years before having to stop because we were all skint - and just at the time when the band had their first top 20 hit in the Indie chart. Such a shame, but didn't we have a nice time.*

Possibly our most gruelling tour was of Germany in April 1990. The thing was, even though we got on fantastically well, there was a certain strain being cooped up in each others' company for a whole month with only two or three other English speakers - from our hosts, the congenial German punk supergroup "Sumpfpapste" (The Swamp Popes). We only knew a few words of German; the numbers one to six, "bier" and the German for "buttocks" - which didn't amuse our hosts nearly as much as it tickled us at the time - we gave up on their finding fun in the name of the local beer "Dinkel Acker".

Anyway as with the stereotypical English abroad the "decent cup of tea" factor kicked in within hours of arrival at Micha Schmidt's flat. And, yes, the local supermarket had boxes marked up as English Tea; but it's not the same when the water is boiled in a saucepan and the milk is pasteurised.

Over the course of the month we came to miss other bits of English life - British toilets, beer and bread. English newspapers, when we found them, were enthusiastically pored over. In one such paper we learned of the plight of Luton Town and their battle against relegation. The Town had been beaten 3-0 at Nottingham Forest and now had, just about, got to win their last three matches to stand any chance of staying up.

We were on the outskirts of Munich, for a gig in a punk rock club in a heavily graffittied portacabin. The band had, unfortunately, been billed a "punk rock" band in Germany - so invariably the audiences, some of whom had stereotype Mohican haircuts (or "parrots" as we called them) wanted to hear songs like those of The Clash or The Pistols - and wanted to know from us such details as the political leanings of the lead singer of Disorder. But, on the whole, they were nice enough people (Micha would explain to us that this was because they were "fun punks"). At the appropriate time I rang Simon to ask what the score was, and was ecstatic when he told me Luton had won. He, on the other hand, seemed most unimpressed; "We're still going down" he said, pessimistic git. But to Steve and I it was great news and we decided to go to the last two games of the season. There was a glory hunting element to that decision, but it basically meant that we were mad keen on football again. (28/04/90).

Score: 2-0. Town scorers – Dowie, Black
Attendance: 11,595

22/4/97: Luton Town v Bury

Terrible match. A game which, beforehand, is set up as the match of the season. There is a feeling of anticipation in the pub. Steve Tyler hasn't apparently caught the mood of the moment. He's put a bet on Luton v Bury and Leeds v Whoever ending 0-0. He'll be a few hundred quid better off if the bet comes in and, although we're all sure the Town will pull off a win, the Leeds bet looks pretty safe. Since taking over at Elland Road George Graham has built a great defence...... and sod the attack. Bury, on the other hand, don't let in many.

It isn't until the match starts that we find out why. Bury are a despicable team - full of the usual second division cloggers, but happy to keep eleven of the blighters behind the ball at all times. As long as the score is 0-0 they, and their small following, are happy. In the whole 90 minutes Bury don't have one solitary shot. Luton, sadly, again don't seem to have the nouse to beat a team that is playing for the draw.

At the end of the game "Boring Boring Bury" reverberates around the ground and the Bury team are booed off the pitch (after celebrating with their own fans who are, of course, delighted). We're not adverse to congratulating a promoted team if they've played well, but Bury were just awful. It's sad, and an indication of the lack of quality in this league, that such a negative team look like being champions.

We don't see him after the match but it's a pretty safe bet that Steve Tyler is smiling, Premiership bore draw specialists have also done their business. He's in the money, Luton Town are surely bound for the lottery of the playoffs. (*26/04/97*).

Score: 0-0

Attendance: 8,281

    🎩 🎩 🎩 🎩 🎩 🎩 🎩 🎩 🎩 🎩 🎩

24/4/88: The Gamut

Littlewoods Cup Final, Arsenal v Luton Town

1988 *After a long season, mainly concerned with cup competitions, the Littlewoods Cup Final presented the season's last hope for silverware (and even writing the words "hope for silverware" isn't natural for a Luton fan). Having been muscled out of the FA Cup semi-final against Wimbledon had been a terrific blow. Then we had to endure the Simod Cup Final.... So we went to Wembley knowing that, after a great season, we might end with nothing to show for it all.*

Nineteen eighty eight was the last year at Wembley at which fans would stand on the steep upper tier terracing behind the goals. There were a couple of feet between every step which meant there was a brilliant view. A year later the terraces were confined to the shallow lower tier where the view is not so good. And, for this final rather than the Simod competition, the Luton fans had turned out in force. There were, of course, many more Arsenal fans, some in small groups around us, but this was a big day out for Lutonians who turned out complete with Luton-made straw boaters, once popular throughout the British Empire but now only worn by Luton fans on Cup Final days.

Luton played well in the first half and they took the lead on thirteen minutes when Stein scored. Cue lots of celebrating in the Luton end (the "no tunnel" end at Wembley).

The second half was a different kettle of fish entirely as Luton looked edgy and an equaliser looked on the cards. And, just when it looked like we might hold out, a scramble at the Luton goal resulted in the ball being turned into the net by Hayes. Luton promptly fall apart. The next few minutes are horrible, Arsenal are all over Luton and it's no surprise when Smith scores past Dibble who has misinterpreted the shot and dived the wrong way. The siege of the Luton goal continues.... it seems that every other second the bar or the post are hit. All this happens at the tunnel end of the pitch, it's even scarier on telly....how Hayes hit the post from about two yards out I'll never know. Finally there is a moment's respite when the ref gives Arsenal a contentious penalty, Rocastle having mysteriously gone down like a sack of potatoes in the area.

The next minute or so is etched upon my memory - and not for the fact that Dibble's penalty save was one of the best ever seen in a cup final (it was certainly better than Beasant's save for Wimbledon in the FA Cup final that year). No, the time was memorable for my complete and utter dejection. The lowest I've ever felt during a football match.... a match, a season, which had been looking good ten minutes ago was falling apart around us. Arsenal, late as they'd left it, were ripping us apart. If they scored from the penalty, I told my brother, Matthew and Pete, then I was going. They'd have come too. Meanwhile the four or five flag waving Arsenal fans in the lower tier in front of us took the piss relentlessly.

Winterburn's kick was a good one, into the corner, but somehow Dibble, at full stretch, managed to turn it round the post. David Evans has said that once Dibble had saved the penalty, he knew Luton would win. That's surely rubbish. The save gave Luton fans something to cheer and, clutching at straws, a basis for hope, but I was worried that Arsenal would just go and score from the resulting corner. Dibble caught the cross whilst I took the opportunity to let out some of the pent up emotion of the moment (oh yes). I recall shouting something witty like "Get the f***ing thing up here then!"

The penalty save provided the spark which in turn gave Luton the extra bit of confidence needed to make a match of it; and, within a couple of minutes, Arsenal's Gus Caesar made the error that guarantees his place in the history of Luton Town. Under a small amount of pressure from Mark Stein, Gus made a complete hash of a hoofed clearance and fell over. The ball fell to Brian Stein who calmly crossed it for Danny Wilson to score with a stooping header. Brilliant. And now time to shout ourselves hoarse in support of our team for the final three or four minutes before extra time. It's difficult to remember one's feelings, past that of elation, after the equaliser went in. We had by no means won but, if we did lose in extra time, it's difficult to imagine I'd have been any more disappointed than I was at the moment that the ref pointed to the spot minutes earlier.

In the very last minute of normal time, Luton got a free kick on the right wing. Ashley Grimes swung it into the box, from which it's cleared back out to Grimes who ran the ball to the by-line before firing a low cross in for Brian Stein to score the most important goal of his life.

If you watch the tape, as we have done over and over and over since, you might notice the strange, almost muted, tone of the celebrations in the Luton end. The sound, not just of post goal elation, but of pure delirium. We simply couldn't believe it - normal goal celebration went out of the window in the emotion of the moment as we were up in that stand hugging complete strangers. Steiney celebrated the goal by running straight at the part of the terrace where we were jumping around like mad things.

The whistle for full time went seconds later and, once we'd gained a bit of cohesion, the Luton fans sang "we won the cup, we won the cup, eee-eye-addio, we won the cup" over and over again. Such a daft song, one which I've only ever sung once - when Fozzie went up to get The Littlewoods Cup.

That day will live in the memory long after the last eight minutes of the game, continuously played on the video since then, fade away.

Score: 3-2. Town scorers - Brian Stein (2), Wilson.
Attendance: 95,732

It couldn't get better and the match marked the effective end of my supporting Luton Town for about three years. I had decided that sometime previously. There were a few good reasons: I couldn't agree with the David Evans' regime, football was deeply untrendy at the time and the Indie pop scene was far more cool and exciting (and "dancing" at gigs, as I told my brother Simon was "like when Luton score - but all the time").

My last official engagement as a Luton Town supporter was to join the thousands outside Luton Town Hall and unwittingly help to trample the flower display outside as the victorious Town side paraded the trophy; my own act of distracted vandalism was matched by the players and officials inside as they managed to break bits off the Littlewoods Cup. David Evans, waving the cup around at the balcony, managed to drop the lid on the pavement below - damaging that too.

Overall it was a great evening, a celebration almost unheard of in Luton, and a great way to sign off. (9/4/89).

26/4/80: The first game I went to
Luton Town v Wrexham

1980 *My brothers tell me how good it is so, for the last home game of the season, I deigned to attend with them a meaningless second division match. And, POW, I'm hooked. Much more than the result, it was the assault on the senses which hit me for six. The partisan crowd, the noise, the smell of fags and burgers and beer - left indelible impressions. It might be a dying art for clubs to seduce young fans, kids these days are turned on by the glossy second hand allure of Man Utd mags and vids rather than matchdays at their local club, but that atmosphere immediately made me a Luton Town fan. I was gripped with the emotion; I wanted to care as much as those around me.*

Pretty soon I was kitted out with scarf and badges, pleading with Dad to take us to the match and in the market at school for handing over pocket money payment in exchange for the elusive Panini Luton badge "gold" sticker. The "going with Dad as a treat" remained, with a few notable exceptions, until about 82/83 when we started going with Andrew's older schoolfriends - Stuart Mattheson, Stuart Kedge (West Ham fan/Luton supporter), David Dawn and Andy Overall - standing in the middle section of the Oak Road terrace where all the singing and swearing came from, and the only part of the terrace which afforded a decent view of both goals.

I think Dad had stopped going to the football in the late sixties when hooliganism started creeping in and he, like thousands of others, decided it really wasn't worth the bother. Even so I think he was happier that we go with friends of our own, like he had done in the 50's and 60's, than make a point of coming along with us to create the ideal nouveau traditional family at football matches. We also delighted in Dad's absence, because it meant we could join in all the songs without having to worry that Dad might hear. And so we did, shouting ourselves hoarse every match, ripping our pre pubescent voice boxes to shreds - only able to speak in whispers for a day or so afterwards. (30/04/82).

Score: 2-0.   Town scorers - Moss, Brian Stein
Attendance: 9,049

26/4/97: Peterborough Utd v Luton Town

Very important match this one, one which Luton had to win to stand a chance of automatic promotion.

Putting the match to one side for a moment, some places are strange aren't they? Some places seem to have their own weird feeling. I've read that the site of Auschwitz is still an extremely unnerving place. The strangest place I've ever been to (twice, with the band) is Nuremberg in Germany. I was aware before we went of the city's history, but never expected that the place would be particularly "spooky". On our first visit the band played in a room within a massive Cathedral like art centre in which, it seemed, everyone was drunk. A few, Germans and American squaddies alike, wanted to talk - which was OK really, apart from the fact that, friendly though they seemed, they got decidedly nasty once they caught on that a) no, they couldn't have a swig of our beer or b) the band weren't going to do any Pistols numbers. Outside the venue on that night, we saw rats scurrying about as we loaded the equipment away. On our second visit, where the band were billed to play at the HQ of an anarchist organisation, Mick and I took a walk about the town and thought the Third World War had started when the sky lit up and we heard loads of gunfire. It was, of course, just military exercises. We stayed that night in the loft of the HQ, in horribly cramped conditions, like a hideout from Secret Army. We were awoken in the morning by a record, at tremendous volume, which began, for a good minute or so, with the sound of an air raid siren. Again, it wasn't WW3, but it wouldn't have surprised me. Strange place Nuremberg, as my friends concur.

Claire and I visited an old SS prison camp during our visit to the Czech Republic. That was a strange place too but, perhaps because I expected it, it didn't have the same effect on me as Nuremberg did.

Maybe ghosts do affect the aura of such places.

Then there's Peterborough, whose inclusion on the weird place list would seem to blow the theory out of the water. OK, so it isn't as unnervingly odd as Nuremberg, but some funny things have happened there in the past. Thrilled Skinny did two gigs in Peterborough. They were the only two gigs (of approaching 200) which provided the soundtrack for a significant brawl in the audience. The second gig was a great night, the band's biggest ever earner, there were loads of people there, on a night which (apart from the fight, which was pretty nasty and bloody) was notable for the fact that loads of us managed to hop over a wall and muck about in the town's open air swimming pool. It was a balmy summer's night and, even at 1.30am, the water was lovely. No-one died. Peterborough then is, for me, a place where highs and lows are perversely acute.

And so it came to pass. Mick, having passed his test recently, was driving. Up the A1. Slowly. The General Election just days away, we left the urban areas, where the red posters ruled, and drove past farmers' fields where newly erected billboard holdings displayed big blue Vote Tory posters whilst every post on the side of the road had little posters with the same request, seemingly becoming more desperate as the fields started to give way back to red urban sprawl - vote Tory....vote Tory...vote Tory..vote Tory.*please* vote Tory.

Peterborough had to win to prevent relegation to the Third Division. Luton had to win to stay in with a chance of automatic promotion; a big game for both teams but, driving towards the ground to hunt out a parking space, it was all Luton fans.

Luton's away support circa late nineties is an enigma in itself, and suffers, albeit to a lesser (and not so outwardly aggressive) extent, from the Millwall big match syndrome. The Luton support can decide to give itself the status of an invading army, with a certain amount of menace, prepared to make a mark. It's an attitude that's embarrassingly outdated, but still sadly in evidence whenever we play at Watford and lately at other away games too.

We parked in a pub car park. The pub was packed out with Luton fans. Singing and surging and trying to get to the bar - it would have been horrible to be a local.

The LT Supporters Club had got a lot of money together to buy hundreds, possibly thousands, of orange, blue and white balloons, which everyone was blowing up ready to release. It was all very colourful, quite cheery, but the undercurrent (perhaps fuelled by my own Peterborough paranoia) was still there. I watched a fan, a few metres to my left, who had a Luton flag. As he was waving it about a couple of blokes tried, albeit in a guise of larking about, to take it off him. He was effectively being mugged but, after a tugging match, he managed to keep hold of his flag which he proceeded to tie with a tight knot around his neck. Unable to trust his fellow Luton fan not to steal it.

Such things are, I feel, also indicative of Luton's support in the late nineties. The club/fan division of the 80's also set fan against fan. If anything, with the Club in its current state of limbo, there is even more fan disunity.

There used to be a respect amongst Town fans. Even when we had hooligan groups (or "firms" as they used to call themselves) following the Club, they had nothing to do (and would have nothing to do) with the regular fans. They would just fight it out with the opposition's hard cases.

I can remember in the mid eighties that there were far more eccentric types who used to be at every game - and especially visible at away games. Sadly in recent years, I've heard an (obviously eccentric) old boy, who always used to go the matches, have the piss ripped out of him by a group of lads. I've heard a Luton fan shouting thinly veiled racist abuse at a group of Asian Town supporters. I myself have been set upon by a group of Luton fans, having been recognised via my column in the Luton News. It's not the sort of thing that makes you feel empathy with your fellow fan. It makes you think about packing it all in.

The match was tight, but Luton were obviously better than Peterborough. Fotiadis scored in the second half, keeping alive Luton's promotion hopes and relegating The Posh. We came out of the ground cheerful. Again, it seemed to be all Luton fans, and we happily talked over the big match against Stockport.

"You won't beat Stockport" chipped in a bloke in front of us.

"No?" said Simon looking toward him.

"No, 'cause you're f***in' shit" said the bloke. Presumably an unhappy Peterborough fan. With a skinhead. Simon walked on, head down.

"Yeah, that's right, you keep walking or I'll kick your f***ing head in".

Claire and I walked past too (not the nicest thing for my girlfriend to have witnessed) and, once I was past Simon's new mate, I let my brother know he was alright. Like gunge at the bottom of a pond, such behaviour still lingers on in the lower leagues.

Thankfully matey didn't try and follow up his threat. We got to the car and drove off. Past groups of Luton fans, singing and shouting. We crawled in the traffic past a shop; there were the Luton fans outside hurling thinly veiled sexual intimidation at the young girl serving behind the counter. It was pretty sad.

Maybe it's just Peterborough and maybe, looking back, I may well have been especially paranoid because I'd taken Claire along. It was a great result but, on balance, it might have been better coming from Teletext or James Alexander Gordon.

Score: 0-1. Town scorer – Fotiadis
Attendance: 9,499

And so the scene is set for the final day showdown with Stockport County at Kenilworth Road. Stockport are just a point ahead of Luton and, as long as they don't win their penultimate game at Chesterfield (who will surely be fighting like demons as they are still in with an outside chance of the play-offs themselves) on Monday evening 28/4/97, a Town victory would see us snatch second place. Kenilworth Road's poxy capacity of less than 10,000 quickly sells out. (*28/04/97*).

28/4/90: Wanting to kiss Iain Dowie
Luton Town v Crystal Palace

 The second part of the, highly unlikely, 1990 relegation battle. Steve's and my return to supporting the Town. All we needed to do was win to take the fight on to the final match at Derby. **1990** *Against Palace, who would be concentrating on their impending Cup Final against Man Utd far more than this meaningless match, and Luton in high spirits, it was going to be easy.*

But Palace are one of those dogged, unfancied (unfanciable), teams. It was all pretty much one way stuff - with Palace occasionally frightening everyone with counter attacks - but we just couldn't score. They just wouldn't let us win. The swine!

In the end, having heard that Sheffield Wednesday (the only team we could hope to climb above) had won away at Charlton, we knew that unless we scored we were relegated.

Up pops Dowie, a minute into injury time, and scores. The crowd goes wild. Luton Town live to fight another day. Simon, sitting in the Oak Road with his date, claims that (in his lovelorn state) he didn't realise the gravity of the situation, how close the Town came to grief at the jaws of relegation, until he saw the frenzied reaction to Dowie's goal at the Kenilworth Road end of the ground.

So, we escaped. A bumper away following for Derby the next week was guaranteed. (5/5/90).

Score: 1-0. Town scorer - Dowie
Attendance: 10,369

28/4/97: Chesterfield v Stockport County

After all the goodwill I'd wished Chesterfield's way during their FA Cup semi-final, I thought they might have done us a favour by avoiding defeat.

Score: 0-1
So, Luton are stuck in third place whatever happens on Saturday.
(*3/05/97*).

30/4/82: When we last won promotion
Luton Town v Shrewsbury Town

1982

The `81/82 season was great for Hatters fans.   At the beginning of the season I had got a copy of "Roy of the Rovers" which included a season planner, which you filled out to include all the results and scorers and league position. The league position graph for that season is an almost unbroken line at the top of the league.

Our promotion winning side was a classy one. It wasn't as good as the side John Moore inherited from Pleat in `86, but it was great to watch - and obviously too good for second division football.

Promotion that year was almost inevitable, and the evening when it was sealed was wonderful. We went along with a kid called Mark Dicker, and his older brother and stood on an Oak Road side section.   After an undeniably tense first half, Luton steamrollered Shrewsbury in the second half and the joy from the terraces was tangible.

Strangely Mark's brother seemed almost over keen to get away after the match and, although we were right next to a gate, we didn't run onto the pitch and celebrate like everyone else did at the end. We read about the extended celebrations in the local press later. Perhaps he was worried about losing us, or wanted to set a good example by obeying the daft "please keep off the pitch" requests read over the tannoys.

A few days later Luton played FA Cup Finalists QPR to win the Second Division Championship and end Rangers' own dwindling promotion hopes. That was a much better, and tougher, match on the pitch. Rangers' Glenn Roeder was sent off, and was suspended for the Cup Final, and Luton ended up winning 3-2. Another great night from Luton Town's last promotion campaign. (12/03/83).

MAY

2/5/92: Luton Town - The Club that cried "Wolf!"
Notts County v Luton Town

1992 *The subtle irony of the relegation season, and the fact that it was the first season back on grass at Kenilworth Road, was that it was Luton's away record that saw them relinquish top flight status on the eve of the Premier League, and Sky's huge cash handouts to the clubs involved therein. Luton didn't win an away game all season, yet the home record was good enough for us to stay up if we won the final away game.*

It didn't happen. Oh, the injustice of it all! It was also a season where (again away from home) we managed to lose points in the final five minutes with alarming regularity. Poring over the statistics thereon I worked out that, if we could have held onto the points we'd lost whilst the fat lady was clearing her throat, Luton would've been a top six side. And oh, how the words "top six side" would haunt us in years to come.

Anyway, prior to the game we were as cocksure as we'd ever been before a last game of the season "do or die" away game. Unlike Man City in `83, Notts County were already relegated and so only had pride to play for. And, unlike at Derby `90, we weren't relying on a third party doing us a big favour by losing at home. We just needed Coventry City to lose at Aston Villa - something that happens year after year. Yes, we had to win away for the first time in ages but, given the circumstances, it wasn't exactly beyond the realms of possibility.

Luton fans travelled in their thousands to Nottingham, taking up noisy residence in several pubs along the road to the ground - dressed up (the official end of season theme was to dress up as Eric Morecambe) and raring to go.

However, inside the ground it was a little bit strange. The original Town allocation had been about 1500 tickets because the normal open away terrace was due for demolition. The club objected and a further 4000 approx tickets were released as Notts County decided to hold off the bulldozers for a couple more days. So, inside the ground Luton fans had a bit of the main stand (where we were stood) and half the old away end - and were separated by the other half of the terrace where the plant machinery and a few workmen stood. It felt strange to be segregated from our own supporters.

The match started well for Luton fans when, within a minute, those with trannies pressed to their ears reported news from Birmingham that Villa had gone 1-0. So soon. Really? After all the duff reports on the Derby terraces a couple of years before, it sounded a little dodgy although it turned out to be accurate.

And pretty soon, true to the script, James scored for Luton and we all went mad in time honoured fashion. Notts County equalised before half-time, through debut boy Rob Matthews, a University Graduate, but that wasn't necessarily a disaster. It was worse at Derby; it just meant that we'd have to come out with all guns blazing in the second half.

It never happened. Matthews scored again, a looping curling shot which seemed to be in the air for ages. "That's in" said Simon as it curled towards the goal. He wasn't wrong.

We had to win, and an equaliser never seemed likely. Coventry were doing their part, losing 3-0 at Villa. In the `91/92 version of The Great Escape Luton cast themselves as Steve McQueen. Powerful bloody motorbike, but it's never going to get over that fence....... Nick Hornby wouldn't have struggled so long with such a second rate metaphor would he? Sorry.

Relegation was something that neither I, nor hundreds of others who hadn't been about for the `74/75 season, had seen. It was a right sod. We stayed and applauded, notably towards Brian Stein and Mick Harford who had given us so many good times over the past ten years, and towards John Moore who was busy instructing

167

disheartened players to go back to the Town fans to register their support.

A sad sad day. There were people sat on the terraces, crying their eyes out, disconsolate, getting sympathetic pats on the back and ruffling of the hair from their fellow fans. I tend to try to be deliberately upbeat in such situations, in a forlorn attempt at lifting the gloom. It never works, even after pints aplenty. One is still left with a sad empty feeling during the days after. (15/09/92).

Score: 2-1. Town scorer – James

Attendance: 11,380

3/5/97: Luton Town v Stockport County

So, the most important game of the year becomes a run out in the sun.... but at least it's quite a good match. Stockport, gawd bless 'em, try and play good football. Unlike Bury. Stockport score from a penalty in the first half, sending their supporters into a contrived frenzy, before Luton take a hold in the second half and eventually equalise through a great goal by Andrew Fotiadis (again).

It's an odd sort of atmosphere inside the ground. The packed Stockport end had obviously bought their tickets thinking they'd be for a "do or die" (i.e. miss out on automatic promotion) battle. The Town fans on the other hand attempt to show they don't care "We're going to Wembley - you're not" that sort of thing. There is however a spark of wit in the Luton Maple choral society as we goad the packed ranks of Stockport fans with "Man U - you all support Man U". It's pretty clever by Luton standards, and succeeds in winding up a few of the opposition supporters - it's not so effective after the fourth or fifth airing mind.

Anyway, in the second half it's the Luton fans who are making by far the most noise - with some new happy clappy song nicked from the continent - quite drowning out the Stockport promotion party which must have had its finest moments in Chesterfield the Monday before.

At the end of the match there's a nice show of mutual appreciation. Most of the Luton fans stay behind to clap Stockport off the pitch - then both sets of fans applaud each other - and finally we applaud the Town team on a strangely premature lap of honour. As we wait, and clap lots, the news comes through via blokes with trannies, that it's Crewe in the play-offs. The consensus of opinion is rather them than Bristol City.

Score: 1-1. Town scorer – Fotiadis
Attendance: 9,499

The bad thing is, ticket wise, that Crewe's ground is so darned small, with a capacity of about five and a half thousand and less than one thousand for away fans. At a conservative estimate Luton might have expected, in a decent sized ground, to have a following for this match of four and a half thousand fans..... Even so, we could have got our hands on the tickets if we'd tried. But I've gone to Crewe once, it's a long boring drive, the Luton allocation will be snapped up so they won't miss me. And I'm skint. (*11/05/97*).

5/5/90: Day of the trannie
Derby County v Luton Town

1990 *It's difficult, looking back, to justify the amazing sense of optimism that travelled up the M1 with the 5000 Luton fans that day. I suppose, when your team looks dead and buried, which it had appeared Luton were before they beat Arsenal and Palace, one clings doggedly to the last hope. Sheffield Wednesday had suffered an amazing dip in fortune over the past few weeks, although their win at Charlton as the Town played Palace seemed to have put an end to that. Luton's only chance of First Division survival was through winning away at Derby and relying on Nottingham Forest, who had nothing to play for, beating Wednesday at Hillsborough. It was a terribly long shot but, although I made the point that we were likely going to Derby to say good-bye to the First Division, there was a certain amount of expectation.*

The away end at Derby was packed with Luton fans on a very hot afternoon. The atmosphere on our terrace was loud, defiant, and when Tim Breaker scored in the first minute from a stupendous range, frenzied. Kingsley Black made the score 2-0 after twenty odd minutes, before Luton managed to lose the lead before half-time.

The news from the guys with the trannies pressed to their ears was good, although rumour was rife, the Chinese whisper network indeed suggested that Forest were beating Wednesday.

It was all looking good, all it needed was another Luton goal. Our play in the second half (the break having thankfully held up Derby's comeback) suggested that we would score. I remember hoping that the goal came quite late, because I had more confidence in Luton's ability to score than to hold onto a lead.

Black's second, and eventually winning goal, crept in (painfully slowly, down by the post) with fifteen minutes to go.

The rest of the match went by in a blur. Derby had a Mark Wright looping header go close (a chance which was apparently reported as an equaliser at Hillsborough), but the ref didn't play loads of injury time. The final whistle was greeted with wild celebrations on the terraces as the players danced on the pitch. The queue out of the carpark was slow and noisy, with Luton fans bibbing horns incessantly. It was still hot and one fan was leaning out of his car window to drink from the window wash jet. The joy and camaraderie on the terrace was mirrored all the way back to Luton on the motorway. An excellent day and, as a result, a good evening too.

Score: 2-3. Town scorers – Breaker, Black (2)
Attendance: 17,044

My Dad was working over in Italy at the time and was watching live coverage of the Sheffield Wednesday v Notts Forest. Not fully understanding the commentary, he wasn't sure what was going on but told us that, towards the end of the match, the pictures were all of distraught Wednesday fans. Whilst he couldn't understand the commentary he guessed, with the regular mention of the words "Luton Town", that the Hatters must have avoided the drop. (08/09/90)

11/5/91: Yet another bloody Houdini act: plastic pitch and Levi Jean rippage. Luton Town v Derby County

1991 *I can't remember the exact mathematics of the escape act this season. It was another, could go down if they don't win, scenario but without the drama. Derby were bottom, already relegated, and Sunderland needed to win away at Man City to stand a chance of staying up. Only two teams were to be relegated that season. I can't remember why.*

We didn't really want this to have to happen. There was a thought that Jim Ryan's side might be given a chance after the heroic effort at the back end of the season before. Instead, he had to sell Tim Breaker and Danny Wilson. The players obviously played their hearts out for the popular Ryan, but Luton Town were a weakened team that season.

We stayed up through an own goal by Mick Harford (who joined us again next season) and Lars Elstrup. Sunderland, roared on by a massive support at Maine Road, went down.

Score: 2-0. Town scorers - Harford (og), Elstrup
Attendance: 12,889

Given the squad at his disposal, this was a creditable result for Jim Ryan who was rewarded with the sack amidst allegations that he had refused to allow the Chairman's three year old daughter into the changing room before this particular match. And so a low key relegation escape had been turned into farce by the club.

And, talking of farce, this was the last match on Luton's plastic pitch - so the brief for the pitch invasion included an interest in ripping off a bit of the plastic for posterity. But would the pitch tear nice and evenly? Would it 'eck. It was next to impossible to get up. In the end I found out that bits could be ripped off the frayed edges of the pitch at the front of the Oak Road terrace. So, no player ever stood on my substantial chunk of plastic pitch, it was still displayed proudly on our mantelpiece for ages. It's somewhere in the loft now.

More easily ripped, I found to my disdain, were my fairly new pair of 501s which suddenly couldn't take the strain of my cavorting about the stand. They were "distressed wash" jeans, and I was pretty distressed too - having to walk out of the ground with much of my arse hanging out of my trouserware. I complained to Levis, who explained

that this was now a discontinued line and sent me a new free pair of
501s. Which was very good of them. (14/09/91)

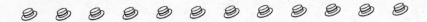

11/5/97: Crewe Alexandra v Luton Town

The First Division play-offs, first leg, are on the Saturday whilst
everyone else's are on Sunday. Sky show Brentford beating Bristol
City away (good) in the morning but the Second Division play offs are
largely ignored by the media, and Sky in particular, when it's time to
concentrate on the fantastic battle at the bottom of the Premiership
(Sky's millions having been part of the reason why there isn't a battle
at the top of the league). I must admit I hope that Middlesbrough end
the season with nothing, although I've had nothing against them in the
past (and indeed had friends who produced their fanzine "Fly me to
the moon". The "Shrug" boys. Hallo. Remember Peterborough
swimming and the caff we took you to in Luton?), it'll give me some
pleasure to see all that money win them nothing but relegation....
Turning to the Teletext I see that Luton have taken an early lead
through David Oldfield. Wa-hey. Then I settle back to watch Sky's
Relegation special - thinking that, if I ignore what's going on at
Crewe, it'll all work out alright.

But, foolish me, I can't help myself, whilst listening to Five
Live's commentary on Leeds v Middlesbrough it occurs to me that
Three Counties Radio (our local BBC station) will probably have
coverage from Crewe. I could really do without the tension, but I tune
in anyway only to find out that Crewe had just equalised - and Julian
James has been sent off. Balls. Back to Five Live until curiosity gets
the better of me again and I switch back to hear the aftermath of
Crewe's second goal. I switch off Three Counties again, vowing not
to do that again and to make better use of my time by sulking and
worrying a bit.

Oh well, at least I'm not a Middlesborough fan; one of the
poor sods that Sky delight in picking out at the end of their brief but
exciting stint in the Premiership. Claire comes in and expresses her

derision that they should take football so seriously (when there are people starving in Africa etc). It's a fair point, but part of the package of being a true football supporter is abject misery at big time loss. I've never gone as far as crying at a football game but I can sympathise, every time, with those who do. (*14/05/97*).

Score: 2-1. Town scorer – Oldfield
Attendance: 5,467

14/5/83: Raddy scores. Pleat jigs. Luton Arndale cheers.
Kids skip with joy in Slip End, South Bedfordshire.
Manchester City v Luton Town

1983 *A match rated, amongst many of the 8000 fans who went up to Maine Road that day (including The Luton News' Brian Swain who has been to every Town match for years), as the most glorious Town match they ever witnessed. That it should beat the 1988 Littlewoods Cup Final in such polls might be down to the feeling that relegation battles, rather than cup finals, are Luton Town's natural forte. Of course I'd vote for the cup final every time - I wasn't at Maine Road in 1983.*

Whilst Watford kicked and ran their "route one" way up to second place in the First Division after promotion, David Pleat's Luton scored and conceded more goals than anyone else - darlings for the Match of the Day and Big Match cameras - but slipping down the table.

The situation on the last game of the season was simple. Man City would stay up, and send Luton down, as long as they didn't lose.

We listened to the match on the radio, for as long as we could bear it, but as time slipped away we decided to save ourselves the tension and went to play headers and volleys at the chalk outlined goal in the garages instead. We played with quite a few of the other group of pre-teen Slip End Town fans, trying to make out that we were "not bothered" about relegation.

I can't remember where the information came from but as soon as we heard the rumour that Luton had scored we ran to get confirmation. Once we got the news that Raddy Antic had indeed scored we listened for the remaining few minutes and then, on hearing we'd won, proceeded to run round the estates of Slip End. Cheering loads.

Score: 0-1. Town scorer – Antic
Attendance: 42,843.

David Pleat meanwhile was doing his famous jig on the pitch (we've grown sick of the clip now) towards captain Brian Horton. What the Match of the Day cameras missed was the assaults that some of the other Town players received from Man City fans who had invaded the pitch.

As young supporters we had, of course, absolute faith that Luton would get a result. The mood of the supporters, even as read by a fan who at the time only went to games once in a blue moon, seemed so defiant that defeat (or failure to win) seemed inconceivable. I remember how we told Colin Malam, chief sports writer for The Telegraph who used to go to the same church as Dad made us go to, that Luton Town would stay up. He sympathetically told us that, more than likely, they would go down. We really wanted a top sports writer to agree with us, but Colin relented - and credit to him that he kept his patience with our continuing pestering that he admit that Luton would avoid relegation. The day after the Man City game, with me bleary eyed having been allowed to stay up to watch Match of the Day, Mr Malam happily took up every opportunity we gave him to eat his words. (12/11/83)

14/5/97: Second Division Playoff Second Leg
Luton Town v Crewe Alexandra

For a good, honest and pessimistic opinion on how the Town would get on I asked my little brother Simon on the afternoon before the match "What do you reckon?". His answer was predictable, made up of the same fears that I had. We could beat Crewe. The six-nil score was no fluke, even if they did have two players sent off - they were 3-0 down before the first. When it comes down to it, out of two teams that try to play good football, Luton are better. But.... the big match scenario... "We'll f*** it up" he says, and I concur.

But Mick, who has come up from London, is pretty confident and the atmosphere in the pub is expectant. We're all quite excited.

In the ground the atmosphere is, not surprisingly, a little bit more tense. Crewe haven't even sold the 2000 tickets in the Oak Road end. The 1500 (generous estimate) they have bought along suffer some quite pitiful baiting by the Luton fans. Our songsmiths follow up the success of "You all support Man U" against Stockport with, "You all support Man U" at the Crewe fans. As if this isn't irrelevant enough, they then inexplicably drag up the 80's terrace standard "What's it like to have no job?". The Crewe fans remain, understandably, bemused.

The game is tight and tense and then POW! a defensive blunder in the Crewe defence lets in Oldfield who scores expertly.

Joy in the stands but the underlying trend for Michael is that of tension. He's wound-up for this one. Uptight. A little bit too roity-toity. And, when the linesman doesn't give an offside against Crewe (who are looking a bit too tasty for any comfort), he runs down to berate the hapless official. Bloody fool - I shout at him not to be such a twot, but he's a man on a mission. So, he gets down as near as he can to the touchline and is promptly told to sit down and shut up by the nearest police sergeant. So Michael, in a terrific act of making a bad situation worse, proves his dolt credentials by blowing the policeman a kiss before skulking back to his seat. The policeman follows him up the stand and warns him that he's in for a life ban if he so much as moves from now on. It had to happen. I'm just surprised it took so long. Michael apologises to the copper and then attempts to justify himself with us....without much success ("we're laughing AT YOU Michael, not with you").

And then, all of a sudden, Oldfield gets a second and it seems we're Wembley bound. We celebrate as heartily as a goal of such importance warrants - except for Michael, looking shiftily over at his friend the policeman, who just claps lots.

Sadly our ovation is cut short in it's prime, "Going to Wembley" songs dying in our throats, by Crewe's next attack which ends with their scoring.

At 2-1 up at half-time we try and keep our spirits up by saying we're in better shape now than we were at the beginning of the match. But the truth is that Luton aren't playing very well.

The second half is a big disappointing blur. From the Kenilworth Road we see Feuer go for the ball, miss it, and Crewe score. It looked, from where we were, that he must have been fouled - it later transpires that he had in fact flapped at the ball. A terrible mistake in a terrific season for our massive American keeper. The match goes on with Luton trying, ever more desperately, for a goal to take the match into extra time. Lawrence puts on every attacker available. But it's hopeless....... we simply don't deserve to win. In the end we've missed promotion by failure to win at home against Wycombe, Bristol City and Bury.

Score: 2-2. Town scorer - Oldfield (2)
Attendance: 8,168

On the final whistle a group of lads congregate near the tunnel and talk of "getting the fu***in' ref". They obviously have no aim in that direction, more than likely because of the police presence around the tunnel, so they go down to near the front and start arguing with a little old lady instead. It's only a game, boys. There's a pitch invasion at the end, with a gaggle of fans trying to comfort the inconsolable Feuer, whilst the boys who appeared at the end, apparently hell-bent on mayhem, bounce off in what they hope is a threatening manner towards the Crewe supporters.

And hundreds of Town fans move in the same direction - up to the Crewe end (which is protected by the police). But the bad boys' menace is instantly diluted to nothing by the honest applause and congratulation heaped on the Crewe fans by their, bitterly disappointed, Luton Town counterparts. It's a moment which typifies the way fans behave these days, but is heartwarming all the same.

Had the police and stewards kept us off the pitch then that moment wouldn't have been allowed to happen. Opposing football supporters are no longer automatically regarded as warring factions and, as long as we're not, the battle against the hooligans is being won in the stands. So, we enjoyed a good few minutes of mutual appreciation with my good faith in my fellow Luton Town supporters, which I had called into serious question at Peterborough, at least partially restored

The Crewe fans, as I'd noticed earlier in the season, seem a really friendly bunch. As we troop, dejectedly, off the pitch they're singing "Luton Town". Bless their cotton socks.

But, bloody hell, the disappointment. It's not a bad taste in the mouth it's a bad feeling in the head. Depression, not helped by the fact that you know you shouldn't take it so seriously. We've had worse, and seek solace in that fact on the way out of the ground. "It makes the good times all the better" I offer. Chris tells us that, since he's been going, there have been no "good times". I tell him they really are good, those good times.....

So, Second Division, Third Rate, football again next year - which is a real downer. (*25/05/97*)

18/5/96: England, their England
England v Hungary

1996 *I've only been to Wembley to see England twice. The first time, the qualifier against Poland for the 1994 World Cup Finals, was great. England still had a chance of getting to the USA, a quest later dashed in the episode now available on video as "Do I not like that", and the spirit was excellent. Wembley was packed, the crowd was loud and the atmosphere was good. My own slight parochial problem was occasionally hung up over cheering for a team managed by Graham Taylor but, above all, there was the feeling that the Nation was behind the team. And I was privileged to be at Wembley that night. England expected, and the team delivered with a 3-0 win.*

We managed, quite easily, to louse up our chances of going to the Euro '96 games. I picked up the leaflets over a year before the tournament - but it all seemed like so far away, and so expensive. Instead, and as a very poor substitute, I paid £56 for a couple of tickets for the England v Hungary friendly. The atmosphere, predictably, wasn't so good. But worse than that, it was altogether nastier. On the train into Wembley there was a group of blokes. Tottenham. Nasty looking stereotypes, no hair, twenties/thirties, trying to suss out allegiances amongst the other passengers. Staring and sneering. It was hard to ignore them but, luckily, they were quite a way away from us. Instead they took part in some, decidedly dodgy, "banter" with some northern fans (can't remember the particular team they supported) before they started ripping into some poor old boy, nothing to do with the football, who had been too near and too old or scruffy or strange to escape their attentions. He got off a few stops before Wembley, with all his bags, to the sound of their moronic laughter and insults.

Inside Wembley was awful. Cold, uncomfortable, extortionate prices for snacks and no edge to make the match interesting. The stadium was three quarters full, and the crowd was made up of three groups. Parents. Their kids. And bigots. We sat near a group of parents/kids in the upper tier behind the West End goal, looking down on our nearest band of bigots. They were busy having a go at the small band of Hungary fans ("who the f***ing hell are you?") and looking forward to Euro '96 with "We hate Scotland and we hate Scotland". A couple of Wembley stewards, who should have ·been doing the rest of us a favour by chucking these idiots out, stood in attendance nearby - laughing along with them.

So we sat, shivering, our ears being bashed by high pitched screams from the kids behind us and the shit wit of the idiots in front entertaining the grinning stewards with "Let's go f***in' mental".

Patriotism is a strange thing, very rarely justified and more often tarred with the same brush which marks out its ugly bedfellow Nationalism. I'd like to be proud to be English, even though I'm not at all sure that this is a worthy ambition. It's easy to wrap oneself up in the flag - it's a national institution - to well up with emotion, let one's heart swell to the tune of "Rule Britannia". We're encouraged at birth to bask in the reflected glory of two World Wars, one World

Cup, Wellington, Nelson, Churchill and The Empire. Glories and heroes of years long past, before many of us were born. I prefer to draw patriotism from our perceived national characteristics of honesty, humanity and fair play – our love of animals, afternoon tea and the freedom of speech. Even so, as a kid, the favourite game (apart from football in the garages) was "WAR". As a scout I saluted the flag and promised to do my duty to God and the Queen – that duty, for past generations has included dying in the mud of the Somme. Still, given that Britain were the undisputed goodies against Hitler in the war, it's no surprise really that we feel some sort of proud emotion when watching old Johnny Mills films on the telly. It might have something to do with Britain's fight against fascism during the last (world) war that I feel particular disgust when I witness England fans parading the full nationalist bit. Although there are probably only a very few fully signed up fascists at England matches, there is an obvious air of nationalist hatred at Wembley internationals.

As for away matches - the travelling contingent still needs to be transformed into supporters who respect the country and the residents of wherever they're playing. There may be some of you, reading this, who go to England matches with this conversion very much in mind - and are upset by my observations, made from my armchair/barstool courtesy of Sky TV coverage. Of course the FA also have a job to do (though they obviously can't be trusted to do it) and the local police are often awful, but this just makes the need for change all the more pressing. Hopefully, one day, England fans will travel abroad seeing themselves (and being seen by the authorities) as ambassadors and not an invading army.

Football supporters have, in general, grown up a lot since Hillsborough. It's a shame then that, though we've reclaimed the national game - we've not been able to do the same for the national team. When Saturday Comes, the fanzine which has been credited with saving the soul of football in the late eighties and early nineties, is still going strong - and often offers its readership special holidays out to see the Africa and South American championships. When they also do trips to see England play away, perhaps it will be a time when supporters will feel able to see their national team, and retain their pride, at away matches. (8/6/96)

Score: 3-0

25/5/97: Second Division Play-off Final.
Brentford v Crewe Alexandra

I make a point of missing this on the telly. The attendance was less than 35000, which is particularly rubbish. Had Luton been involved then Wembley might at least have been half full. And we'd have worn straw boaters, which would have provided a talking point for Sky's eight hours of coverage.

It's good to hear that Crewe won - nice to see that two of the three teams going up (Stockport and Crewe) are proper football sides. (*the end*).

Score: 0-1

BACK TO JUNE AGAIN

8/6/96: International Competition - at last
England v Switzerland

We had picked up the colourful Euro `96 leaflets in the LTFC ticket office months ago and during the weeks leading up to the competition Simon and I moaned that we had been stupid to miss the chance. Mick, Martin and Mally, the canny swine, had got around to buying tickets to all England's first round matches. But, at the time, if truth be known, we didn't have the disposable income to buy the tickets. What we did have, which also didn't help, was a feeling in the back of the mind that the FA were trying to rip us off again. Still, if we'd been real football fans, we would have managed to find the money somehow.

1996

England had not had a competitive match since Graham Taylor ignominiously toddled off into obscurity. Two years of meaningless friendlies later we finally had real international competition to watch.

I carefully and deliberately missed the boring opening ceremony. It's a policy I've taken into watching live games on Sky, the games usually starts at 4pm or 8pm, there's rarely any reason to tune in beforehand for the banal "build up" coverage.

Watching England on telly was very much how I remembered it; over hyped, tense and annoying. Perhaps the low key start wasn't a totally bad thing, it acted as a calming influence throughout the nation, and held up the triumphalist rubbish from the tabloids for a few days.

Score: 1-1

15/6/96: Trobb's wedding
England v Scotland

My colleagues, the charming Miss Tina Robbins and Mr Cliff Keen (tall geezer), had chosen the 15th June 1996 for their wedding date. I was amongst the first to tell Trobbins what a daft day it was to be married.

Apart from their wedding day, it was a ver ver special day in the British sporting diary. The clash of the Auld Enemy no less. It always means more to the Scots than it does to the English. Unrequited hatred. I, like quite a lot of Englishmen I suspect, have a soft spot for the Scots; unless they're playing England, when their traditional feelings towards the tie make them horribly tricky opposition. I envy their fans for the way that they behave abroad in supporting their ragamuffin team. They seem to charm their hosts wherever they go, managing the neat trick of getting drunk with dignity.

My girlfriend Claire doesn't give a monkeys about football normally, but, because she has Scottish parentage, she's very interested in this match, probably to wind me up more than anything, she hasn't showed any interest in their games before or since.

We watched the first half at home and at half time made our way to Dunstable to go to the wedding after catching the second half in a town centre pub. It was horrible in there. Dunstable is normally a quiet little town, it might even be described as quaint if it wasn't so near to Luton - a town that many Dunstable residents view with loathing. Many regard Luton, especially at night, as a strictly "no go" area. But, when England play, the pubs in Dunstable become uncommonly involved and unpleasant. In the pub we went into, the lads were staring up at the tellies on the walls and cringingly joining in the chants.

We missed the first Shearer goal but after Scotland's missed penalty and after Gazza's goal, they were jumping around like mad things - like they imagined people do at football matches.

Claire, who had been willing McAllister to score from the spot, was hurt by their tiny minded anti-Scottish abuse and had a silent tear. It was a small over reaction on her part, the lads of sleepy little Dunstable were good for much more than that.

The wedding was nice. Everyone was cheerful (had England lost, it would have been more like a wake), and it was a lovely day. The winos in the church gardens playfully shouted "Ingerlund" which, to their credit, was at least topical. Thankfully the lads stayed in the pub.
Score 2-0

England v Holland

Simon and I watched the Holland game in a pub in Slip End. An entirely different atmosphere..... it was really quite dull. Fantastic game though.
Score 4-1

With England safely (or gloriously, depending on which paper you read) into the quarter finals, the national ground swell of enthusiasm was well underway.

A good cup run, in a national sense, is a fine thing - there's just so much good feeling in the air and everyone wants a slice. The mass popular interest in England, once they have progressed to the knockout stage of major competition, is entirely different. We don't follow England because they are good; over the years, apart from 1966 (lest we ever forget), they haven't been. We follow England because we're born into it. It's the same deal that sees traditional fans (many of whom aren't as bitter as I am) support our clubs. When England do well the reaction is the same, albeit amplified many thousands of times, as when Luton Town get to Wembley and thousands of local people who never usually go to Kenilworth Road buy straw boaters and beat a path to the twin towers.

The feel good factor when England do well is enjoyed throughout the country. Mass elation isn't something one normally associates with the England football team. Far more representative, especially in the eyes of the media, is the mindlessly boring violence slant to the national side's support. Our culture has a lot of down points, the police baton charge or the bloodied face of a football fan are highly photogenic illustrations of that. But, at rare times, during the knockout stages of the World Cup and European Championships, for example, there is surely evidence, if we had time to consider it, that the game can do an awful lot of good for the morale of the nation.

22/6/96: Jerusalem
European Championship Quarter-Final. England v Spain

Andy and Max and Claire and I were in Brighton, on a whim, for the weekend, staying at the cheapest available B&B we could find in the brochure. Quite possibly the worst B&B in town too. Still, it was good fun. We like Brighton. Unlike the vast majority of our seaside resorts, it's lively but not vulgar. It's a cool place... and then, of course, you can quote Quadrophenia. I usually leave that to the others, whilst I make the point that the so-called "Ace Face's", apparently amazing scooter was in fact not nearly as good as the Lambretta Jimmy wrecked in the accident which culminated in his stunning shout of "Piss off Postie".

"Going shopping" was the plan, as arranged with the girls at breakfast. The Lanes have some nice little shops, though Andy and I were more concerned with finding a decent pub to watch the match in. We found one which was all right and we settled down as the pub filled out. The game was horribly tense. England, having played Holland off the park, were struggling against the Spanish who, for their part, seemed annoyingly reluctant to play their part and be beaten.

It must be a strange, almost surreal, sight to anyone who didn't know what was going on (though I seriously doubt that there were many such people in England that day); a packed pub with the eyes of everyone therein glued to one of four TV sets dotted about the beams and rafters - groaning and shouting in unison. Very little animation, save for the rush to the bar when the ref blows his whistle for the end of the first half, second half and first period of extra time.

Unlike Dunstable, mercifully, there was little effort to join in with the ubiquitous "football's coming home" and the songs sung at Wembley. In fact there was hardly any singing until the second period of extra time when a group of about a dozen lads behind us started to sing Jerusalem. They knew all the words too, it was excellent. In retrospect it was moving; at the time I was too preoccupied with the match, and biting my nails to the bone, to care. Apart from that, I was a little sorry that I didn't, and don't, know the words.

There was of course the usual raucous elation when England won through in the penalty shoot out. After that it was just nice to get out of that bloody pub and into the bright Brighton sunlight, a good evening guaranteed.

Score: 0 – 0 (after extra time). England won 4-2 on penalties

26/6/96: Return of the Dunstabilious
European Championship Semi-Final. England v Germany

Semi-Final heartbreak. I've yet to see a team I support, Luton Town or England ("support" is used loosely in regard to the latter....I've been to a couple of games, bought a few replica shirts....hope they do well etc..), win a proper, stand alone, semi-final. The Town in the Simod Cup doesn't count because:-

1) It's a Mickey Mouse competition and

2) I'm not sure I was there...

though I seem to remember a half hearted pitch invasion.

The feel good factor in the run up to the Germany game was a little spoilt by the horribly jingoistic hype screaming from the front pages of the tabloids. The Mirror quickly apologised for their "...Fritz, zee War is over" cover and admitted they hadn't caught the public mood. No, they'd misread the situation, and perhaps the majority of English people really aren't anally retentive fascists.

But, in truth the hooligans at the tabloids were but a minor embarrassment, it was still a day of great expectation. The match would, in my eyes, be too tense to watch in the pub so I sat at home with beer, and Martin. I can't remember why he came around, though I doubtless invited him. When Shearer scored we jumped into the air, like millions of others around the country. We broke no bones, but our reaction came as something of a shock to our cat Molly, who never sits on my knee usually, and picked a bad time to start (she's learnt her lesson, and now only registers grudging affection at food time).

A few minutes of elation before Germany equalised, then loads of minutes of anguish. Extra time, as you'll remember, was painful. How did Gascoigne and Anderton miss?

By the time of the penalties our lounge was full. Claire and Andy and Max had all come around at some stage during the match, I must have let them in myself, but had hardly appreciated their presence until I took to pacing around the room, and into the hall, during the penalties.

Penalties aren't the best way to end a cup tie. When your team wins a shoot out, it's high drama - if they lose it's downright unfair. Especially against the Germans. Again. At the time I was sure that, when Stuart Pearce exorcised the ghosts of his 1990 miss (he'd scored in the shoot-out against Spain too - but that was just a rehearsal now), England would win. But the Germans, them darned penalty taking machines, obviously had no time for such sentimental irony.

The tale of ten blokes taking penalty kicks in a highly charged atmosphere might have very little to do with the perceived national characters of the countries they represent..... but if the cap fits.... Germany's ruthless efficiency and nerves of steel played their part but so did the good old English sense of heroic failure. Young Aston Villa defender Gareth Southgate steps forward to serve Queen, Country and Football Association.

At our flat Martin, our Villa expert, shrieks "not Southgate", as he walks forward to the penalty area. Martin's pessimism was, I was sure at the time, misplaced.

Southgate shot, weakly, and the penalty is saved. Despite the catcalls of almost everyone at Wembley, and the negative force transmitted from the rest of the country (and Uri Geller), the German chap scores and England are suddenly out of the competition.
Score: 1-1, Germany won 6-5 on penalties.

Still, it was great while it lasted. Now it's over there is the usual trouble around the country and England's lads once again show that they can't take defeat in anything near good nature. Dunstable town centre is hit again, as it was in 1990. Youths run amok, smashing windows in the High Street. Moore's, the town's department store (and a real throwback to times past), had had a charming window display put up featuring St George's flags and "Good luck to England" messages. The windows were all put through, and the flags nicked. There are claims that the trouble had something to do with police provocation after the Spain match on Saturday; even so the trouble is sickeningly predictable.

Disturbances like those in Dunstable were mirrored throughout the country that evening (though there were no major incidents in Luton), a reaction which cannot be blamed on football, the clubs or the FA.

Although it is creeping back, especially in the lower leagues, hooliganism at football matches is still unfashionable. The vast majority of fans have realised that, as a social group, the football supporter had to grow up and take account of itself after the Heysel and Hillsborough tragedies; and in the main that has happened. The atmosphere of menace that used to be part and parcel of every away excursion in the 80's has, in all but a very few extraordinary cases, disappeared. Drinking in pubs, and chatting with home supporters, is now very much on the cards.

Outside, sometimes immediately outside, football circles is the wider English lad culture. The "Brits on the piss" types who swarm in to Ibiza of a summer to stage their own British invasion. Drink, drugs and sex (hopefully with someone else) would all appear to be higher on the list of priorities of the stereotype '90's lad than football. But in general, they like, or they like to be seen to like, their sport. They must enjoy the Euro96 ride with England and want to let it be known, bigtime, that they don't like losing.

Football supporters took the defeat with sad resignation. Perhaps, at the risk of sounding ridiculously superior, we've learnt to see through the hype and know in the end that it's just a game. It was those who knew no better, who didn't know how to behave, who took to the streets with bits of concrete looking for a window to smash.

It could be argued that the tabloids, general content, and especially during the Championships, fired up nationalist feeling in the country. It certainly didn't help, but people (however appalled they say they are) still go and buy the papers.

I would go further and suggest that, even after disasters which have shown that there is no place for football hooliganism in the modern game, the British public still feel relatively comfortable with this particular form of youth folk devil. Football hooliganism follows a fixture list that is quite easy to follow - West Ham v Millwall - not best day for a quiet lunchtime drink in East London. The press can be there in good time to get some gory action photos and footage for the next documentary.

Football hooliganism is usually nicely localised. It won't leave syringes in playing fields or condoms in your hedge. Even so football, and football supporters, generally have no time for aggro anymore - yet we have clearly still not seen the last of it. Does the British media and public regard football hooliganism as a socially acceptable form of civil disobedience?

The post Euro `96 documentary expose featured Luton three times. The first was in Wembley stadium during the Swiss game when the security staff were looking at a problem over seats. It was Mick and Mally whose tickets for the match, sent through the post, had mysteriously found their way into the hands of a Swiss travel agent. As a couple of stewards took up their case with the Swiss fans, Mick could be seen waiting in the aisle wearing his 1974 replica Luton top.

The second came from a secret camera hidden in a Luton town centre pub where, the producers had thought, trouble would "go off" when England were defeated. It didn't. But, give the programme its due, people did look unhappy.

The third was from a policeman at the bottom of the M1, announcing that it had "gone off Bigtime" in Luton. The trouble was in fact in Dunstable. In Luton town centre the result of the carnage after the match, as far as I could see the next morning, was limited to a burnt out bin in the town centre. Meanwhile, hot on the heels of the police, in Dunstable came the emergency force of glaziers.

England's defeat set our thoughts scurrying frantically toward some source of comfort. So, we started looking towards Luton Town's impending season - and the fact that we would have to purchase our student season tickets (we're not strictly students - but one never stops learning really does one?) before the end of June to get the maximum discount available. Had England won through to the final, we would surely forgotten all about it until it was too late. (29/6/96)

AWAITING
PUBLICATION...

Some pre-public inquiry publication thoughts on the subject of relocation, with historic reference to the reasons why club and Supporter sometimes appear divided on this and other issues.

Kenilworth Road is certainly one of the most cramped football grounds in the country. Boxed in by housing on two sides and by the old Luton-Dunstable railway (and new relief road) by the main stand, the Club have long looked at relocation as the only way forward. Relocation has been mooted at the club at least since the 1950's, when the ground capacity of just over 30,000 was simply too small on many occasions. Those were the days.....

Milton Keynes was a small village of little note back then, but since the new town was built a succession of Luton Town chairmen and directors have had their eye on moving the Club to a place which is crying out for the free publicity that a League Club affords a town. The Milton Keynes issue has unquestionably soured relations between the Club and its supporters.

Back in the 1930's the Luton Town Supporters' Club gave the Football Club the equivalent of millions in today's money from their own pockets to renovate the ground. Thus The Bobbers stand, so called because it used to cost a bob to get in, was built; a shallow row of terracing along the touchline with a low roof. It was converted to seats in the 70's and, by the mid-eighties the football club had put in the current ridiculous looking row of executive boxes. The old Bobbers Club bar under the stand is still open on matchdays - although it now only serves an ever decreasing number of businessmen who hire the boxes out. Meanwhile The Bobbers Club has been moved to under the Oak Road stand, which houses away fans - so the bar is shut on matchdays.

Sadly the treatment of the Bobbers seems indicative of the Club's attitude towards its supporters. It's a shame because, before then, the club were the model of the "happy, family club" image, with genial manager Harry Haslam at the helm and (our hero) Eric Morecambe giving the Hatters almost weekly mentions on the classic Morecambe and Wise show.

In 1976 Luton Town nearly went to the wall. The club had to sell Peter Anderson to Antwerp to survive, but also called upon the fans once again to dig deep into their pockets to keep LTFC afloat. After the immediate danger was averted, there must have been a time when the fans and the club looked together with optimism, born out of adversity, toward the future.

By the early 80's it became obvious that the Club, led by chairman Denis Mortimer (and not including Eric Morecambe who had left the board a few years earlier), were looking towards the future in a northerly direction, up the M1 a few junctions, to the new town of Milton Keynes. The actual news of the Club's despicable ambition in that direction was leaked on the very day that Luton Town stayed in the First Division at Maine Road in 1983. The excuse they gave for the urgency of relocation was a new relief road running alongside the existing (long redundant) Luton-Dunstable railway line. The new road, the Club informed us, would make it impossible to hold matches at Kenilworth Road.

The seasons which followed were soured by bad feeling between club and supporters. The supporters, adamant that the Club belonged to the town - not to the directors - produced the fore-runners of fanzines and organised rallies. Planes flew over Kenilworth Road followed by "No to Milton Keynes" banners, club AGMs turned into shouting matches whilst many fans boycotted the ground. The club, ironically, pointed at the low crowds (caused by the boycott) as another reason why the Club had to move.

A siege situation was instilled within those employed by the club whose loyalty was with the Club - not with the town of Luton (although some resigned). Meanwhile the fans, although basically united, were fragmented by their own paranoia - members of some branches like the official Supporters' and Bobbers' Clubs, with their long histories of working together with the Club, were viewed with suspicion.

Denis Mortimer was eventually ousted and replaced by David Evans, who still had Milton Keynes on his mind. Eventually it was Milton Keynes council, lobbied by the local NIMBY groups - and by Luton Town fans - who chucked the plans out.

Meanwhile, even though the Milton Keynes issue was out of the way, the wounds still had to be healed. Many of the club officials still held an unhealthy disrespect towards the supporters (who themselves weren't universally prepared to let bygones be bygones) and "The Luton Town Story", brought out to mark the club's centenary in 1985, although an impressive tome and a good reference guide, betrayed the town and Luton Town supporters by berating the fans' attitude towards the Milton Keynes issue.

The new relief road, which the club had led us to believe would mean the end of football at Kenilworth Road was built, and named Hatters Way. And in the corner nearest the road the club have managed to find room for a new (albeit small) stand.

Evans went on to show a contempt towards football supporters by masterminding the away fan ban, and to Luton Town fans in particular by selling the ground to the council. He used the money to pay off his, and other directors', loans. With interest - but less, he delighted in saying before he walked away from the club towards a colourful political career, than they would have got at a building society.

Next in the chairman's hotseat were Messrs Nelkin and Kohler. One of their first jobs was to boot out popular manager Jimmy Ryan and replace him with "prodigal son" David Pleat - a hero in his time at Kenilworth Road, but very much a villain when he left. Not an altogether popular move.

Nelkin eventually left and Kohler went ahead on his own. With no money to spend on players and as chairman of a Club on the plummet he too has been subjected to the fans anger.

But Kohler, apart from being something of a breath of fresh air on the PR front, has the ambitious (and/or mad) dream of building a multi-purpose domed stadium on the outskirts of the town, near junction 10 of the M1.

The scheme has caused excitement in the town and uproar in the villages around the site - Slip End (the nearest village) in particular. The NIMBY protest groups, although massively outnumbered by people in the town in favour of the scheme, gained the support of Luton South MP Sir Graham Bright - in one of his last acts in the job before he was voted out by the local electorate.

His intervention meant that, despite Luton Council's unanimous support for the scheme, a public inquiry was called. At the time of writing, no decision has been made - although pro-domers have been encouraged by the Labour election victory.

The current clamour of football clubs trying to better themselves with new stadia has uncovered another seemingly inherent problem - that of the risks of taking a Club out of its traditional home, usually in the heart of the town or city which bears its name, and onto an out of town lot; surrounded by ample parking in the case of the big clubs or on an industrial estate/retail park for the minnows. In either case the new stadium trend means that home fans have to travel out of town to see their football. Only time will tell whether relocation of football grounds will have a detrimental effect on the standing of a football club in the town it supposedly represents. Hopefully very few clubs will be like Wimbledon. They stopped playing in Wimbledon less than ten years ago, are now playing in that South London crater known as Selhurst Park, but are already talking about moving to Dublin (apparently oblivious of the wishes of their small army of supporters). British football certainly doesn't need the grotesque franchising operation that means that US gridiron Clubs can up sticks and move to another town if and when they feel like it.

The proposed Kohlerdome would face the same dilemma, if that's what the future holds. Although I, like the majority of Lutonians (gawping in fascination at the plans and models), have jumped headlong onto Mr Kohler's bandwagon, I do have reservations about the travel implications. Of course there are plans for "Park and Ride" schemes, but these have gone down like lead balloons in many towns (including Luton) in the past. The site is uniquely served by the motorway (so away fans should be alright). Fleets of buses would have to be used to ferry home fans to and from the ground...... although personally I'd like to see a mono rail or cablecar link between Luton Station, via Gypsy Lane, and the stadium.

Kenilworth Road is an amazingly cramped ground, as embedded in the local community as a third rate football ground could possibly be. If the Club is to hope to compete in the future then Luton Town must move to the new site (and, even if the stadium is built, that remains a big "If" now that the top Premiership Clubs are so far ahead). In fact the wrench from the bosom of the local community woould not upset Luton Town too much. Kenilworth Road is in the middle of the Bury Park Asian community and, over the years, the club has failed to raise significant support from the people on its doorstep. It's a national trend; the vast majority of football supporters in this country are white blokes. But, that said, there was a time when there were hardly any women going to football matches. I don't know what the situation is in other football towns with large Asian communities (Bradford springs to mind, but we tend to miss them in the league) but based at Kenilworth Road you'd think that Luton Town had a marvellous opportunity to buck the ethnic trend.

There are some Asian Luton fans and I'm always delighted to see their presence in the ground or wearing Luton shirts in town., Because they're such a small group, I'm pretty sure that the bigots in the crowd (who would, sadly, still outnumber them) don't make them that welcome. However the Asian community continues to present a largely untapped resource for the football club, and even if we're only at Kenilworth Road a few more years, the Club should do its utmost to foster support in every community in our cosmopolitan town.

In short the Club want to relocate. The fans are happy to accept that the Club has to relocate - but struggle to trust Club officials whom many still see as the enemy of football in Luton. Perhaps the Asian problem, if anyone at the LTFC even feels that there is one, is indicative. How far can the fans trust the Club to do what's best for the Town, when it can't attract the very people living on its doorstep? Even so, and even though David Kohler may turn out to be an Avengers style diabolical mastermind and/or the antichrist, the Junction 10 site and Kohler's Dome dream seem worthy of fan support. The public inquiry will, with a bit of luck, be published sometime in 1998 (it's taking an obscene amount of time). The permutations, even given that the inquiry will presumably give a straight yes or no, are endless. In the meantime, it's the wait that's killing us.

KENILWORTH SUNSET?

Kenilworth Road is a hole. It's too small, too cramped, the facilities are second rate and the view from the majority of seats in the main stand are obstructed by stanchion posts and floodlight pylons. Few fans would argue against the fact that the club needs to relocate, as soon as possible. Indeed some (myself included in some ways) see the slump in the team's fortunes over the past few years as a symptom of the general malaise caused by the painfully slow progress of the public inquiry over the Kohlerdome proposal at Junction 10. The fans want the stadium there, so do the club, so do the majority of Lutonians - but as long as uncertainty hangs in the air, the club will suffer. News that the scheme has got the go-ahead would instantly create an atmosphere which, I feel, would be enough to give the club and the fans a renewed sense of spirit, which in itself would be enough to get the team out of Division Two. In the meantime, with the future of the club in the balance and the spectre of Milton Keynes again waiting in the wings (as is Kohler's Plan B threat), relegation to Division Three looks more likely.

If the public inquiry is released tomorrow (hopefully, by the time this book is published it will have been), the dome - which will likely be sponsored "The easyJet Dome" or "The Whitbread Inns Dome" - will obviously take a while to be built. Kenilworth Road will surely creep into the 21st Century as the home of Luton Town. After that it'll be good riddance, and time to get a dome bound bus to J10..............

Accepting that the public inquiry goes in our favour (and not my Dad's), I shan't be crying when Luton play their last game at the Kenny. I don't show that much emotion at matches. Still, there likely will be tears and a decent pitch invasion to include our ripping up chunks of turf for our gardens (like we did in 85 after the "last game on grass"). Hopefully by that time the new stadium will be near completion, I've little time for thoughts of ground sharing with anyone.

Luton will then historically move on to the Dome, the fantastic new stadium which, though it only holds 20,000 people, will make the club tons of money from its myriad of other uses. The Luton Blockers ice hockey team, Luton Griffins basketball side, Who reunion concerts and the glitzy launch of Vauxhall's new people carrier 73% powered by electricity. Meanwhile the glorious Hatters, under the managerial skill of the super tactical computer - the Pleatatron 2000 - will storm up the leagues, winning the club's first FA Cup as Shearer and Beckham (both now 73% bionic) vow to see the last 50 years of their careers out at Luton Town.

Oh yes, if I allow myself time to dream, the future can look pretty damned rosy.

We'll look back at the good times at Kenilworth Road but if the stadium, and more importantly the team that plays in it, is any good, we won't miss it. That in itself will be a shame. In common with most old grounds in the country, Kenilworth Road was built piecemeal over the years - with the fans of the time coming up with the money for improvements. The history of the ground is interesting in itself. Most Town fans know that the main stand came from Kempston race track, but until I visited the club statistician (or historian as he'd rather be regarded, with good cause) Roger Wash, I really had no idea how the ground had taken shape. The chunk of stand bought from Kempston provided only part of what we now know as the main stand, from the tunnel to the new main stand. For a time in the thirties, there was a grass back between the main stand and the Oak Road terrace. This area was called Scotch Corner, as were the houses beyond Maple Road and the railway line, due to the high proportion of Scots who had moved to Luton to work in some sort of factory on Dallow Road at the time. The wing stand was bolted on in the late 30's and the wooden rows on Oak Road were concreted over (then roofed over as well) a little time later.

The evolution (and recent decline) of Kenilworth Road has been almost continual since then; from the smallest of adjustments, to the adding of function rooms, to the seating over of terraces and the

the adding of function rooms, to the seating over of terraces and the Bobbers stand being converted into executive boxes. It's an amazing story.

It does seem a major departure from this type of evolution, to the new vogue manner of all new stadium construction. The fans have little or no involvement, other than they are expected to be excited and delighted by the new instant stadium when it's built and ensure that their bums are on the seats when their team plays. The history of the club that they support is all but forgotten amidst the clamour of club officials, players, sponsors and (lastly) fans offering the "you've never had it so good" line. And, if the history of a club is forgotten then so is the spirit of what brought the club to life in the first place. In many ways the traditional values of the game are much more visible in a ramshackle old ground like Kenilworth Road than it is in a brand new corporate super stadium like, for example, the Cellnet Riverside (Middlesbrough) and The Reebok Stadium (Bolton).

The English game is, as Mr Kohler accepts, nothing like the franchisee attitude to sporting institutions of NFL American Football Teams. But when business takes over and the fans are forgotten, this is the direction it is going in.

The worst example of this attitude is at Wimbledon who left Plough Lane years ago and are currently sharing Selhurst Park. The club heroically cling onto Premiership status but, by openly looking into the chances of bigger crowds and revenue that moving to Dublin might offer, have shown that they don't give a damn for the feelings of the few loyal fans that they do have. Wimbledon FC can still (at the time of writing) be saved for Wimbledon, but those who care will have to move fast to dissuade those in the club who want to see the club in Ireland. Even Joe Kinnear, their manager, has said that he'd like the club to go to Dublin. Like when Pleat, after months of sitting on the fence and burying his head in team affairs, eventually came out in favour of the MK move, Kinnear's dereliction of duty towards Wimbledon is totally despicable.

In Luton's case the Junction 10 plan, though it moves the club outside the town centre, is welcomed by the fans - and the Townsfolk. It really would be a boon for the town. Hopefully, when it is built, Luton Town FC will be the very obvious focus of the development. Planning permission, granted unanimously by Luton Borough

Fans and council should be careful that the name of Luton Town FC is prominent amongst' the host of big corporate sponsors who might wish a slice of the limelight.

In the meantime, if these seasons are to be the last at Kenilworth Road, we should endeavour to regard it with the respect that it, and the Hatters fans from years gone who created it, deserve. There were times during the Oak Road days when, shutting up for a second, one could be quite amazed at the noise that was coming out of the terrace. We enjoyed watching our football there immensely. Refreshment facilities were next to non-existent and the toilets (a urine stenching room with no windows or any lighting at all) were disgusting, and funny as a result (the toilets in the Bobbers stand were, according to Roger Wash, worse). I sat in the Bobbers stand once, on my second and last stint as a programme vendor, and was amazed at the fans therein. From the Oak Road their programme waving reactions looked funny to us young kids but sitting amongst them I saw that they really were getting at the ref. At the game I viewed from there he was actually attempting to justify his decisions to them! The main stand enclosure, when it was terracing, could be a good place to watch the match and we had some mighty fine moments on the Kenilworth Road terrace right into the early 90's.

The sense of camaraderie between the fans at these times created a real sense of extended family at the ground. In my case these people have been, at various times:-

My brothers Andrew & Simon; Stuart, Kedgie, Andy, Dawnie, Scho', Elaine, Warren, Matth', Pete, Beece, Brian, Stan, John, Steve, Andy, Bob, Michael, Chris, Mick, Keith, Ian, Dave, Geoff, Jez, Steve, Mark, Andy, Mark, the girls who wore straw boaters and the woman with the Birds Eye gloves.

The "family" may have changed over the years (through their losing interest, moving away, joining the army, or whatever), but the home has always been Kenilworth Road. Since I've been supporting Luton Town I've lived at four addresses, but have always gone to the same place to see my football....... apart from the away games obviously, but you get the point. My abiding memories of Kenilworth Road will be of the big cup games against Arsenal, Watford and West

Road will be of the big cup games against Arsenal, Watford and West Ham, and the glory promotion nights against Shrewsbury and QPR (though I was probably too young at the time to fully appreciate them). The single best moment at Kenilworth Road would probably be the moment when Wayne Turner slid in to score the winner in the second replay against Watford in `85. We had far better players than Turner. There were hundreds of better games. When we travelled away with Luton we saw far better grounds than our own. Despite that fact, and the feeling that the away fan chant of "Shit ground, no fans" sums the current situation up pretty well, Luton Town fans will be able to look back at Kenilworth Road days with a great deal of fondness.

END BIT

So, that's it folks, it's all over, can we have you making your way to the doors now please. I hope you've had a jolly nice read and, just maybe, might want to read it all again one day..... maybe whilst sitting in your luxuriant bucket seat at Luton Town's new stadium on Junction 10?

I've been concerned that this book might read like an epitaph to a once proud, now sinking and bitter, little team that had its moment in the sun in the 80's. There is an element of that; you may have noticed that the recollections beyond the original First Division are pretty scant. The recollections do come from a better time, but the overwhelming hope is that Luton Town can do it all again after the move to the new stadium. We're not pretentious enough to call ourselves "sleeping giants" but our club, with a bit of luck, might just get on with the job when we get the chance and not spend years and years moaning on about potential. In the meantime, the diary of the 96/97 season will, I trust, provide a record of a season in the small time league. I would be very interested to read the same sort of account by a fan at the time of Luton's previous slide into the lower leagues in the 60's. I hope that this book is available to be taken out of the attic in years to come, so that the 21st Century Hatters fan can read what it was like at the Luton v Peterborough match in October '96. Amidst the recollections of the memorable games, it's honest and representative to show how basically mundane the average run of the mill match is.

Matches in our league obviously aren't hyped as heavily as their Premier League counterparts. Fans will turn up to the matches knowing that they probably won't be made happy by the standard of play or the result. The times we've talked up a game, walking towards the ground, only to spend most of the match staring blankly at the pitch and wondering where it's all going wrong. Moribund is a word that doesn't feature much in football highlight books but, in terms of Luton Town over the past few years, it certainly seems apt. So, given that the footballing fayre is so sub-standard these days, why do we bother?

We bother, as we all know deep down, because we care. And, because we enjoy it. We enjoy moaning and sulking, the expectation and the feeling of the common cause. I love going down the pub before a match, asking if so and so is fit yet, meeting my mates, talking down our chances for the benefit of away fans, whipping up a bit of enthusiasm and getting two pints pissed before the match.

Even so there is more to fear about the way our club, and football in general, are going than to be optimistic about. Football has undoubtedly lost its way to crass commercialism. Meanwhile, in the lower leagues where fans are feeling increasingly alienated and disaffected, hooliganism is creeping back. Even at Luton, which still regards itself as a forward thinking club, the fans are causing concern again. The recent lowpoint (during the current `97/98 season, which has so far seen the club slide into the relegation places) was when Watford won 4-0 at Kenilworth Road. And Luton were lucky to only concede four. It had taken Watford ten years to beat us, and there were a disturbing number of Hatters fans who simply couldn't take the defeat and went out of their way to cause trouble. Against the backdrop of a thrashing from the local rivals it was pretty sickening. The Luton/Watford rivalry is something that I've turned to a lot in this book, and the nastiness of the recent feeling (especially, it has to be said, from the Town fans) made me think about altering what I'd written about the matches. There is after all, little doubt in my mind that Luton's band of trouble makers have been wound up by the hooliebooks written by a couple of Watford fans (who can't bear to even write Luton, they put L*t*n, so it's obviously the vowels they despise the most).

Oh yes, I hate Watford. Instinctively. Luton Town fan/Watford hater - they're the two sides of the same coin - but that hatred is no more than tribal ceremony. I've nothing, but pretend sympathy and incomprehension, against Watford fans. My own fave

Watford fan, as I've written somewhere in this book, was a guy called Peter at school who understood as well as I did that one or other, or both, of us would rip the piss out of the other on Monday morning. We were good friends on the understanding that we hated each other. I only know one Watford fan now. He's a bloke at work called Roy who is altogether too nice and has no time to even mention the rivalry. He goes on about "my lot" and "your lot" with no malice, he honestly wishes "my lot" well. We've had some good chats lately, even if I still have to prefix any praise of Watford's league position with "I hate to say it but....." (and I really do hate to say it). Luton will beat Watford again, and Watford will beat the Town again. I hope that, next time it happens, it can do so with good grace on both sides.

The trouble at the England match in Rome has made me fear for the World Cup in France. We saw the match in a pub in Bedford with Tony, who obviously wanted Italy to win. The defiant roar that went up from the lads when they saw pictures of the trouble was indicative of how deep set the problem is in English psyche. It's gone on too long now. The known trouble makers should be made to wear tracers so that the police can make sure they don't get to France. Yes, it will violate their civil liberties but for how long do we have to sit back and watch them disgrace us? Why the hell, after seeing England heroically qualify for the World Cup Finals, should we have to worry about fans' behaviour at the matches? By the time you read this book, you'll know what happened in France. Hopefully the England team, rather than the fans, stole the headlines. More than anything, I can't help thinking, wouldn't it be brilliant if England won the World Cup?

On the 18th July 1995 Luton Borough Council passed the unanimous descision to grant Luton Town FC permission to build a new stadium, the "Kohlerdome", on land adjacent to the M1 Junction 10 at the south of the Town. Thanks largely to opposition from the then MP for Luton South, Graham Bright, the government launch a public inquiry.

This book was started, and written throughout, in the belief that, when it was finished the public inquiry would have been published and the future of Luton Town Football Club would be a little clearer. Not only would the club's future have been clairified but, on a more personal level, the whole mood of this book should have been set by the findings of the public inquiry and LTFC's reaction to it. Now, almost three years after the council backed the stadium plans, this book will be published with the decision still pending and the club's future still in the balance. In one way, in that this has been the situation for the last 15 years or so, I suppose that this state of affairs is at least that which Luton Town fans are familiar with. However, first and foremost, the uncertainty is a major pain in the backside.

The 97/98 season was diabolical for Luton Town. Dogged by injuries throughout the season (Paul Showler played once, as sub), trounced 4-0 at home to Watford, beaten 1-0 at home to Torquay in the Cup, selling Tony Thorpe to nouveau riche Fulham (who proceeded to keep him on the bench and avoid promotion via the playoffs) and only narrowly avoiding relegation after David Pleat stepped in to loan us young Spurs starlet Rory Allen. Watford, meanwhile, went on to win the Second Division Championship.

Luton's Second Division survival was ensured after a 2-2 relegation showdown against Brentford, who were relegated. That was one of the two away games I went to during the season. The other, up at Carlisle, was a lovely away trip on a Tuesday night including B&B, drinking until closing and a 1-0 win. I didn't go to Watford. I really didn't want to see them do the double over us, even though, in the end, Marvin Johnson scored to earn a creditable 1-1 draw. But there was also the question of the intensity of rivalry that had caused some nasty incidents at the Kenilworth Road match, with some Luton fans unable to take defeat. The big match ill-feeling towards supporters of the other team was evident at Brentford. "You're going to get your f****** heads kicked in" sang a section, albeit a tiny one, of the Luton support. I've never heard that before from Luton fans away. It was sickening. It was surely also, as I've warned somewhere else in this book, an indication of disillusion, disaffection and disenfranchisement felt amongst fans. Luton Town are no longer players, however unlikely, in the big league. Whereas, ten years ago, Luton fans away from home were a cheerful and cocky bunch – living in eternal hope rather than expectation of an an away win at a big club, there is no such potential glory in trips to Walsall, Wigan, Blackpool and Brentford. Whilst most of us merely stand and stare, waiting for a spark, there is sadly an element who decide that – even if the team is rubbish – there is kudos (in certain sad circles) in having some tough fans.

Luton Town fans need to reinvent the atmosphere again, it's an easy enough thing to do. The club has simply been sinking for far too long – good news in relation to the club will do wonders to change an atmosphere in which antisocial behaviour has started to re-establish itself.

The mood of relief after the Brentford game threatened, in the evening, to become that of celebration in the pub. I propped up the bar with Jeff, a "Mad as a Hatter" stalwart and a diehard in his own right, who quite rightly argued that for the club to be involved in a Second Division relegation in the first place was reason for despondency. I agreed, to an extent, but argued that the publication and a result – any result – of the public inquiry would be a relief.

Of course the outcome I, and thousands of other townsfolk, are hoping for is a "yes" vote. No doubt there would be some major questions to be answered like "When?", "How much?" and "So, who exactly is paying?". I suppose the answer to the last question would involve a big sponsorship tie-in which may well involve the stadium having an even more ridiculous name than "Kohlerdome". Oh yes, I can see myself in the future arguing for the soul of the club. At the moment I'd just love confirmation that that argument will be aimed at Luton Town FC - a newly affluent club, and their corporate pals, at Junction 10.

A "no" vote would be a terrific blow to the ambitions of the football club in the foreseeable future. A move out of Kenilworth Road seems the only chance that the club have to compete with bigger sides. Even so, if David Kohler, on publication of the inquiry, carried out his threat to take his ball away and up the M1 to Milton Keynes, I would certainly not follow. The Council's decision to back Kohler, is proof that the town has done all it can to help the football club – that he is still prone to talk up a move to Milton Keynes is nothing short of insulting. "No man is bigger than the club" David Kohler once told me (playing down his own egotism if I remember), he was right even if I don't think he really believed it himself. However, it would also be right to say that no club is bigger than the community it serves. Luton Town FC belongs not to David Kohler, but to Luton town.

If it came to it, and I don't believe it will, I would never go to Milton Keynes to support the club if it moved there. I would rather support a new Luton Town side, playing in Luton (possibly at Kenilworth Road), at the bottom of the football pyramid than go to Milton Keynes FC; even if they were playing Premiership football against Manchester United.

Still, I don't want to end on a sour note. We're all really looking forward to the World Cup and the new season after that - we're renewing our season tickets and, because we feel guilty (and because this book exposes the sham), we'll be paying full price for our season tickets this year. Micheal Flaherty is, as I write these words, on a jumbo jet on the way back to his native Australia; where he's going to live. We'll miss him chunks – but he says that he'll be wearing a Luton top during the next Adelaide test against England, so watch out for him there.

Well, that's about it folks. Thanks for reading this book, I hope you've liked it and now feel, frankly, not ripped off having bought it. Now you've finished it – why not read it again or go back to the bit you liked best. Thanks again and, if you've enjoyed this book, why not consider covering it with attractive paper? Bye bye, see y'later and, don't forget, sing your hearts out for the lads!

 COME ON YOU HATTERS!*

* Team encouragement suggestion - serve vigorously prior to Town corner kicks.

APPENDIX 1

Luton Town managers since 1978

David Pleat: 24/1/78 - 16/5/86

When David Pleat took over from Harry Haslam in '78 he was one of youngest managers (if not the youngest) in the League. And so began the Pleat dynasty. Pleat's teams played with passing play and tremendous flair. It was great stuff to watch. His promotion side in '81/82 was obviously too good for Division 2, but was shown to be too lightweight for the top flight. So, Pleat bought (on a budget of course) a strong "backbone", hardy players like Steve Foster, Peter Nicholas and Mick Harford. It was a tremendous team, and so it was a genuine surprise when Pleat accepted the offer from Spurs. Pleat immediately became Lutonian enemy number one although, in fairness, his first term as manager did wonders for the club.

	Played	Won	Drawn	Lost	Goals For	Against	Points
1978 – 1986	402	158	107	137	604	543	581
Average		39%	27%	34%	1.50	1.35	1.45

The figures come courtesy of the, extremely useful, Definitive LTFC book and the modern day miracle that is Microsoft Excel. Cup games are included. Wins (even prior to '81/82, and including Cup matches) are marked as 3 points. This guide, of course, is just a comparison bit of fun; and although stastically accurate (well, we've checked it twice) it obviously doesn't take into account players that the managers have had at their disposal at any one time..... now, read on. Average scores for goals and points are totals divided by games played.

John Moore: 3/6/86 - 16/6/87

True, John Moore did inherit a fantastic team (even after Pleat nabbed Mitchell Thomas for Spurs - in a transfer that was billed in Luton, somewhat hysterically, as the crime of the century), but he also made the team defensively tougher. Under Moore, Luton Town finished 7th in '86/87 our best ever league position. Sadly, Moore wasn't keen on the admin and media sides of the job and resigned after a year in charge. He's been back at Luton Town now, and remains a backroom hero for the Club.

	Played	Won	Drawn	Lost	Goals For	Goals Against	Points
1986 – 1987	47	19	15	13	52	13	72
Average		40%	32%	28%	1.11	0.28	1.53

Raymond Harford: 16/6/87 - 3/1/90

Strange one, Raymond. Although it was another promotion from within, no-one really seemed to know that much about Ray. He never played for the Town. In any case, he too inherited a good team, and in his two full seasons in charge the Hatters got to the Littlewoods Cup Final twice (winning once of course). He was sacked at the beginning of 1990 because, apart from a disastrous start to the season, he "didn't smile enough" according to David Evans. It's hard to say, I wasn't really around at the time, but his comment that the 1988 Littlewoods Cup Final was "the worst day of his life" always seemed a little bit strange....

	Played	Won	Drawn	Lost	Goals For	Goals Against	Points
1987 – 1990	133	51	34	48	191	186	187
Average		38%	26%	36%	1.44	1.40	1.41

Jimmy Ryan: 3/1/90 - 13/5/91

The tabloids asked "who is Jimmy Ryan?" when he was appointed, but the fans knew. Ryan was a Hatters favourite between 1970-75, coming from Man Utd; and was back coaching at Kenilworth Road when Harford was sacked. Luton's First Division survival in 1990 was miraculous and, although his side was forever being weakened by the club's "sell to survive" policy (otherwise known as "sell up & slide") it was obvious that the players he did have were eager to play for him. A level headed Scotsman, he was asked to comment after the `91 escape on how disastrous relegation would be. He replied that a "disaster" was something like the recent flooding in Bangla-Desh, and shouldn't be used in the context of a mere football match. Great bloke. Sadly, Nelkin and Kohler didn't agree. They sacked Ryan in favour of the Prodigal Pleat. Jimmy Ryan's career never recovered after his move from Luton and, needing a job, he found himself having to take up a coaching job back at Old Trafford.

					Goals		
	Played	*Won*	*Drawn*	*Lost*	*For*	*Against*	*Points*
1990 – 1991	64	18	16	30	77	106	70
Average		28%	25%	47%	1.20	1.66	1.09

Again, the point has to be made here - these statistics are relative.... Jimmy Ryan was a much better manager than these figures suggest he was.

David Pleat: 7/6/91 - 11/6/95

The Return of the Old Master. There's little doubt that Pleat wouldn't have been the choice of the fans, but to Messrs Nelkin & Kohler he was obviously the box office name indelibly linked with Luton Town's *Football Focus* halcyon days. They probably weren't wrong. Pleat bought back Brian Stein and Mick Harford.....which was a bit sad (especially in Steiney's case), and despite his "well, I've not yet been relegated" comments to the media, the Town slid quietly into the new First Division; maybe a sacking offence for a mere mortal - but not for our living legend. The club still had to fulfill their role in resurrecting Pleat's career again and, eventually, managed it when

Pleat took up the job at Sheffield Wednesday. We quite forgot to be outraged this time.

	Played	Won	Drawn	Lost	Goals For	Against	Points
1991 – 1995	207	55	69	83	232	299	234
Average		27%	33%	40%	1.12	1.44	1.13

Terry Westley: 3/7/95 - 18/12/95

Oh you can't blame Terry, who was appointed to be manager from Youth Team Coach on David Pleat's recommendation. It's just..... that he seemed totally unprepared for the job. In TV interviews he had something of the startled rabbit look about him, he really couldn't work out why Luton were losing. His favourite saying was his insistence that Luton were a potential "top six side", as we careered down the Division One table. His inevitable sacking came, cruelly, just before Christmas. It was already too late by then.

	Played	Won	Drawn		Goals For	Against	Points
1995	28	5	7	16	26	47	22
Average		18%	25%	57%	0.93	1.68	0.79

Lennie Lawrence: from 21/12/95

Lennie Lawrence is, at least, a "brand name" manager. Known for his successful relegation battle heroics with Charlton in the 80's (they weren't as good at it as Luton became..... but there you go). The Hatters put on a spurt after he became manager, but it was clearly a case of too little too late. The idea of bouncing straight back up in '96/97 looked a good one for quite a time, but that too proved too much. He's going through a pretty rough patch with the Town at the time of writing (four straight home losses hasn't done him many favours) and if he's still the manager if and when this book is published then he'll have done well. The figures below are up to and including the `96/97 season - of what you have been reading about in much of this tome.

	Played	Won	Drawn	Lost	Goals For	Against	Points
1995 – 1997	85	33	25	26	115	103	124
Average		39%	29%	31%	1.35	1.21	1.46

APPENDIX 2

1996-1997 Football League Division 2 - Final Table

		Played	Home					Away					Points	LTFC points
			W	D	L	F	A	W	D	L	F	A		
1	Bury	46	18	5	0	39	7	6	7	10	23	31	84	2
2	Stockport County	46	15	5	3	31	14	8	8	7	28	27	82	2
3	Luton Town	46	13	7	3	38	14	8	8	7	33	31	78	-
4	Brentford	46	8	11	4	26	22	12	3	8	30	21	74	3
5	Bristol City	46	14	4	5	43	18	7	6	10	26	33	73	1
6	Crewe Alexandra	46	15	4	4	38	15	7	3	13	18	32	73	4
7	Blackpool	46	13	7	3	41	21	5	8	10	19	26	69	4
8	Wrexham	46	11	9	3	37	28	6	9	8	17	22	69	1
9	Burnley	46	14	3	6	48	27	5	8	10	23	28	68	3
10	Chesterfield	46	10	9	4	25	18	8	5	10	17	21	68	1
11	Gillingham	46	13	3	7	37	25	6	7	10	23	34	67	6
12	Walsall	46	12	8	3	35	21	7	2	14	19	32	67	3
13	Watford	46	10	8	5	24	14	6	11	6	21	24	67	2
14	Millwall	46	12	4	7	27	22	4	9	10	23	22	61	3
15	Preston North End	46	14	5	4	33	19	4	2	17	16	36	61	3
16	Bournemouth	46	8	9	6	24	20	7	6	10	19	25	60	3
17	Bristol Rovers	46	13	4	6	34	22	2	7	14	13	28	56	3
18	Wycombe Wanderers	46	13	4	6	31	14	2	6	15	20	42	55	4
19	Plymouth Argyle	46	7	11	5	19	18	5	7	11	28	40	54	2
20	York City	46	8	6	9	27	31	5	7	11	20	37	52	4
21	Peterborough United	46	7	7	9	38	34	4	7	12	17	39	47	6
22	Shrewsbury Town	46	8	6	9	27	32	3	7	13	22	42	46	6
23	Rotherham United	46	4	7	12	17	29	3	7	13	22	41	35	6
24	Notts County	46	4	9	10	20	25	3	5	15	13	34	35	6

APPENDIX 3

The following matches are referred to in this book.

Date	Home Team			Away Team	Competition
26 Apr 80	Luton Town	2	- 0	Wrexham	Football League
30 Apr 82	Luton Town	4	- 1	Shrewsbury Town	Football League
12 Mar 83	Nottingham Forest	0	- 1	Luton Town	Football League
14 May 83	Manchester City	0	- 1	Luton Town	Football League
12 Nov 83	Luton Town	1	- 1	Birmingham City	Football League
3 Dec 83	Luton Town	2	- 4	Coventry City	Football League
2 Jan 84	Luton Town	2	- 3	Nottingham Forest	Football League
14 Jan 84	Luton Town	1	- 2	Arsenal	Football League
8 Dec 84	Luton Town	1	- 0	Aston Villa	Football League
15 Dec 84	Leicester City	2	- 2	Luton Town	Football League
26 Dec 84	Luton Town	2	- 0	Coventry City	Football League
2 Mar 85	Luton Town	2	- 1	Sunderland	Football League
9 Mar 85	Luton Town	1	- 0	Watford	F.A. Cup
13 Mar 85	Luton Town	1	- 0	Millwall	F.A. Cup
13 Apr 85	Everton	2	- 1	Luton Town	F.A. Cup
21 Apr 85	Luton Town	2	- 1	Manchester Utd	Football League
17 Aug 85	Luton Town	1	- 1	Nottingham Forest	Football League
5 Oct 85	Luton Town	1	- 1	Manchester United	Football League
19 Oct 85	Luton Town	7	- 0	Southampton	Football League
9 Nov 85	Tottenham Hotspur	1	- 3	Luton Town	Football League
23 Nov 85	Watford	1	- 2	Luton Town	Football League
4 Jan 86	Tottenham Hotspur	0	- 0	Luton Town	Football League
5 Mar 86	Luton Town	3	- 0	Arsenal	F.A. Cup
6 Apr 86	Birmingham City	0	- 2	Luton Town	Football League
6 Sep 86	Chelsea	1	- 3	Luton Town	Football League
18 Oct 86	Manchester Utd	1	- 0	Luton Town	Football League
28 Jan 87	Luton Town	3	- 0	Liverpool	F.A. Cup
6 Oct 87	Luton Town	4	- 2	Wigan Athletic	League Cup

27 Oct 87	Luton Town	3	- 1	Coventry City	League Cup
17 Nov 87	Ipswich Town	0	- 1	Luton Town	League Cup
19 Jan 88	Luton Town	2	- 0	Bradford City	League Cup
10 Feb 88	Oxford Utd	1	- 1	Luton Town	League Cup
28 Feb 88	Luton Town	2	- 0	Oxford Utd	League Cup
27 Mar 88	Reading	4	- 1	Luton Town	Simod Cup
24 Apr 88	Arsenal	2	- 3	Luton Town	League Cup
9 Apr 89	Nottingham Forest	3	- 1	Luton Town	League Cup
21 Apr 90	Luton Town	2	- 0	Arsenal	Football League
28 Apr 90	Luton Town	1	- 0	Crystal Palace	Football League
5 May 90	Derby County	2	- 3	Luton Town	Football League
8 Sep 90	Luton Town	1	- 0	Leeds Utd	Football League
11 May 91	Luton Town	2	- 0	Derby County	Football League
14 Sep 91	Luton Town	2	- 1	Oldham Athletic	Football League
2 May 92	Notts County	2	- 1	Luton Town	Football League
15 Sep 92	Watford	0	- 0	Luton Town	Anglo-Italian
20 Feb 94	Cardiff City	1	- 2	Luton Town	F.A. Cup
23 Mar 94	Luton Town	3	- 2	West Ham Utd	F.A. Cup
9 Apr 96	Luton Town	1	- 2	Stoke City	Football League
30 Jul 96	Hitchin Town	0	- 0	Luton Town	Friendly
3 Aug 96	St Albans City	3	- 2	Luton Town	Friendly
5 Aug 96	Luton Town	4	- 2	West Ham Utd	Friendly
7 Aug 96	Luton Town	2	- 0	Norwich City	Friendly
17 Aug 96	Luton Town	1	- 2	Burnley	Football League
20 Aug 96	Luton Town	3	- 0	Bristol Rovers	League Cup
24 Aug 96	Brentford	3	- 2	Luton Town	Football League
27 Aug 96	Bristol City	5	- 0	Luton Town	Football League
31 Aug 96	Luton Town	1	- 0	Rotherham Utd	Football League
4 Sep 96	Bristol Rovers	2	- 1	Luton Town	League Cup
7 Sep 96	Wycombe Wanderers	0	- 1	Luton Town	Football League
10 Sep 96	Luton Town	2	- 1	Gillingham	Football League
14 Sep 96	Luton Town	0	- 1	Chesterfield	Football League
17 Sep 96	Luton Town	1	- 0	Derby County	League Cup
21 Sep 96	Bury	0	- 0	Luton Town	Football League
25 Sep 96	Derby County	2	- 2	Luton Town	League Cup
28 Sep 96	Luton Town	1	- 0	Blackpool	Football League
5 Oct 96	Luton Town	3	- 1	Walsall	Football League
12 Oct 96	Shrewsbury Town	0	- 3	Luton Town	Football League
15 Oct 96	Stockport County	1	- 1	Luton Town	Football League
19 Oct 96	Luton Town	3	- 0	Peterborough Utd	Football League
23 Oct 96	Wimbledon	1	- 1	Luton Town	League Cup
26 Oct 96	Luton Town	2	- 0	Bournemouth	Football League
29 Oct 96	Watford	1	- 1	Luton Town	Football League

2 Nov 96	Plymouth Argyle	3	-	3	Luton Town	Football League
9 Nov 96	Luton Town	2	-	0	Notts County	Football League
12 Nov 96	Luton Town	1	-	2	Wimbledon	Football League
16 Nov 96	Torquay Utd	0	-	1	Luton Town	F.A. Cup
19 Nov 96	Preston North End	3	-	2	Luton Town	Football League
23 Nov 96	Luton Town	2	-	1	Bristol Rovers	Football League
30 Nov 96	Bournemouth	3	-	2	Luton Town	Football League
3 Dec 96	Luton Town	2	-	2	York City	Football League
7 Dec 96	Luton Town	2	-	1	Borehamwood	F.A. Cup
10 Dec 96	Luton Town	2	-	1	Leyton Orient	M.Mouse Cup
14 Dec 96	Luton Town	6	-	0	Crewe Alexandra	Football League
18 Dec 96	Millwall	0	-	1	Luton Town	Football League
26 Dec 96	Gillingham	1	-	2	Luton Town	Football League
18 Jan 97	Luton Town	0	-	0	Wrexham	Football League
21 Jan 97	Luton Town	1	-	1	Bolton Wanderers	F.A. Cup
25 Jan 97	Bolton Wanderers	6	-	2	Luton Town	F.A. Cup
27 Jan 97	Luton Town	0	-	0	Watford	Football League
1 Feb 97	Notts County	1	-	2	Luton Town	Football League
4 Feb 97	Northampton Town	1	-	0	Luton Town	M.Mouse Cup
8 Feb 97	Luton Town	2	-	2	Plymouth Argyle	Football League
15 Feb 97	Bristol Rovers	3	-	2	Luton Town	Football League
22 Feb 97	Luton Town	5	-	1	Preston North End	Football League
1 Mar 97	York City	1	-	1	Luton Town	Football League
4 Mar 97	Chesterfield	1	-	1	Luton Town	Football League
8 Mar 97	Luton Town	0	-	2	Millwall	Football League
12 Mar 97	Wrexham	2	-	1	Luton Town	Football League
15 Mar 97	Crewe Alexandra	0	-	0	Luton Town	Football League
21 Mar 97	Luton Town	1	-	0	Brentford	Football League
29 Mar 97	Burnley	0	-	2	Luton Town	Football League
1 Apr 97	Luton Town	2	-	2	Bristol City	Football League
6 Apr 97	Rotherham Utd	0	-	3	Luton Town	Football League
8 Apr 97	Luton Town	0	-	0	Wycombe W.	Football League
12 Apr 97	Walsall	3	-	2	Luton Town	Football League
15 Apr 97	Blackpool	0	-	0	Luton Town	Football League
19 Apr 97	Luton Town	2	-	0	Shrewsbury Town	Football League
22 Apr 97	Luton Town	0	-	0	Bury	Football League
26 Apr 97	Peterborough Utd	0	-	1	Luton Town	Football League
3 May 97	Luton Town	1	-	1	Stockport County	Football League
11 May 97	Crewe Alexandra	2	-	1	Luton Town	Football League
14 May 97	Luton Town	2	-	2	Crewe Alexandra	Football League

ACKNOWLEDGEMENTS

A number of people have helped, some of them unwittingly and not necessarily directly, in the publication of this book. I would like to thank the following people:-

My brothers Andrew and Simon.
Andy, Chris and Michael.
The Thrilled Skinny pop group (1987-1992).
John Buckledee, Geoff Cox and The Luton News folk.
Keith Hayward and the "Mad as a Hatter" boys.
Roger Wash for access his fascinating LTFC archives & memorabilia.
Paul Bowes and Trevor Wood from The Book Castle.
Steve Bailey, Brian Elliss & Alan Shury, whose book, the Definitive Luton Town FC proved invaluable in the later stages of compiling this book.
Andy Whiting (again) and Susan "Sledger" Ledger for proof reading.
John Hegley for his limerick.
Alison, Nick and the staff down the pub. For they sell me nice booze.

And a special mention to me old man Dave. Despite being a confirmed NIMBY type in relation to the new stadium, he and his expertise in Microsoft Word have been extremely helpful in putting together this book – printing draft copies aplenty and filling the book with sexy hat and hourglass graphics.

Books Published by
THE BOOK CASTLE

COUNTRYSIDE CYCLING IN BEDFORDSHIRE, BUCKINGHAMSHIRE AND HERTFORDSHIRE: Mick Payne.
Twenty rides on- and off-road for all the family.   1 871199 92 1

PUB WALKS FROM COUNTRY STATIONS: Bedfordshire and Hertfordshire: Clive Higgs.
Fourteen circular country rambles, each starting and finishing at a railway station and incorporating a pub-stop at a mid-way point.   1 871199 53 0

PUB WALKS FROM COUNTRY STATIONS: Buckinghamshire and Oxfordshire: Clive Higgs.
Circular rambles incorporating pub-stops.   1 871199 73 5

LOCAL WALKS: North and Mid Bedfordshire: Vaughan Basham.
Twenty-five thematic circular walks.   1 871199 48 4

FAMILY WALKS: Chilterns South: Nick Moon.
Thirty 3 to 5 mile circular walks.   1 871199 38 7

FAMILY WALKS: Chilterns North: Nick Moon.
Thirty shorter circular walks.   1 871199 68 9

CHILTERN WALKS: Hertfordshire, Bedfordshire and North Buckinghamshire: Nick Moon.   1 871199 13 1
CHILTERN WALKS: Buckinghamshire: Nick Moon.   1 871199 43 3
CHILTERN WALKS: Oxfordshire and West Buckinghamshire: Nick Moon.   1 871199 08 5
A trilogy of circular walks, in association with the Chiltern Society.
Each volume contains 30 circular walks.

OXFORDSHIRE WALKS: Oxford, the Cotswolds and the Cherwell Valley: Nick Moon.   1 871199 78 6
OXFORDSHIRE WALKS: Oxford, the Downs and the Thames Valley: Nick Moon.   1 871199 32 8
Two volumes that complement Chiltern Walks: Oxfordshire and complete coverage of the county, in association with the Oxford Fieldpaths Society. Thirty circular walks in each.

JOURNEYS INTO BEDFORDSHIRE: Anthony Mackay.
Foreword by The Marquess of Tavistock, Woburn Abbey. A lavish book of over 150 evocative ink drawings.   1 871199 17 4

JOURNEYS INTO BUCKINGHAMSHIRE: Anthony Mackay.
Superb line drawings plus background text: large format landscape gift book.   1 871199 14 X

BUCKINGHAMSHIRE MURDERS: Len Woodley
Nearly two centuries of nasty crimes.   1 871199 93 X

HISTORIC FIGURES IN THE BUCKINGHAMSHIRE LANDSCAPE:
John Houghton. Major personalities and events that have shaped the county's past, including a special section on Bletchley Park.   1 871199 63 8

TWICE UPON A TIME: John Houghton.
Short stories loosely based on fact, set in the North Bucks area.   1 871199 09 3

MANORS and MAYHEM, PAUPERS and PARSONS: Tales from Four Shires:
Beds., Bucks., Herts., and Northants.: John Houghton
Little-known historical snippets and stories.   1 871199 18 2

MYTHS and WITCHES, PEOPLE and POLITICS: Tales from Four Shires:
Bucks., Beds., Herts., and Northants.: John Houghton.
Anthology of strange, but true historical events. 1 871199 82 4

FOLK: Characters and Events in the History of Bedfordshire and Northamptonshire:
Vivienne Evans. 1 871199 25 5
Anthology about people of yesteryear – arranged alphabetically by village or town.

JOHN BUNYAN: His Life and Times: Vivienne Evans.
Highly-praised and readable account. 1 871199 87 5

THE RAILWAY AGE IN BEDFORDSHIRE: Fred Cockman.
Classic, illustrated account of early railway history. 1 871199 22 0

GLEANINGS REVISITED: Nostalgic Thoughts of a Bedfordshire Farmer's Boy:
E W O'Dell. 1 871199 77 8
His own sketches and early photographs adorn this lively account of rural Bedfordshire in
days gone by.

FARM OF MY CHILDHOOD, 1925–1947: Mary Roberts.
An almost vanished lifestyle on a remote farm near Flitwick. 1 871199 50 6

BEDFORDSHIRE'S YESTERYEARS Vol 2: The Rural Scene:
Brenda Fraser-Newstead. 1 871199 47 6
Vivid first-hand accounts of country life two or three generations ago.

BEDFORDSHIRE'S YESTERYEARS Vol 3: Craftsmen and Tradespeople:
Brenda Fraser-Newstead. 1 871199 03 4
Fascinating recollections over several generations practising many vanishing crafts and trades.

BEDFORDSHIRE'S YESTERYEARS Vol 4: War Times and Civil Matters:
Brenda Fraser-Newstead.
Two World Wars, plus transport, law and order, etc. 1 871199 23 9

DUNNO'S ORIGINALS: Facsimile of 1821–2: New introduction by Vivienne Evans.
Anthology of prose, poetry, legend. 1 871199 19 0

DUNSTABLE – TOWN AND CHURCH IN TRANSITION,
Little-known part of Dunstable's heritage: 1550–1700: Viviene Evans.
Wealth of original material as the town evolves without the Priory. 1 871199 98 0

DUNSTABLE WITH THE PRIORY: 1100–1550: Vivienne Evans.
Dramatic growth of Henry I's important new town around a major crossroads. 1 871199 56 5

DUNSTABLE DECADE: THE EIGHTIES: A Collection of Photographs: Pat Lovering.
A souvenir book of nearly 300 pictures of people and events in the 1980s. 1 871199 35 2

DUNSTABLE IN DETAIL: Nigel Benson.
A hundred of the town's buildings and features, plus town trail map. 09509773 2 2

OLD DUNSTABLE: Bill Twaddle.
A new edition of this collection of early photographs. 1 871199 05 0

BOURNE and BRED: A Dunstable Boyhood Between the Wars: Colin Bourne.
An elegantly written, well-illustrated book capturing the spirit of the town over fifty years
ago. 1 871199 40 9

ROYAL HOUGHTON: Pat Lovering: 0 9509773 1 4
Illustrated history of Houghton Regis from the earliest times to the present.

THE STOPSLEY BOOK: James Dyer. h/b – 1 871199 24 7; p/b – 1 871199 04 2
Definitive, detailed account of this historic area of Luton. 150 rare photographs.

THE CHANGING FACE OF LUTON: An Illustrated History:
Stephen Bunker, Robin Holgate and Marian Nichols.
Luton's development from earliest times to the present busy industrial town. Illustrated in colour and mono.   h/b – 1 871199 66 2; p/b – 1 871199 71 9

THE MEN WHO WORE STRAW HELMETS:
Policing Luton, 1840–1974: Tom Madigan.
Meticulously chronicled history; dozens of rare photographs; author served in Luton Police for fifty years.   h/b – 1 871199 81 6; p/b – 1 871199 11 5

BETWEEN THE HILLS: The Story of Lilley, a Chiltern Village: Roy Pinnock.
A priceless piece of our heritage – the rural beauty remains but the customs and way of life described here have largely disappeared.   1 871199 02 6

KENILWORTH SUNSET: A Luton Town Supporter's Journal: Tim Kingston.
Frank and funny account of football's ups and downs.   1 871199 83 2

A HATTER GOES MAD!: Kristina Howells.
Luton Town footballers, officials and supporters talk to a female fan.   1 871199 58 1

LEGACIES: Tales and Legends of Luton and the North Chilterns: Vic Lea.
Twenty-five mysteries and stories based on fact, including Luton Town Football Club.
Many photographs.   1 8711199 91 3

LEAFING THROUGH LITERATURE: Writers' Lives in Hertfordshire and Bedfordshire:
David Carroll.   1 871199 01 8
Illustrated short biographies of many famous authors and their connections with these counties.

A PILGRIMAGE IN HERTFORDSHIRE: H M Alderman.
Classic, between-the-wars tour round the county, embellished with line drawings.   1 871199 33 6

SUGAR MICE AND STICKLEBACKS: Childhood Memories of a Hertfordshire Lad:
Harry Edwards.   1 871199 88 3
Vivid evocation of those gentler pre-war days in an archetypal village, Hertingfordbury.

SWANS IN MY KITCHEN: Lis Dorer.
Story of a Swan Sanctuary near Hemel Hempstead.   1 871199 62 X

THE HILL OF THE MARTYR: An Architectural History of St. Albans Abbey:
Eileen Roberts.   h/b – 1 871199 21 2; p/b – 1 871199 26 3
Scholarly and readable chronological narrative history of Hertfordshire and Bedfordshire's famous cathedral. Fully illustrated with photographs and plans.

CHILTERN ARCHAEOLOGY: RECENT WORK: A Handbook for the Next Decade:
edited by Robin Holgate.   1 871199 52 2
The latest views, results and excavations by twenty-three leading archaeologists throughout the Chilterns.

THE TALL HITCHIN SERGEANT: A Victorian Crime Novel Based on Fact:
Edgar Newman.   1 871199 07 7
Mixes real police officers and authentic background with an exciting storyline.

THE TALL HITCHIN INSPECTOR'S CASEBOOK:
A Victorian Crime Novel Based on Fact: Edgar Newman.
Worthies of the time encounter more archetypal villains.   1 871199 67 0

Further titles are in preparation.
All the above are available via any bookshop, or from the publisher and bookseller,
THE BOOK CASTLE
12 Church Street, Dunstable, Bedfordshire, LU5 4RU Tel: (01582) 605670